The Framework of Legal Evolution

The Framework of Legal Evolution

Proefschrift

ter verkrijging van de graad van
Doctor in de Rechtsgeleerdheid
aan de Rijksuniversiteit te Utrecht,
op gezag van de Rector Magnificus
Prof. dr. Sj. Groenman,
volgens besluit van het College
van Dekanen in het openbaar te verdedigen op
woensdag 6 februari 1974
des namiddags te 4.15 uur
door

Leopold Willem Rosdorff

geboren op 16 april 1931
te Rotterdam

Springer-Science+Business Media, B.V.

Promotor: Prof. mr. J. J. M. van der Ven

ISBN 978-90-268-0734-3 ISBN 978-1-4899-6028-3 (eBook)
DOI 10.1007/978-1-4899-6028-3

To my parents

ABBREVIATIONS

D	- Digesta
Eur. Conv.	- European Convention on Human Rights
G.	- Gaius
H.L.R.	- Harvard Law Review
H.R.	- (Supreme Court of the Netherlands) - Hoge Raad der Nederlanden
N.J.	- (Dutch Judgements) - Nederlandse Jurisprudentie
U.E.	- Ulpiani Epitome
Un. Decl.	- Universal Declaration of the Rights of Man

CONTENTS

Foreword

I am greatly indebted to the principal supervisor of this dissertation, Prof. Dr. J.J.M. van der Ven, and the readers, Prof. Dr. J.Ph. de Monté verLoren and Prof. Dr. J.P.M. Geurts. Accordingly, I would like to thank them in the Dutch language

Als mijn promotor hebt gij, Hooggeleerde van der Ven, Uzelf veel moeite getroost om met mij mee te denken over de materie van het onderwerp. Vanuit de rijkdom van Uw grote kennis en ervaring, ook buiten de rechtsphilosophie, gaf U mij vele inspirerende adviezen. Uw hartelijke belangstelling was voor mij een grote morele steun.

Veel aanmoediging om met deze dissertatie de weg te gaan, die ik voor mij zag, ondervond ik van U, Hooggeleerde de Monté verLoren. Met U mocht ik vele juridische kernproblemen bespreken en gij kon deze vanuit Uw zeer uitgebreide rechtshistorische kennis op een verrassende wijze in een nieuw licht stellen. Dat U het manuscript in de eindphase hebt doorgelezen geeft mij nog extra redenen tot dankbaarheid.

Uw betrokkenheid met deze dissertatie, Hooggeleerde Geurts, kwam pas tot stand in het laatste stadium. Ook van U mocht ik vele nuttige raadgevingen ontvangen. Vanuit Uw theoretisch-physische achtergrond, die geschraagd wordt door een groot philosophisch inzicht, hebt gij Uzelf in deze juridische dissertatie verdiept. Voor de grondige wijze waarop gij deze arbeid verricht hebt ben ik U hoogst erkentelijk.

I. General introduction

(I.1) Problem and Purpose. At present, in the second half of the twentieth century, it is a realistic attitude to suppose that there is hardly any self-conscious human being on earth, who may not once in his life-time be confronted with a change in law. There is no doubt that such a change with respect to the individuals involved might cause emotions of dramatic character and that a change intended as an improvement might be experienced, either deservedly or not, as a deterioration.

Dramatic emotions may however originate as well, if individuals want a change in law and such a change is not effected. So, even if a law-giver acts with the best possible intentions, it might happen that his attitude is not appreciated by those for whom he works.

It appears from experience that it may only be possible after one or two generations of men to establish whether a certain attitude towards a certain change or non-change in law was just or not. Such a historical approach however is determined by its own time, place and conditions, and its results are actually not foreseeable. Similarly it is time, place and conditions which might change a certain opinion on a historical event.

Nevertheless, we do find legal changes in the course of history, which are unanimously considered as improvements, e.g. regulations abolishing slavery, or introducing protection of women and children. In spite of the fact that legal changes in a reverse direction have occurred as well, legal historians generally devote their studies to what they call development or evolution of legal phenomena.

It may be clear that for the purpose of concluding whether legal provisions or even whole legal systems have gone through or are meeting with a process of evolution- a criterion or touchstone is needed describing what legal evolution is. The problem now is that one meets with difficulties as soon as the question is posed of a specification of a criterion for legal evolution. The reason for this is that such a criterion is dependent on subjective opinions concerning law and society, which in their turn are dependent on subjective religious or philosophic convictions.

Comparison now of distinguished opinions on legal evolution might lead to the formulation of a catalogue of principles, common among men of different religious and philosophic convictions, by which specified objective criteria for legal evolution could be established.

However, one can raise serious objections to such an approach. The criterion, thus found, necessarily forms a minimal body, only selected because it is the expression of common ideas among different subjective convictions. It might be that something objectively true is omitted because it is not commonly shared. In as far as the discovered criterion is based on religious opinions, it is based on ideas which one should presumably believe implicitly without any actual opportunity to check them by scientific methods. In as far as the found criterion is based on philosophic ideas, it indeed in principle might be subject to scientific researches into its justness, but such researches are frequently impossible because the actual stages of knowledge and experience may not yet permit them.

Another approach towards a solution might be an investigation into the principles of legal evolution which is based on scientific data and theories, as well as that part of philosophy which is based on results of science.

As to a scientific theory, naturally in this respect the restriction has to be made that it is not a pure speculation, but a hypothesis based on facts and therefore, in principle, suitable for control. Moreover, if there is competition between more theories on the same subject, a choice has to be made between these theories on scientific grounds. A possible foundation of principles of legal evolution on a scientific theory can therefore never attain the same justness and objectivity as such a foundation on scientific facts, but such a foundation on scientific theories could certainly be more just and more objective than a foundation on metaphysical convictions.

The question now arises whether there indeed exist scientific facts or theories which can be used for the foundation of such a hypothesis. For trying to find an answer to this question we have to look at the sciences which are relative to investigations into human beings. Then we meet:

1) biology, studying human organic life in relation to non-human life;
2) paleontology, studying human life in the periods of its beginning;
3) history, studying human life during its movements in

time;
4) psychology, studying all internal and external human activity;
5) sociology, studying actual human behaviour in community-life;
6) the sciences of information and communication which study the nature and transmission of information both in living nature - human societies included - and in the physical area;
7) auxiliary sciences like ethnology and formal logic.

The progression of these sciences has been purposely chosen for demonstrating their relationship. In this progression one may distinguish the various sciences from each other, but it is impossible to separate them: they shade off one into another. This close relationship of sciences makes us wonder whether they could not have something in common that might be useful in approaching our aim of finding the principles of juridical evolution.

At this point of our investigation we indeed have the opportunity to meet a conception in which all these sciences participate and which is moreover one of the greatest conceptions of science - namely ..... the conception of evolution.

It is in this conception, which embraces scientific theories as well as scientific facts, that we might succeed in finding the elements necessary for basing principles of legal evolution on results of scientific investigations. This expectation might be enlarged because of the fact that both biology and paleontology, on one side, and the social sciences on the other, have developed theories of evolution covering both the biological as well as the social area; in fact, theorists of evolution have been, and still are, searching for one universal body of principles governing evolution not only in the areas of biology and social sciences, but in those of the physical world as well. Examples of such endeavours are the conception of Ernst Haeckel discussed in *(I.C.5)*, the search for a unity of sciences by the Wiener Kreis and the field theory of Albert Einstein.

Our purpose being to discover principles of juridical evolution we thought it therefore worth-while to investigate whether biological and social theories of evolution might provide us with materials for the attainment of this end.

During our investigations it appeared that even in modern theories of evolution, principal aspects of reality are not treated. A similar conclusion was reached when studying fundamental structures of law. In both groups of theories it was the results of the modern theories of information and communication that appeared still almost completely lacking.

Integration of theories on information and communication, especially theories concerning cybernetics, with data derived from biology, social sciences and law, brought about as a consequence the necessity of formulating new conclusions. This consequence resulted in a new theory of evolution, applicable in the area of law and based on principles of value in both biology and social sciences. Another consequence of this study was the necessity of exposing fundamental structures of law in, to the average lawyer, a somewhat unusual shape, by application of cybernetics and formal logic to juridical constructions. It might be that this approach offers some perspectives for the solution of centuries-old fundamental problems of legal theory and practice; the interested reader is referred to the chapters relating to this matter.

It is with feeling of gratitude to the great theorists of evolution that the following pages are presented. That their theories are not all treated equally is due to the principle of selection that was applied with respect to the final cause of this study, viz. the search for principles of legal evolution.

(I.A) THE BIOLOGICAL CONCEPTIONS OF EVOLUTION

(I.A.1) Introduction to the notion of Biological Evolution. In biology the notion of evolution *(1)* means that the different forms of life actually have a structure and a position in nature which are due to a development from other forms. This development generally is called phylogenetic because it concerns the development of species, or phylogeny; in biology the notion of evolution is not related to ontogeny, or development of individuals, except for the individual's qualities as a member of his species.

Evolution of species may be considered as a deviation from the principle of heredity. By this principle we understand the phenomenon that ancestors, parents and progeny show identical or similar features, as well as the process by which these features are transmitted from one generation to a following; this following generation may, but should not necessarily, be the next one in succession.

The conception of evolution arose during the 18th and 19th centuries as the result of a growing critical attitude towards a literal interpretation of the biblical creation-story, discoveries of fossils from apparently extinct living beings, attempts to make classifications of living species, both animals and plants, and new discoveries in the areas of physics, chemistry and medicine as results of new scientific methods.

The growth of this conception of evolution has up to now not resulted in one theory providing for a universally appeasing explanation of phylogenetic phenomena. It is a regrettable fact that we must still distinguish principally between three philosophical branches into which the conception of evolution actually has resulted, viz. a materialist direction (neodarwinism: a.o. J.S. Huxley), a finalist direction (a.o. Bergson, Driesch, Teilhard de Chardin) and a direction with both materialist and finalist features (neolamarckism).

Finalism and neolamarckism are now in fact seldom upheld by modern biologists; finalism however remains of great importance as a source of inspiration in biology.

The distinction between the three schools can be reduced to differences of opinion as to the reasons why, within species, deviations may occur from the principle of heredity. Such deviations presumably originate from influences of the species' environs or the species' individuals upon each other, with results ultimately determined by pure change (materialism) or by a final cause (finalism) or by both (neolamarckianism). According to this last school, the final cause is selected by the organism from various opportunities on a base of free choice; the finalist schools teach that the final cause determines evolution into one direction; Bergson moreover teaches that final causes can be moulded anew in a further evolutionary direction.

The three main directions within the conception of evolution should be distinguished from the three methodological starting-points in biological research. In that area three approaches are possible, based on mechanicistic, historical or finalist methods.

The mechanicistic approach is founded on the idea that with respect to all occurrences in material systems, physical-causal explanations should be searched for. The historical approach is a search to explain unique and irrepeatable particular occurrences of certain places in certain times. The finalist approach as a search to explain why a certain organic structure has a special appropriateness with respect to a certain purpose or multiple of purposes.

Actually the finalist approach is based on the method of static teleology; it only looks after teleological appropriateness of an organic structure as such and does not - contrary to dynamic teleology - consider such an appropriateness to be due in addition to a presupposed activity of unknown nature *(2)*.

The three methodological approaches are all useful for the description of biological phenomena; these phenomena can be considered either as causally ordered, or as ordered according to historical criteria, or as having a finalist order. These three ways of arranging phenomena are based on different axiomatic principles, but not on the idea that one order should exclude the possibility of considering the same phenomena as arranged within one of the two other orders: the three methodological approaches are relative to each other not exclusive, but complementary. Only by applying them together to the same phenomena may the result be a complete image of these phenomena *(3)*.

Before entering into a deeper analysis of problems of biological evolution I shall first devote a few words to the schools of neodarwinism and finalism.

(I.A.2) Finalism and Neodarwinism. Modern finalist theories of evolution should of course take that of neodarwinism into account. Finalism can at present not

deny that a selection of the fittest should be a regulative factor behind evolution. The separation-point between neodarwinism and finalism is now the question whether it is determined by pure chance or not that a certain mutation or recombination of genes might bring about an individual which is better adapted to its environment than was its ancestors. The finalist theories reject the principle of pure chance alone as driving force behind such mutations and recombinations of genes and they teach that this process is mainly due to a well-determinable cause; they fundamentally differ in opinion as to the nature and the working of this cause; the only thing in which they agree is that the cause is final.

As neodarwinism grew towards a hypothesis of a more and more appeasing probability, its postulates became, among its theorists, especially C.H. Waddington, G.G. Simpson and J.S. Huxley, the motive to work out its principles into new reflections on fundamental problems of human life; this gave rise to the school of evolutionary humanism. Within the framework of this study Huxley's ideas especially will appear to be of interest to us for finding relationships between fundamental problems of biological, social and juridical evolution.

We should however take into account that the neodarwinist hypothesis has not succeeded in building a methodological approach which is pure mechanicistic and free from all teleology. Notions like "struggle for life" and "survival of the fittest", i.e. survival of the *best adapted* forms, have a meaning which one cannot but consider other than as representing a final cause. Already therefore, we cannot leave finalism out. The finalist theories are moreover important because of their relations to religious and philosophic questions and because of their relatedness to possible applications of cybernetics *(1)* to evolutionary problems, including those of legal evolution; e.g. whatever the cause of gen-mutation or gen-recombination, a species may change its phenotype by selection of appropriate genetic information and such processes are supposed to be due to biological evolution. We will see in *(III.B.5)* ff. that such a process can be considered as a learning-game and that learning-processes of fundamentally similar nature occur in non-biological phenomena of evolution.

(I.A.3) Conceptions of Finalism

(I.A.3.a) The Conception of Entelechy. The idea that evolution's direction might be determined by a final cause can be traced back to Aristotle (384-322). Modern finalist theories can be considered as variations on this philosopher's teachings; Aristotle's terminology is still frequently used in teachings of finalism, but sometimes with meanings deviating from the original. For a clear understanding of problems of finality in respect to evolution it therefore appears necessary to treat Aristotle's theory.

Aristotle came in contact with problems of evolution through his work on animal-classification. His observations had caused him to reject the older ways of classifying animals, based on placing animals in contrasted groups, like land and water animals. This principle led, as he noticed, to separation of closely related animals. He therefore drew up a new classification in which the related animals were ordered according to the greatest possible number of distinguishing qualities. Aristotle was himself aware of the fact, that his classification demonstrated progressions from lower to higher developed organisms. He rejected however the theories of the natural philosophers for the explanation of the order which he had discovered; Aristotle used his biological findings for his own metaphysical theory, in which an explanation is given of nature's movements.

This theory is based on the idea, that everything in the world is compressed by an inner force to become somewhat greater than it is. Everything is cast or reality, originated from its raw material; any thing which is a cast has in its turn the capacity to be the raw material of a higher cast. The embryo is the raw material from which the child is a cast; the child is raw material in relation to the cast of the adult. Matter is the cast's potential (δυναμις).The cast is both matter's completed reality and the realization of matter's potential (ἐνερχεια or ἐντελεχεια) *(1)*. Nature is the cast's victory over matter.

If every thing strives naturally towards realization of the potentials within it one may establish that the final cause, which determines the purpose of realization, is the most important and decisive of all causes by which an occurrence is brought about. It is this final cause which determines that from a chicken's egg not a duck will develop, but a chicken. If not a chicken, but a monster results, then such a development is due to matter's slowness, which is a handicap to the cast's constructive activity.

A chicken's egg is the chicken's entelechy: the egg has its purpose within itself. Nature's entelechy is God, who moves the world as the object of his love; God is nature's cast and the ultimate final cause of all things. He is not so much a person as a magnetic force.

Modern conceptions of evolution are not contrary to Aristotle's theory that matter has eternally existed as a potential of being which God started to move at a certain moment and during this movement the casts were made. Aristotle however does not explain the existence of related species as a development of one species from another *(2)* : the different species were in his opinion originated by spontaneous generation.

Modern revivals of the Aristotelian conception of entelechy can be found in the schools of vitalism and neovitalism. Both schools were a reaction against 19th-century Darwinism to which living organisms were nothing but pure mechanisms, like watches. The distinction between vitalism and neovitalism was drawn in 1856 by Rudolf Virchow (1821-1902). Both directions postulate that processes in a living organism are regulated according to special laws, which are neither physical nor chemical.

Vitalism assigns the regulation of these processes to the independent activity of a particular vital force, which somehow organizes the physical and chemical potentials according to its own laws; neovitalism does not assign this regulation to a force, but to a principle.

It was the principal representative of neovitalism, the biologist and philosopher Hans Adolf Eduard Driesch (1867-1941), who identified the neovitalist vital principle with a notion of entelechy based on that of Aristotle. Driesch called entelechy "the unextended, spaceless, immaterial, individual, energies suspending, regulating, forming principle of life"; to him it was an agency of nature ("*Naturagens*"), the "*Individualitäts-konstante*" of the organism; or more simply: a driver on a machine.

Driesch' definition of entelechy indeed already contains categories for a cybernetical explanation of fundamental problems concerning the nature of life. Driesch did not however discover the principles of cybernetics, possibly because of the neovitalist thesis that life's laws are different from those of physics and chemistry.

Neovitalism postulates that an organism is more than the sum total of its elements; it emphasizes that towards these elements an organism's totality is irreducible. Neovitalism differs from 20th-century holism (a.o. J.B.S. Haldane, H.J. Jordan, J.C. Smuts) in this respect, that while accepting the postulate that an organism is more than the sum total of its elements, holism studies the organism's elements and processes in their interrelationships without a notion of entelechy.

The conception of life as held by neovitalism is similar to that which Gierke took as an argument for his theory that a legal person is a really living organism. Attention will be given to Gierke's theory in *(III.C.4.a)*.

(I.A.3.b) Finalist Conceptions of Evolution. The French philosopher Henry Bergson (1859-1941) was inspired by Driesch' exposition of the notion of entelechy to develop his own vitalist conception on this subject *(1)*. Besides the fact that Bergson's entelechy is not a principle, but energy, it principally differs from preceding conceptions by the idea that final causes may be moulded anew. Bergson's notion of entelechy is embodied in a theory of evolution of great importance, also with respect to the later development of cybernetic, which will be treated in *(III)*.

Another direction in finalism has been developed by the Jesuit priest and eminent paleontologist, Pierre Teilhard de Chardin (1884-1955). His theory is vitalist and his conception of vital force lies at the base of an extremely original theory of evolution. Teilhard de Chardin believed that the vital energy should be of psychic nature, but he assigned properties to it which do not absolutely correspond to results of modern research in psychology and psychiatry *(2)*. The final cause towards which the working of psychic energy is directed is in Teilhard's theory a kind of mystic unification of mankind at a point as close as possible to God. In spite of its controversial postulates Teilhard's theory does belong to the greatest theories of evolution. Moreover it is a theory with some social and legal implications and therefore well-worth treating within the framework of this study.

As reaction to the daring hypotheses of Teilhard de Chardin new endeavours have been made to integrate the undeniable results of materialist biology with less speculative solutions for problems concerning relations between mind and matter. Neodarwinism having provided explanations for phenomena which vitalism and neovitalism could only assign to the mystery of life, this mystery has in fact developed into the mystery of all reality, either living or not. This stage of development was certainly already reached by Bergson and Teilhard de Chardin: both have seen the problem, but their solutions are in the direction of vital energies which are relatively superior above matter. The recent development of cybernetics is of great help for the finding of common principles to which both living and dead matter might be subject.

This development however does not exclude the fact that within living reality there is a dimension still insufficiently explained, viz. that of interiority. Modern evolutionists are inclined to consider a teleological framework in the increasing inward orientation on the line from lower animal to man. One of the principal representatives of this direction is the Dutch philosopher A.G.M. van Melsen (born 1912) *(3)*. This finalist school has not yet progressed to the point of developing principles concerning social evolution.

Because of reasons already stated in the preceding alineas the theories of Bergson and Teilhard de Chardin will now be treated on the following pages.

(I.A.3.b.1) Bergson's Theory of Evolution. Bergson's vision on evolution was a reaction against Darwinist materialism. His approach of reality deserves well of 20th-century science.

The essence of reality is to Bergson similar to becoming, which is a continual and active process, that of creative evolution, stimulated by the life-impulse *(1)*. Matter *(2)* is to Bergson the sum total of all images (a *"système d'images"*), which present themselves as expanded within their own coherences. These images are perceptive notions (*"perceptions"*) in relation to all possible activities of the organic body.

Matter originates - according to Bergson - from life when life's tension is released, i.e. when the life-impulse (*"élan vital"*) ceases to continue its activity. Life then sinks away and externalizes itself in space to a diffused progression of homogeneous conditions. Bergson did not see any essential difference between matter and mind, matter only being distinguished from mind by the criterion of time.

Human behaviour was to Bergson only to a certain extent determined by mechanic principles and he was of the opinion that to a great extent the human will is free;

therefore indeed a large number of human acts are chosen by reason; other human acts however find their origin in the life-impulse. Bergson distinguished the acts originating in the life-impulse from those related to mind and those related to matter. When related to mind, acts are arrangeable in an ascending order: science, arts, morality, religion. When related to matter we find an order of descent: instinct, the life of plants and dead matter.

Reason has not the capacity to maintain an understanding of the unity of both the ascending and descending aspects of life, because of the physical notion of time *(3)*, but it is intuition which grasps for reality's duration and so for reality's unity. Intuition now is used when leaving the area of mathematics and physics for that of life and consciousness: then we have to make an appeal to the notion of "meaning of life", which cuts right across reason and finds its origin in the "*élan vital*", which is a vital impulse of the same nature as instinct, although instinct itself is something else *(4)*.

Evolution is therefore, according to Bergson, not the result of the mechanism of natural selection as painted by Darwin and Spencer. Moreover, Bergson finds in the results of biological researches other objections to a mechanical explanation of evolution:

(1) The origin of instincts cannot be explained by natural selection. Instinct must already have been in full existence before the development of the species started, because otherwise it could not have been of benefit to the surviving fittest.
(2) The existence of complicated organs, e.g. the eye, cannot be considered as a result of natural selection: such an organ was not yet able to function during its development and it could only start to fulfill its function after completion of its development.
(3) Natural selection cannot be considered as the cause of equal results, generated by different means on different lines of evolution. So the eyes of molluscs and vertebrates are of the same construction *(5)*.
(4) The theory of natural selection provides no solution for the fact that, when an important organ within an organism is lacking, another organ is sometimes able to fulfill the same task as the missing organ and even to build up the same accessories of this missing organ *(6)*.

Bergson therefore concludes that life embraces more than a mechanism of material accessories *(7)*: Life is a power with the capacity to grow, to re-establish itself and to create, according to its own will to a certain extent, surrounding circumstances as it desires. Therefore Bergson characterizes the notion of evolution as creative (*"l'évolution créatrice"*). Creative evolution however is not directed towards an external purpose: such a finality would mean an inverted mechanism, as well as a fatalism destructive to human initiative and creative evolution itself. Bergson solves this problem by stating that creative evolution is directed towards a purpose within itself and is to be understood as an entelechy. This means that creative evolution is the self-conscious energy of free activity, actually realizing the potentials which it already possessed in its origin; this realization is the purpose or *causa finalis* which determines what actually is occurring; thus it is the acorn's entelechy which makes an oak grow from the acorn; creative evolution is in the same way life's entelechy or life-impulse (*élan vital*); creative evolution is moreover the entelechy's realization of life itself.

To this point Bergson's entelechy seems to have developed with Aristotelian features, but creative evolution is not only pre-determined to realize itself: it is the self-conscious energy of free activity, able to re-establish itself according to its own will in a new direction if it cannot proceed further *(8)*. Then the results of life's new establishment cannot any longer be considered as realized purposes, which were already existent before their realization *(9)*. As soon as life's new establishment is realized, however it appears to us not as a result, but as a realized purpose, which could be explained as being already in existence before its realization. But this would not be a just explanation, for life is free to establish itself in a new direction according to its own will, making a choice from differentiated opportunities. This freedom of choice is only limited by the fact that creative evolution can but proceed in one direction: forward. It is in this way that creative evolution has the capacity to mould its own final causes anew *(10)*. Bergson saw the proof of this new conception of entelechy in the existence of similar results on different lines of evolution, caused by different means: both molluscs and vertebrates have eyes of similar construction *(11)*.

Life now, is to Bergson nothing less than God; God and life are one and the same *(12)*. The evolutionary God is not almighty, but limited in his power by matter, and not omniscient, but slowly growing in consciousness and knowledge *(13)*.

Bergson sees the process of evolution as a development, caused by the life-impulse, from safety to freedom. So there are three directions to be distinguished in evolution: that of the plants, which have remained in safety; that of the insects, who chose freedom, but whose spiritual development remained at the stage of pure instincts; and that of the vertebrates, where, among the mammals, it was the human species which succeeded in domestication of its instincts and development of thinking. Evolution here has led to continuously higher shapes of spiritual development, resulting in an ever increasing controlling power in the areas of mind and matter.

Bergson only devoted very few words to the application of his theory to social evolution; what he did say is well worth citing: *"L'animal prend son point d'appui sur la plante, l'homme chevauche sur l'animalité et l'humanité entière, dans l'espace et dans le temps, est une immense armée qui galoppe à coté de nous en avant et en arrière de nous, dans une charge entraînante capable de culbuter toutes les résistances et de franchir bien des obstacles, même peut-être la mort" (14)*.

Bergson's special notion of entelechy's purpose as a final cause which has the capacity to become moulded anew, does express a finalism which can be built within a cybernetical machine *(15)*. It was nevertheless not given to Bergson to disclose the area of cybernetics. There are three reasons to which this might be due.

First of all it was Bergson's conviction that the real nature of his entelechy could only be grasped by intuition; this opinion may have prevented him from attempts to express the *élan vital* in the image of a mathematical model. Secondly Bergson had a vitalist conception of life, which means that his notion of entelechy was a particular force, somehow organizing within a living organism, physical and chemical opportunities according to its own laws. Thirdly Bergson actually did restrict the presence of his entelechy to organic life dead matter according to his opinion being generated when the *élan vital* falls out. Modern conceptions- in which cybernetical theories are applied, teach however the unity of organic, and in any case relatively greater structures of inorganic nature, by holding that atoms, molecules, living cells and organisms are all to be considered as servomechanisms *(16)*, with among their properties those of growth, a trend towards restoration after deviations caused by external factors, and even mutation.

(I.A.3.b.2) Teilhard de Chardin's Theory of Evolution. Not much imagination is necessary to understand that among men of theology, Bergson's evolutionary conception should have clinched the matter. For Bergson had not only gone as far as to formulate a conception of evolution directly opposite to the biblical creation-stories, but he had even ventured to make evolution literally equal to God Himself.

It was now Teilhard de Chardin who decided to search for a solution of the arguments between the theories of evolution and theology, convinced as he was that the truths of Roman Catholicism and science cannot be contradictory. As a philosopher he was not however appeased by a simple reconciliation of differences of opinion between theology and science, and he introduced in both science and theology original opinions of his own initiative. Thus he succeeded in creating a new synthesis between controversial ideas concerning the universe, which in spite of the controversies which it caused in its turn, among theologians as well among scientists, has earned admiration throughout the world.

Teilhard de Chardin explains the origin of life by presupposing that matter has both an outside and an inside structure. Any atom is to him composed of a mechanic stratum, which covers a biologic stratum. The latter stratum he called consciousness; by the notion of consciousness is meant any kind of psychic life, ranging from the atomic pre-vital stage to the human phenomenon of thinking. Therefore spiritual perfection, which is concentration of consciousness, and material synthesis, which is complexity (*"complexité"*), are two aspects or connected sides of the same phenomenon *(1)*.

So the internal side of matter is invisible at the beginning of the development of the universe, when its materials are still characterized by relatively simple atomic structures. But gradually universe develops itself to a structure, characterized by a smaller number of more and more complicated structures, which have, according to their complexity, a greater psychic stratum. It is according to this law that the universe developed from its original physical phase to the biological phase, recently culminating in the growth of man.

In order to explain this development Teilhard de Chardin makes the two sides of matter correspond with two kinds of energy. Corresponding with matter's mechanical side is the energy known from physics. This energy causes a certain structure to behave like all other structures of the same complexity and concentration; it leaves its source and

and vanishes for ever in the universe; therefore Teilhard de Chardin calls it *centrifugal*. But next to this physical energy he distinguishes physic energy *(2)*, which is centripetal and becomes accumulated. It is this latter kind of energy, which draws a structure in the direction of a more and more complex and *"con-centrated"* condition. This centripetal energy now is the driving force behind evolution: when psychic energy has been sufficiently accumulated within a certain con-centrated and complex condition, this condition suddenly crosses a threshold and a new stage in evolution is reached.

So in its pre-vital stage the earth gradually became covered by a stratum of mega-molecules - result of chemical reactions on the terrestrial surface - which formed together a mass of very small centres, however already of a much greater complexity than atoms. This growing stratum of mega-molecules meant a growing accumulation of psychic energy he distinguishes psychic energy *(2)*, which is via the intermediate form of the virus. From the physical point of view this meant the possibility of new types of complex and concentrated organization of innumerable different kinds of matter; from the psychical point of view, a new type of conscious activity and singleness of purpose *(3)*. From its pre-vital stage the earth by this mutation passed into that of "biosphere".

The cell's equilibrium is, contrary to the molecular structures from which it originated, not stable; the cell is continuously adapting itself to its surroundings, and at a certain moment, in order to keep its structure together, the cell has to divide itself into two new cells. This reproduction not only results in the structure's continuation, but also in its multiplication. Multiplication in its turn leads to variation into gradually different kinds of cell-structures. Hereafter follows the phenomenon of two cell-structures also reproducing and multiplying themselves, which results in a much greater variation in posterity. The fact that they are living together, forces the cell-structures to adapt themselves to a certain specialization within the group in which they are accumulated. This situation we see e.g. among the corals. Above this stage grew that of the *metazoa*, cells of cells, where an autonomous centre functions above an organized group of living particles;this is the stage of animal life. Above this stage nature developed with changing successes, societies of free *metazoa*. These latter groups in their turn tend towards super-complex unity *(4)*.

This development could not be reached just by cross-breeding of hereditary qualities; such a cross-breeding only gives variation in the same horizontal stage. But the mutations towards a new horizontal stage are caused by accumulation of new qualities in the same genealogical progression. The struggle for life determines, by the natural selection which it causes, that genealogical progression, which shall reach a new stage in evolution.

As evolution continues in its different branches, psychic energy or consciousness accumulates on the top. In the branch of the mammals it was finally in the primates that evolution became centered around the brain; consciousness was growing in each further developed species. Mammals seem to have reached the highest possible grade of consciousness: they know, but they don't know that they know. Then at a certain moment a new threshold is crossed: there is a primate who knows that it knows. This is what Teilhard de Chardin calls "hominization"; in a wider sense however hominization is a spiritualization of all forces of bestiality in human civilization. Development of human civilization caused, according to Teilhard de Chardin, in a relatively very short period, a greater change on earth than ever before; geologically the new period is given the name of "*psychozoicum*". The new stage into which the earth passed as a result of hominization is called by Teilhard de Chardin, *"no-osphere"*; this term is explained in *(I.B.1)*.

No-osphere, the earth's present stage, is however, according to Teilhard de Chardin, not yet the end of evolution. His argument is this: evolution is the same as ascent of consciousness; ascent of consciousness is the same as preparation of unity. Therefore Teilhard de Chardin foresees the development of a super-order, a "mega-synthesis" *(5)*, a collectivation *(6)*, which has already started in the evolution of the technical means of communication. Here a new type of human being, the "*homo progressivus*", will be the new master of the world. Teilhard de Chardin reckons among the homo progressivus all who are "possessed by the demon (or angel) of research".

Mega-synthesis will create a still greater complexity and therefore a still greater amount of consciousness: this centripetal energy will then become accumulated in one point, which Teilhard de Chardin calls Omega or God-Omega *(7)*; this accumulation of psychic energy in God-Omega will lead to a reversal of equilibrium between matter and consciousness; the latter will leave its material mould and will rest on God-Omega only. This will be the end of the world, and this end will be reached in peace, in spite of the highest possible tension by which it is accompanied, provided that in the future, evil *(8)* will not develop in the same way as good. In the latter case the world's end might be more according to traditional apocalyptic prophecies.

At present however the earth is already tending towards collectivation. This will imply that besides individual thinking a collective thinking will originate, which is destinated to rule the super-organism of collectivated individuals *(9)*. Teilhard de Chardin is himself well-aware of the dangers of collectivation, leading to loss of personality.

These dangers however may be corrected by the *spirit of evolution*, suppressing that of egoism. The spirit of evolution, makes human individuals strive after unity by means of two kinds of feelings of sympathy within them. The first feeling of sympathy is of a great "quasi-worshipping" nature and directed towards the evolutionary movement which carries man away to collectivation. The second feeling is of brotherly sympathy of each human being for the most original secret of each of his fellow-beings with whom he communicates, not only in the same act of vision, but also in the same living subject, the super-organism. This is an attitude of love, and love means freedom. There will therefore be no fear of slavery or exploitation in the super-organization, but on the contrary, the spirit of evolution will lead to a further human personalization and at long last to "deification" in point Omega.

As a consequence of his theory concerning future human development Teilhard de Chardin has stated his opinion on the development of fundamental human rights: this opinion will be treated in *(I.D.3)*.

It will appear in *(IV.B.3.b)* that, in spite of great admiration, I cannot but reject some basic postulates of this theory. However it will also appear from this study that the distinctions which Teilhard de Chardin introduced into the conception of evolution are perhaps of still greater value than this theory.

The theory of Teilhard de Chardin appeared to be a biological theory with human social implications; it has been treated here because of its finalist nature. In *(I.C.6)* its connections will be discussed with Huxley's materialist conception of evolution. First however it is necessary to expose the main ideas of those who consider human social evolution as a phenomenon which is completely or anyhow almost completely subject to principles other than evolution of organisms.

(I.B) THE CONCEPTIONS OF SOCIAL EVOLUTION

(I.B.1) Introduction to the notion of Social Evolution

(I.B.1.a) The Social and the Non-Social Conceptions of Evolution. Human evolution can be studied either from the biological or from the social point of view. In the first case the attention is drawn to developments of the human species, in the second case it is developments of human society to which notice should be paid.

Developments of human society can be studied either integrated with or distinguished from - although not absolutely separated from - biological researches into developments of the human species. Both approaches have resulted in interesting hypotheses but the scientific data for checking the justness of their postulates are perhaps only sufficient for concluding that a certain hypothesis does not agree with social reality.

Scholars of various branches of science have been searching for a satisfactory explanation of the causes, the nature and the goals of social evolution and this has resulted in a great number of theories which are hardly comparable because of differences in terminology, starting-points, frame-works of larger conception, assimilation of information on social phenomena and interpretation of such information. Within the framework of this study it is therefore impossible - if only because of reasons of space - to give a complete description of all these theories, to analyse their origins and their influences and to state opinions on their justness. Moreover, this is not necessary; in this study the problems of evolution are approached from within a different framework to that of previous authors, viz. from the point of view of cybernetics.

This does not however exclude the possibility that a brief sketch of the actual results of considerations on social evolution could give the reader an introduction to the problems which a theory of social evolution might face.

Here, in *(I.B)*, I restrict myself to the theories in which social evolution is treated as a phenomenon which is not in principle subject to laws similar to those of biological evolution. The other group of theories, in which social and biological evolution are considered as fully or partially regulated by identical laws, is treated separately in *(I.C)*, for it is especially from this group of theories in this study that a cybernetic approach is developed towards evolutionary problems.

The ideas concerning social evolution as a phenomenon regulated by its own laws are developed in theories within frameworks based usually on approaches which are either historical, sociological or economical. I will try to give now a systematic survey of the main questions with respect to basic problems concerning social evolution, together with the main proposals for their solution. The model of this system is developed by introducing a certain kind of order to the number of considerations put forward by various theorists on social evolution. This arrangement appeared necessary because, as the reader will notice, there is no theory of social evolution that treats all the points which proved to be of interest within the framework of such a theory. We have tried to integrate these considerations, as far as possible, into our conception of no-ospheric evolution. The term "no-osphere" is related to the ancient Greek words for mind (νους) and sphere (σφαιρα) and originates from Teilhard de Chardin. The conception of no-ospheric evolution, developed in *(III.B)* and elaborated in *(IV.B)* is a theory of social evolution based on the common cybernetic foundations of social and organic life.

Social evolution and law have connections of various nature. The relations between no-ospheric evolution and legal evolution are treated in *(IV.A)* and *(IV.B)*; legal evolution is indeed a part of social evolution, but no-ospheric evolution is in its turn a legal value and a source of legal values. We will see in *(IV.E)* that promotion of no-ospheric evolution is expressed as a duty of States and International Organizations in some of the main documents of present day's International Law *(1)*.

(I.B.1.b) Denial that Social Evolution is possible. A theory of social evolution denying the very phenomenon of social evolution might be looked upon as a "stunt", but this was certainly not the intention of Ludwig Gumplowicz *(1)* (1838-1909) who seriously posed such a theory within the framework of his social philosophy. This sociologist put forward a theory of continuous conflict between the main groups of human beings, viz. races, classes and states. Processes of conflict lead to suppression of the weakest by the strongest groups. It is in this way that Sovereignty and the National State originate. In the course of history this process was indeed subject to a transformation by social evolution, for general massacre was commuted into slavery and economic exploitation. However, this transformation resulted in the natural consequence that a

State is a composite of heterogeneous racial and social elements. Conflicts between races and classes may eventually result in emancipation of the conquered majority and its assimilation with the ruling minority. Then indeed social and political evolution reach their final outcome, the "folk-state" or nation. But a state has an inevitable tendency to either expand or decline; there is no midway to Gumplowicz: states which do not attempt to conquer other states will become increasingly weaker in comparison to states continuing this activity and will ultimately become conquered themselves. So the state must begin new conquests and become heterogeneous again; this implies that the process of development of a nation must start anew. If a state does not follow this law of nature but obeys ethical laws, then internal decay is the natural result. Social evolution is therefore in the long run as impossible as swimming daily across the Channel.

Certainly there is truth behind the idea of conflict as a dynamic force in social history and we will consider this idea in *(I.B.3.d)*, *(IV.B.3.e)* and *(IV.B.3.g)*. Gumplowicz' fatalist notion of State was determined by what he saw in the Austrian-Hungarian monarchy under which he lived. This theory is for the rest a curious hybrid between Marx and Macchiavelli.

(I.B.1.c) Rejection of Similarity between Social and Biological Evolution. The theories of social evolution which are dealt with in *(I.B)* are not based on the idea that social and organic evolution proceed according to similar regularities. An explicit rejection of such similarities has been given by Charles A. Ellwood *(1)* (1873-1946). This writer placed organic and social evolution in opposition to each other as respectively an automatic process and a consciously chosen human mental action. This action consists of inventions in the mental and social realm and in distributing the inventions from the inventor to the user by means of communication. Social evolution is therefore a result of a psychological process and this result is described by Ellwood as collective adjustments. Organic evolution, on the other hand, as an automatic process of variation, heredity and selection, has nothing in common with the human social process of communication and interlearning. The only relationship between organic and social evolution which Ellwood did acknowledge was that the former affects the latter as a framework.

Ellwood's theory of social evolution will be discussed in *(I.B.2.b)*. At present however a few words may be devoted to the question of whether it is indeed just to make distinctions as extreme as Ellwoods' between organic evolution and social evolution.

It is in fact true that mechanicistic biology considers organic evolution as an automatic process, but it is at least doubtful whether such a notion conforms biologically to finalism. On the other hand, the conscious processes of the human mind, by which in Ellwood's theory social evolution is determined, might appear in future to apply automatically as well, in spite of the fact that man in his actual situation experiences a freedom of choice. If however it will be proved that human individual behaviour is never always predictable, then there still remains the search of innumerable sociologists for methods by which they can foretell the conduct of any human group under any circumstance.

One of Ellwood's merits is that he has clearly seen that transformation of information is a necessary accessory in the process of social evolution; it was not given to him to live long enough to see the discovery that transformation of genetic information might play an analogous role in processes of biological evolution. In this respect also Ellwood's distinction between the learned adjustments of a human being and the results of variation, heredity and selection in biology, seem at present obsolete; now the process of natural selection can be considered as a learning process to which a species is subject, and of a nature similar to that of human learning *(2)*.

(I.B.1.d) Descriptions of Social Evolution. There is no doubt that most writers on social evolution have tried to explain how this phenomenon should be understood. But only one of them did indeed strive to develop a normative description of social evolution. This was the English philosopher and sociologist, Leonard Trelawney Hobhouse (1864-1929).

Hobhouse interpreted evolution as any sort of growth; social evolution includes, in his opinion, both advance and retrogression; the notion of social evolution consequently embraces that of social progress. It was this notion of social progress for which Hobhouse has given three descriptions:

1. social progress is the growth of social life in respect to those qualities to which human beings attach or can rationally attach value;
2. social progress is an increase in the harmonious adjustment of man to society, of the different

types of social organization to each other, and of society as a whole to its environment;
3. social progress is the development of the principle of union, order, co-operation and harmony, among human beings.

In the first description social progress is formulated as growth of social life; this notion of social life needs some explanation. Hobhouse saw as the fundamental fact of social life, as it is reflected in the third description, the interplay of human motives and the interaction of human beings. This interplay and interaction exercise influence on the individuals who take part in them and it is now this process of influencing which constitutes the fundamental fact of social evolution.

What Hobhouse meant by qualities to which human beings attach or rationally can attach value may be understood from his last description: the principle of union, order, co-operation, harmony, among human beings.

We find in Hobhouse's second and third description a notion of social progress connected with an ethical nucleus, viz. the notion of harmony. The introduction of an ethical notion into a definition of social progress seems almost unavoidable, but this implies that such a definition cannot be applied in establishing advance in the area of ethics, which advance is social progress as well: such an application would be similar to climbing one's own shoulders. Objections to the first and the third descriptions are moreover that they only concern relations between human individuals and not between human societies. The second description of social progress might indeed serve as an objective criterion among social scientists; an additional advantage is that it may link up with biological descriptions of evolution. However, it will appear from our treatments in *(I.C.7)* and *(III.B.4)* that Hobhouse's second description does not fit into our cybernetic approach in which another role is attributed to the environment.

Lastly, the distinction which Hobhouse made between social progress and social evolution is somewhat subtle and not in accordance with the customary use of both notions as synonyms. But Hobhouse rightly saw that progress and retrogression are both features of evolutionary processes. This question will be further analysed in *(I.B.3)*.

(I.B.2) Social Evolution and Evolution of differentiated areas of Social Life. In the preceding paragraph the inference was made that it might be possible to describe social progress - we do not mean social evolution - as an increase in the adjustment of man to society, of the different types of social organization to each other, and of society as a whole to its environment.

Within this description it is the notions of man, society and social organization which should each demonstrate an increase in a certain adjustment. The study of such increases must of necessity divide into studies concerning differentiated areas of social life. Evolutionary studies with respect to these areas are usually divided roughly into four branches: evolution of technology, of culture, of property and in politics. It is at this point that dangers of confusion threaten, for the notion of social evolution might indeed cover these four branches, but concentration on one or a few of them might lead to identifying only the studied branches with the whole social realm, and this in its turn might lead, as we will see in this paragraph, to rather one-sided conceptions of social evolution.

I shall not discuss whether this division of the social realm into four areas is just or not; the division is based on the nature of the existing studies concerning social evolution in these branches, not on the nature of society. The branches themselves can therefore hardly be described; they certainly merge with each other and there is no doubt that they cover notions which might deserve to form their own branch, as e.g. interhuman communication, religion, law. In the following four sections of this paragraph I will however discuss social evolution in respect to those four main branches.

(I.B.2.a) Social Evolution and Technology. It was the French sociologist Gabriel Tarde (1843-1904) *(1)* who considered invention as the source of all progress. Invention was to him any form of thought or action which gains expression.

According to Tarde invention may proceed from two origins. The first origin is the thoughts and acts of individuals who are gifted with a high capacity for originality and invention. The second origin is the conflicting imitation of existing inventions, for each invention may cause a wave of imitation, just as a stone cast into the water produces concentric rings.

The discovery of new inventions according to the second process and the spreading of these inventions belong to the social process and according to Tarde the social process consists fundamentally of the intermental activity of a group of associated individuals. This intermental activity takes place through the three fundamental processes of repetition or imitation, opposition and adaptation. It was undoubtedly the Hegelian dialectic of thesis, antithesis and synthesis by which Tarde was inspired; just as the Hegelian synthesis may become a new thesis, new inventions can proceed from an adaptation resulting from an opposition of conflicting imitations.

Tarde indeed was right in emphasizing the role of invention as a source of progress, but it was not given to him to see that it is not the only source. Social improvements are possible without any invention at all, e.g. by means of new social laws. Social improvements as a result of technological developments may indeed be considered as due to imitation of inventions, but the application of existing inventions is generally not the result of a conflict between different alternative inventions. This is due to the fact that an invention in most cases should be considered as the best possible solution for a certain problem at a certain moment and at a certain place, while a search for a still better solution will generally take a long time.

Tarde's idea that the social process fundamentally consists of the intermental activity of a group of associated individuals is in itself not rejectable, but it is now between individuals themselves that it appears impossible to place the development of their relations within a dialectic framework. Neither the triad of Tarde, nor that of Hegel, when applied for example to marriage, leave any logical place for the notorious fact that conjugal conflict does not always result in adaptation or synthesis, but in divorce. In general, adaptation or synthesis can only proceed from a conflict within which polarization does not develop so far as to make reconciliation an impossible thing.

So far as similar problems are indeed solved by different inventions, it may be true that sometimes someone does succeed in bringing their separate advantages together into one new synthesis or adaptation, but mostly a choice should be made between these inventions. Often this choice may lead to application of all these inventions, but in the direction for which they are best fitted.

Technology as the source of social evolution was also the idea of Morgan *(2)*. Morgan did not provide us, like Tarde with a subtle analysis of the origin of invention, but he accepted technological development as a historical fact to which he attached his notion of social evolution which was similar to cultural evolution. This theory will be treated in the following lines.

(I.B.2.b) Social Evolution and Culture. The American pioneer of social sciences, Lewis Henry Morgan (1818-1881), ventured to repudiate the actual theological explanation of savage cultures, holding that they are not the result of degradation after the Fall of Man but represent phases of social evolution which all cultures have to pass through. These phases are dependent, according to Morgan on the technological means at man's disposal.

Morgan was by this conception the first to come forward with a theory of social evolution which was not only purely secular but was also based on a scientific observation and explanation of data without searching for analogies with biological phenomena.

Morgan's theory *(1)* is, briefly, that culture advances as technological means of man's control over his habitat, particularly over his means of subsistence, are enlarged and improved. E.g., metallurgical developments, especially the introduction of iron tools, as well as successes in domestication of wild animals and cultivation of wild plants caused a change from hunting to intensive agriculture. This change produced, according to Morgan, a correspondingly radical change from tribal society to civil society, from clan and tribe to political state.

According to Morgan man originally lived like an animal. By means of articulate speech, however, human beings were able to communicate ideas to each other and from one generation to the next; in this way it was possible for man to elevate himself from the brute level upwards to civilization.

Communication was also considered by Ellwood *(2)* as the most fundamental factor in human social development. He rightly saw that there are other means of communication than speech alone and considered both natural and artificial methods of communication as important in this respect. According to Ellwood it is the web of intercommunication among the individuals of a group, in the form of the social tradition which they accept, that controls their social behaviour and gives rise to all their customs, institutions, and methods of living together.

Following the theory of Ellwood this web of intercommunication is similar to culture and this notion of culture dominates the human social process even to the extent of having the capacity to change human society by means of learned adjustments. These changes result from inventions in the mental and social realm and the diffusion of these inventions from the inventor to the users.

In Morgan's theory culture is not similar to a web of communication which controls society, but to society itself, except for man's technological resources and abilities. Social evolution is, in Morgan's theory, dominated by technological developments and so far as communication is concerned development of speech in this theory should fit into the division of technology.

The notions of culture used by Morgan and Ellwood have both a much longer range than this term in its original meaning of tillage or care and its figurative meaning of civilization. Culture in the sense of civilization is a feature of a society *(3)* and it is evaluated by qualitative criteria; it is as much a feature of a society as the growth of its population which can also be evaluated according to quantative methods; it therefore seems apparently unjust to regard culture in the sense of civilization as being equal to society itself.

Subtraction of technology from this sense of society puts technology outside civilization and this was certainly not Morgan's intention. Considered as a branch of culture with the property of giving rise to developments of other branches of culture, as in Ellwood's system, technology might possibly be identified with Ellwood's idea of culture as a web of intercommunication among the individuals of a group, in the form of the social tradition which they accept; it seems indeed undeniable that culture's nucleus is of communicative nature.

Development of civilization, does indeed determine that of society, but Ellwood did not appreciate that society's development may influence that of civilization as well. A society may however be changed by various causes of economical, political, geographical or climatological origin and there is no doubt that such changes influence this society's culture.

(I.B.2.c) Social Evolution and Property. It was Morgan again who earned recognition by establishing an important influence of accumulation of property on the course of social evolution.

Morgan's theory in this respect *(1)* is closely connected with his ideas on the evolution of the notion of family, which he called a property-making organization because it is in the family that property can be accumulated by inheritance at death.

Evolution of family proceeded, according to Morgan, in

a definite direction: from promiscuity in the original primitive horde through different forms of group marriage and by the restrictions of customs to progressively reduced unions between one man and one female without exclusive cohabitation, until the stage of monogamy was reached.

At present we know that this theory cannot be just; monogamy does exist in primitive society as well, and promiscuity can also be discovered in highly developed society. This does not however exclude the fact that Morgan did demonstrate some processes in his theory which may indeed have occurred.

Morgan sees inheritance at death *(2)* as a problem of little significance in savage society because the few possessions of the deceased were either buried with him or destroyed or simply divided among his close relatives and friends. The problem however becomes important when culture develops and property accumulates. Then, first, property will be inherited by the members of the deceased's clan. Later the heirs become limited to the agnates of the deceased. Ultimately the heirs become restricted to the children of the deceased, the agnates only inheriting if there are no children. Originally this last system was matrilinear, but this changed, according to Morgan's opinion, into a patrilinear system because of the accumulation of property combined with the desires of men to bequeath property to their sons. According to Morgan the increase of property in families exercised a steady and augmenting influence in the direction of monogamy.

One may indeed acknowledge that the influences mentioned by Morgan have contributed to changes from matrilinear to patrilinear systems, without however excluding the possibility of other origins as well. Such changes might be due as well to retrogression in the position of the woman from head of a fatherless family to that of her husband's slave. This retrogression is certainly not favourable to the development of monogamy. Such a change, either retrogressive or of progressive nature might have other origins than accumulation of wealth alone, as for example inventions restricting labour of women, or a long period of peace during which the male population becomes an increasingly essential economic factor in a society where formerly all productivity was in the hands of women, the men's business being war.

In spite of the fact that Morgan's theory concerning social evolution and property may be subject to serious criticism its basic idea is certainly just. Accumulation of property is a factor of increasing importance in social evolution, whether this notion is taken in a sense of progress or a sense of retrogression.

In modern society the importance of the family as a property-making organization has changed and is still rapidly changing. Taxes on inheritance at death generally prevent the passing of great fortunes from generation to generation, the more so where the law provides for division of the inheritance into equal parts among the descendants. However, at present accumulation of property occurs increasingly in big organizations, both of private and of public nature. In the private sector this is due to the development of the limited liability company, which process started in the 17th century, and in the public sector it was due, especially since the 19th century, to the increasing conception that public authorities should be involved in economic and social life in the interest of common welfare.

Accumulation of property in and distribution of new inventions among big organizations working either commercially or exclusively in the public interest, have undoubtedly resulted in more convenience being placed at people's disposal, certainly in industrial society. The development of these big organizations results in the increasing possibility that in industrial societies, either capitalist, socialist or communist, these big organizations could become the main , if not the only employers.

It was Herbert Marcuse (born 1898) who demonstrated *(3)* the danger of this development in that it could deform human individuals into "one-dimensional" types of men who are adapted to the requirements which such organizations necessarily impose upon their employees, even in their private life. Marcuse does not see an alternative solution to this problem.

As a matter of fact it is the problem of every community of men: does the individual exist for the community or the community for the individual? This is a situation of conflict and conflict is one of the driving forces behind social evolution, as we will see in *(I.B.3.d)*, *(IV.B.3.e)* and *(IV.B.3.g)*. The conflict cannot however exist between the organizations and their employees for these have adapted themselves by becoming organization-men *(4)*; the conflict can only occur between the organizations and those who are not employed by them. Actually it seems an irreconcilable conflict between establishment and bohemianism; the future will show how far succesful approaches from the side of establishment and organization will be made towards the training of employees who are thoroughly aware of the fact that life comprises more important dimensions than the organization alone; this might be the best investment of accumulated property.

Accumulation of property being a question with social implications, property itself is both a social phenomenon as well as a juridical construction. In *(III.C.3.a)* we shall see that property may fulfill an extremely important role in a theory concerning juridical evolution. This is not due to the social phenomenon that property has become man's master passion, as Morgan formulated, but to the reality that property is a legal construction fitting into the phenomenon that from a cybernetic approach man and his tool or resource, may form one entirety together *(5)*.

(I.B.2.d) Social Evolution and Political Evolution. An endeavour to define political evolution has been made by Tarde *(1)*. He saw political evolution as the outcome of the various aspects of social evolution and was therefore of the opinion that only a very general formulation could be given. The formula which he devised was obviously inspired by Spencer's "general definition" of evolution *(2)*. Tarde saw the course of political evolution as characterized by a transition from an original disorganized confusion to a harmonious adjustment of differences, in both internal and external political relations, through the operation of psychic forces making for an equilibrium.

The development of this transition proceeds of course by way of Tarde's dialectic triad of repetition or imitation, opposition and adaptation. Application of this principle to the development of internal and external relations of political entities is anyhow not according to historic reality which does show us innumerable cases where the situation of opposition between such entities resulted in destruction of the weakest; if one can still speak of adaptation in such cases then this adaptation is no more than that of the conquered to the requirements of the conqueror. A case where Tarde's dialectic seems applicable is the Conquest of England in 1066.

So far as Tarde's formulation of political evolution as such is concerned - leaving aside its dialectic background - it appeared to be the best possible which could be given in the 19th century and still now it cannot be considered as wrong in its essence *(3)*. We might only doubt whether the origin of political entities, pre-historic gatherings of men in the interest of either all of them or of the mightiest, did indeed generally spring from disorganized confusions, but, except for an increasing respect for the Law of Nations, relations between states can indeed be characterized by the notion of disorganized confusion. Trends towards domination of other states exist side by side with trends towards an equilibrium between all political entities.

In spite of the fact that so many people have tried to describe the manner in which they thought the course of political evolution should proceed, either to Utopia or to another chiliastic empire, only Tarde saw the problem that man should first of all know what is meant by the phenomenon of political evolution as such.

More can be said about this phenomenon. Evolution of states and other political entities is evolution of legal structures. In *(IV.B.3.f)* and *(IV.B.3.g)* this complex of problems has been comprehensively treated with respect to cybernetics and there the reader may discover how, from a cybernetical point of view, political evolution is interwoven with evolution of law.

(I.B.3) The Search for regularities in processes of Social Evolution

(I.B.3.a) Mechanicism and Non-Mechanicism in Theories of Social Evolution. If somebody is struck by the fact that history and prospects in the future demonstrate the reality of a social evolution, and consequently wishes to search for an explanation of this phenomenon, then he can but deny any lawfulness in this occurrence on penalty of not finding an explanation at all. On the other hand, however, if somebody claims to have discovered the mechanism by which social evolution does proceed, then there is certainly place for some objections. Social life as such depends on the interaction of human beings, either as individuals or as groups, both organized and not. Acts of human individuals are actually never fully predictable, although, when taking a large number of human individuals, crowds, associations or organizations, the probability of the majority's behaviour is now able to be predicted with an increasing accuracy. Another objection is that the study of social life of the past, the present and the future periods brings forward such a tremendous complex of problems that one human life seems too short for a scientific treatment of all of them.

The authors on social evolution in the 19th century and the first half of the 20th century have searched for a mechanicistic explanation of this phenomenon; during this period we can notice an increasing consciousness that regularities in social phenomena may exist, but that a pure mechanicistic explanation might not be sufficient. We have seen in the preceding paragraphs some of the approaches of Morgan, Ellwood and Hobhouse; we also considered Tarde's endeavour to put social evolution within the framework of a dialectic triad; the term mechanicistic is traditionally attributed to these systems, although such a use is incorrect. E.g. interplay of human motives and interaction of human beings; to Hobhouse the fundamental fact of social life is certainly not an activity of entirely the same nature as that of a clock-work mechanism.

A turning-point in mechanicistic explanation of social evolution might be found in the works of the German scholar Wilhelm Wundt (1832-1920). His studies on folk psychology, which in fact consisted in thorough analyses of the entire range of social life and of culture, brought him to the conclusion that the regularities, which he had found in this range do not belong to history, but to psychology. This idea means indeed a break with the mechanicistic conception of social evolution because of the fact that Wundt rejected the application of the physical notion of causality to psychological processes. Wundt distinguished between physical and psychic causality. In the former action and reaction are equal and opposite: a cause is equal to its effect and vice versa. In the latter the cause results in a transformation and a growth; the effect is greater than the cause.

Leaving aside to what extent Wundt's distinction between physical and psychic causality might be considered as right or not, Wundt did not consider man as a psycho-somatic entity, like present-day's psychology, but he advocated psychophysical parallelism according to which physical things cause physical things and psychical things cause psychical things, the causality being different in the two domains.

Wundt's merit with respect to the conception of social evolution is the fact that according to his theories social evolution needs a different explanation rather than a pure mechanicistic one; he was however not the first to put this explanation on a psychological base.

Social life being a human phenomenon it is impossible to explain social phenomena without at least some psychological conception in the back of the mind. Even Émile Durkheim (1858-1917) *(2)* who claimed that the social fact should always be viewed as mechanically determined and that it should be explained in terms of another social fact which is not of lower order, as e.g. a psychological or a biological phenomenon, could not escape the necessity of introducing these banished areas from the rear.

Around the turn of the 19th to the 20th century a theory of social evolution, based on a mechanicistic psychological conception, has been framed by the Austrian Field Marshal -Lieutenant Gustav Ratzenhofer (1842-1904). Ratzenhofer's psychology is based on a primeval force *(Urkraft)*, a substance which shows, at least on the surface, much similarity to the vital force of Henri Bergson. This primeval force is expressed in the form of innate interests. Ratzenhofer distinguished five of these interests, which he considered were based on instinctive needs: the procreative interest; the physiological interest which is the interest of self-preservation; the individual interest which is related to self-centered behaviour; the social interest which is determined to develop due to the fact that the procreative interest forces man to a social interaction resulting in a blood bond through consanguinity; the transcendental interest which concerns man's relation to the universe and the infinite.

Ratzenhofer believed that human behaviour could always be reduced to these five interests. Presnt-day psychology does not sustain such a conception; nowadays the influence of the milieu is considered to be a factor possibly even more decisive to human behaviour than innate drives.

Ratzenhofer's psychological conception was the base for an original theory of society. Interest-seeking behaviour to Ratzenhofer motivates all social action. This leads to a number of reciprocal relationships between individuals. The sum total of these relationships is the social process. It is now only in the social process that society exists; society is not an entity, not a being, but a "becoming", a moving complex of reciprocal relationships, the social process itself *(3)*.

The theory of social evolution which Ratzenhofer based on these conceptions was a typical theory of conflict and will therefore be discussed in *(I.B.3.d)*.

Another direction towards a non-mechanicistic approach of social evolution can be found in the theory of Ellwood *(4)* of which some elements already have been discussed in *(I.B.1.c)*. He saw social progress as a process of intercommunication and interlearning, resulting in collective learned adjustments. But Ellwood did not consider society as a mechanism and he was of the opinion that there are various possibilities of learned adjustments which result in a variety of social behaviour.

There is no conflict between this theory and the conception of cybernetics which was disclosed two years after Ellwood's death. Cybernetics is a denial of mechanicism applied to social evolution; it cannot provide us with a detailed theory telling us how social evolution should occur in every situation; a cybernetic approach might however provide us with some general principles which provide a framework for a variety of opportunities of social evolution, the selection of which may depend on various and capricious combinations of definiteness and arbitrariness. A cybernetic conception of social evolution requires both Ratzenhofer's vision of reciprocal relations between individuals as well as Ellwood's ideas on communication and interlearning *(5)*.

(I.B.3.b) Linearity and Non-Linearity in Theories of Social Evolution. We have already seen the distinction made by Hobhouse between social evolution and social progress *(1)*. Social evolution may include, according to Hobhouse, both retrogression and advance; the notion of social progress then concerns advance alone.

Evolution cannot indeed be seen as a process in one direction, only, viz. forward, as it was thought to be during the 19th century and as it was still held in the first half of the 20th century by Bergson and Teilhard de Chardin. Both organic and social life have their retrogressions. If however we take, following Ellwood, social evolution as a learning-process *(2)* - and the same attitude is, according to Wiener *(3)*, permitted towards organic evolution - then we see that retrogressions have a necessary function in evolution, because of the fact that from a retrogression so much can be learned that it could lead to a pattern of behaviour which may be considered as an advance with respect to the retrogression.

Separated from the distinction between progress and retrogression is the problem as to whether the ultimate result of alternations between these two notions, provided that learning indeed did occur and result in advance, is the course of one determined opportunity. In the preceding paragraph reference has already been made to the fact that this cannot be the case; a learned adjustment is the result of a choice between various opportunities and the choice can be based both on conscious selection and on arbitrariness.

One of the merits of the Russian sociologist Maksim M. Kovalesky *(4)* (1851-1916) has been the attention which he drew to the idea that, following Comte's opinion *(5)* that social evolution is due to various and interdependent causes, in different epochs, different factors are apparently dominant. So he saw the political factor as dominant during the periods of Alexander of Macedonia, the invasions of the barbarians, of Napoleon; the religious factor dominated during the conflicts between Pope and Emperor, the Reformation certain periods of Chinese history; the economic factor dominated during the transition from servitude to free labour. Domination of a certain factor does however not imply more than it is; domination always occurs in interdependence with other factors.

This is not the place to discuss whether Kovalevsky's examples are completely in accordance with historical reality; a serious objection to the nucleus of the hypothesis could be the idea that political, religious and economic factors seem to be, if not completely, at least to a great extent, interdependent or even reducible to each other.

These objections need not prevent us from taking social evolution, when considered as a learning-process, as a process in which during different epochs, political, religious or economic learning dominated.

Social evolution then cannot be taken as a development which can be conceived in the shape of one straight line, but as a unit of broken lines, starting anew at different points. The breaks may be caused by retrogressions and by alternations of the dominant factor. The units can follow capricious directions, but only to the limits between which development belongs to the possibilities.

Another question however is, whether such limits determine the course of social evolution in such a way that, in spite of opportunities for selection of various directions, the final destination is definite. In other words: is social evolution a process characterized by determination?

(I.B.3.c) Determination in Theories of Social Evolution. If social evolution is a determined process, then this determination might be either finalistic or not, or intermediary. If social evolution is a process which is finalistically determined then this process should have a built-in purpose; if it is not finalistic then the purpose is lacking.

If we were to acknowledge that social evolution has a certain purpose, e.g. an Utopian world of universal brotherhood, then this purpose would determine the course of social evolution as a final cause. If we however deny the working of final causes in the process of social evolution, then this does not imply that the course of this procedure cannot be determined at all. If.e.g. somebody throws a heavy bag loaded with full bottles on a table, then certainly bangs are heard, but it is difficult to consider these bangs as a final cause of the bag or its contents. That bangs occur, however, is a question of determination by the incident's circumstances. In the mechanicistic theories of social evolution we can find a similar non-finalist determination.

If we take social evolution, as in Ellwood's theory, as a process of learning *(1)*, then we may infer that determining factors are experiences, capacities to learn from these experiences and opportunities for application of the learned data. If indeed the learned data is applied, then absence of retrogression, or advance, may result from this, at least ultimately after correction of possible new unexpected retrogressive factors. The occurrence of these consequences is however not a physical necessity but depends upon the human will. Man has many desires, which in their turn are determined by instincts, traditions, reason and the actual geo-physical circumstances. It depends indeed on the actual human situation whether learned data is selected as suitable for the satisfaction of human needs.

It is a well-known fact that human needs exert an urgent pressure upon human behaviour. It is also true that human needs may be in conflict with each other and that man often has to search for a well-balanced solution for their satisfaction. It is ultimately this essential search for an equilibrium which determines the direction of the learning-process which is social evolution. This search could indeed be considered as social evolution's final cause; it is a goal built within the process.

If we indeed acknowledge the search for a balance of solutions for the satisfaction of human needs as social evolution's final cause, then this search should manifest itself in the distinguished areas of social life.

That a theory of social evolution with respect to social evolution's goal should distinguish between goals of evolution in different areas of social life was a valuable idea of the Belgian sociologist Guillaume de Greef (1842-1924) *(2)*. He distinguished between seven categories of social factors, the first of which were economic phenomena. De Greef saw socialization along Syndicalist lines as the goal of economic phenomena. His sixth factor was juridical phenomena, the goal of legal progress being complete realization of contractual relationships and a restriction of the severity of criminal law. De Greef's theory was a stage-theory and will be discussed in *(I.B.3.e)*. We will not discuss here the problem of division of social life into various areas; within the framework of a modern cybernetic approach however such a division should be developed in accordance with cybernetic principles.

Another problem of determination is that of trends in lines of development. These trends can be formulated as the possible ways along which the final cause can be reached. We can distinguish between convergent trends in social development, e.g. trends towards universal brotherhood, to co-operation between states; we can also distinguish divergent trends, e.g. trends towards hatred between individuals, trends towards conflict between states. Also the last type of trends can be directed towards attainment of social evolution's final cause, as will be demonstrated in *(IV.B.3.g)*. In the next paragraph we will see how various theorists considered social evolution as a process of conflict.

(I.B.3.d) Conflict in Theories of Social Evolution. In *(I.B.1.a)* we saw how Gumplowicz put forward a theory in which denial of social evolution was based on a process of a spiral course of conflicts between races, social groups, or states. According to Gumplowicz conflict was destined to remain a struggle by means of armed violence.

There has been no other theorist on social evolution who, being of the opinion that conflict is an essential phenomenon in social life, considered conflict as destined to remain eternally on the physical plane.

Gumplowicz' theory was partly a literal application of Darwin's biological theory of struggle for life to the human social area; it might be formulated as Darwinism without evolution, the other conflict-theories of social evolution only applying restricted forms of social Darwinism.

This latter group of theories holds that armed struggles gradually become replaced by economic competition, intellectual competition, law-suits, socialization, equilibrium, co-operation or adaptation.

This is not the place to treat comprehensively the ways in which these theories consider evolution of conflict, because of the fact that this may not bring us much further towards understanding the role of conflict in the process of social evolution. A few words however, should be said about those speculations, for the course of conflict's role in social evolution is more complicated than a gradual ascent from cruelty to charity, although the reality of this trend in history cannot be denied. Armed conflict still exists and it is pursued with great cruelty, if not against civilian population then certainly against military colleagues. There is indeed some restraining influence on warfare through the provisions of the Law of Nations. However, the Danis are a stone-age people numbering about 100,000 individuals living in the recently disclosed Baliem-valley in Western Irian, who although often solving tribal conflicts by means of primitive arms, follow restrictive customary rules in their warfare which e.g. limit fighting to traditionally agreed hours and places. It is therefore somewhat doubtful whether pure violence has been the original means of solving conflict among human beings.

So far as the role of conflict in processes of social evolution is concerned I have already discussed the dialectic system as developed by Tarde, in *(I.B.2.a)*. There I stated that neglect of the possibility of polarization is a reason why the dialectic systems of Tarde and Hegel should be considered as insufficiently adequate for a full explanation of conflict's role in social life. Hegel's theory will be treated in the next paragraph, because it is a stage-theory.

A question which follows is whether conflict should be considered as the only driving force behind social evolution. A theory affirmative to this question is that of Ratzenhofer *(1)*. In common with Gumplowicz he saw the genesis of the state in the struggle of races; according to Ratzenhofer this state is also originally a conquest state, but, contrary to Gumplowicz, it develops to a culture state; this culture state is a kind of balance of power mediating between individualization and culture freedom on one side and socialization and subordination on the other side; the former weaken the social structure, the latter consolidate it by means of struggle and war, as regards the outside and by means of an internal struggle of interests.

The theories of Gumplowicz, and Ratzenhofer, his disciple, are theories which consider conflict as the only force behind the course of social life; Ratzenhofer however did not follow the extremely rigid ideas of his master.

The first conception of social darwinism, that of Walter Bagehot (1826-1877), was also less rigid than the later theory of Gumplowicz. Bagehot had been the first to apply Darwin's biological theory to phenomena of social evolution and Darwin himself was greatly interested in this development.

Bagehot was editor of the Economist from 1860 until

his death, and published in 1869 the book "Physics and Politics. Thoughts on the Application of the Principles of "Natural Selection" and "Inheritance" to Political Society". This work had a greater influence on public opinion, at least abroad, than Bagehot's other famous works, viz. "The English Constitution" (1867) and "Lombard Street" (1873). In his "Physics and Politics" Bagehot demonstrated that in the course of human history violent natural selection developed towards a selection by discussion. In the first period *(2)* of history, the "preliminary" age, men were united in small hordes and tribes. Religious and legal customs were considered as sacred, and their rule was absolute. Freedom of opinion and tolerance towards deviating behaviour were impossible. But these conditions did have the result that the whole group exerted itself for a common purpose; an absolute rule of custom was therefore a very important stage in civilization's development. The second period is a period of selection between the local hordes as a result of struggles between them; the groups with the less suited customs being either eliminated or integrated in the group with the best suited customs *(3)*. This is the period of "nation-making". The last period is the "age of discussion"; discussion on the use and necessity of laws and customs cause these institutions to lose their sacred and inviolable character. Only civilizations which have entered the "age of discussion" have the capacity to develop themselves; nations who do not liberate themselves from the absolute rule of their sacred customs will remain in a state of "arrested civilization". The European nations, according to Bagehot, only entered fully into the "age of discussion" during the period of Reformation; nearly all Oriental civilizations appeared to him as being of the arrested kind.

The second author on social evolution who brought a conflict-theory of a lesser nature and the first sociologist framing such a theory, was the Russian writer Jacques Novicow (1849-1912) *(4)*. His theory may be considered as a reaction to the school of Gumplowicz. Novicow indeed recognizes the Darwinian notion of struggle for existence as a social phenomenon. But he also recognizes the reality of alliances as a deciding factor in the process of social evolution. Struggle and alliances develop in a progressive series: physiological, economic, political and intellectual are the successive shapes in which they occur. Intellectual strife will become increasingly dominant, the other types still existing but with increasingly less importance.

Another approach towards the problem of conflict

was made by the French sociologist Émile Durkheim (1858-1917) *(5)*, who as a positivist was of the opinion that all biologism should be banished from sociology. He recognized as did Spencer and the Utilitarian school, that increase in division of labour is an important factor in social evolution. But he refused to see this economic reality as the only aspect. Durkheim saw, as a typical distinction between primitive and civilized society, the type of morals or social solidarity; this ethical factor is reflected in the type of legal codes. In its essence Durkheim saw this reflection with respect to civilized society as an obligation laid upon the individual to individualize himself by intensive specialization in order to make his distinctive contribution to social welfare. Division of labour therefore originates from changes in social structure which in their turn arise from an increase in both material and moral density. But now Durkheim introduced banished biology from the rear by explaining this increase in density as increase in population and the changes in social structure arising from it as an intensification of competition forcing individuals to specialization for survival.

Durkheim's theory is therefore still essentially an explanation of social evolution being due to conflict. He indeed recognized the activity of an ethical factor separated from struggle, but it was to conflict that this factor was ultimately reduced.

Durkheim's theory in this respect was opposed by that of his countryman Alfred Fouillée (1838-1912) *(6)*. As a philosopher Fouillée developed the notion of "*idée-force*" (idea with force), by which he understood a self-realizing physical factor. To him ideas exert force on matter; material forces in their turn influence consciousness. The notion of idea included that of desire; desires were to Fouillée the primary driving force behind human activity. Fouillée left the unsatisfactory dualism of mind and matter as posed by Descartes out of his conception, but did not solve the problem.

It is on the basis of this theory that Fouillée emphasized that, besides struggle in the Darwinian sense, co-operation has been a feature of society from its primitive origin onwards. So far indeed as struggle for survival is concerned there is a progressive adaptation to the influence of ideas of superior force by means of imitation, education, customs, legislation, moral codes, religious beliefs and economic practices.

Fouillée's approach gives a modern impression; the

present theories of information and communication claim that the role of ideas in society can be studied as a physical factor and these theories have developed in cybernetics a conception of self-realization. Moreover modern physics, psychology and psychiatry investigate opportunities of mutual influence and common nature between mind and matter. Lastly, Fouillée's attitude towards so-called primitive society has been justified by later developments in anthropology. Fouillée's merit with respect to the conflict-notion in relation to social evolution, it was Teilhard de Chardin who judged conflict beside other phenomena and that he tried to see these phenomena as independent from the Darwinian struggle for survival.

Fouillée having relegated conflict to a lower position, as being only one of the determining factors of social evolution it was Teilhard de Chardin who judged conflict to be a factor probably destined to disappear totally from the social stage *(7)*. In *(IV.B.3.e)* and *(IV.B.3.g)* the problem of conflict will be treated from the point of view of fitting into the framework of this study.

Actually conflict is the object of various branches of study. Psychology studies intrapersonal, interpersonal and group conflicts. Sociology studies the role of conflict in society. Although it considers conflict as a social pathological phenomenon, it sees as conflict's positive side the opportunities of perseverance which it offers to new ideas and suppressed interests. Psychologists and sociologists are however not the only practisers of conflict-studies: conflictology is now growing towards a field of studies in which contributors from other disciplines (law, economics, politicology, biology, physical sciences) also co-operate; the international meeting point is the "Center for research in conflict resolution" at the University of Michigan. Both the negative and positive sides of conflict will be discussed in various subdivisions of *(IV.B.3)*, intrapersonal conflict in *(IV.B.3.d)*, interpersonal conflict in *(IV.B.3.e)*, group conflict in *(IV.B.3.c)* and *(IV.B.3.g)* and conflict between individual and society in *(IV.B.3.h)*.

(I.B.3.e) Social Evolution as a process in Stages. The idea that social evolution is a process which develops from stage to stage is much older than the conception of social evolution itself. Although the theories treated in *(I.B)* defend concepts which distinguish principles of social evolution from those of evolution in

living nature, they had up to this paragraph the common factor that their origin was somehow due to inspiration by developments in biological speculation. However, from the earliest times onwards human beings have tried to formulate their origin and the meaning of their place at the actual end of a chain connecting them with their ancestors.

Mankind's origin was often formulated in a creation-myth, mankind's destination as a prospect of eternal harmony - sometimes only to be reached after an apocalyptic trial. From the time that man became familiar with facts of history or what he considered to be such, approaches were made to find a meaningful order in these facts; this meaningful order was believed to be represented by the periods of stages into which divisions of the course of history were attempted. We will treat here briefly some principal aspects of these endeavours.

Philosophy of history *(1)* was first practised in theological form, interpreting history's purpose as realization of the Lord's Kingdom on earth. Such was the opinion of St. Augustine (354-430), who saw the development of history as consisting of three periods: the lawless, the lawful and the graceful. Another approach was that of Gotthold Ephraïm Lessing (1729-1781), who, rejecting Christianity's historical foundation, upheld that history is similar to God's education of mankind: the world that God is striving for is one of coincidence of highest reason and perfect morality, in which man will do good because it is good *(2)*.

The first approach to a scientific discovery of a logical order in chronologically arranged events was achieved by Giambattista Vico (1668-1774), whose *"Principi di una scienza nova"* appeared in 1725. He saw that a nation's history is influenced by its milieu, its mental conditions, its interests, its inclinations, its ideas *(3)*. He was the first to teach that each nation's history passes through cyclic periods *(4)*. These periods were to him that of the gods, that of the heroes and that of the human beings; after the actual human period the cycle would recommence with that of the gods.

There is no reason to assume that Vico's "metaphysics of humanity", as philosophy of history was called by him, has influenced the biological theories of adaptation. His ideas were only discovered by German romanticism; he is now considered as the forerunner of the school of philosophy of history *(4a)*.

Immanuel Kant (1724-1804) was of the opinion *(5)* that

history has a fairly regular course, directed towards mankind's advancing cultivation and socialization. Man is driven to culture by "antagonism" in society, i.e. by man's anti-social sociability". The human dispositions only have the capacity of full development within society; mankind therefore approaches nearer and nearer to the purpose of a perfect social order. The ideal constitution of this community is a situation of "eternal peace", provided by a League of Nations, by which all wars and outrages will be excluded and law will rule *(6)*.

Saint-Simon (1760-1825) was of the opinion *(7)* that history should be divided into two principal periods, according to the development of human intelligence. These periods were from Moses to Mohammed and from Mohammed to the present time, both periods comprising 1100 years. The second period is that of a continuous progress of science. These ideas were the background for Saint-Simon's ideas on necessary social-economic reforms.

The culmination of these types of theories is found in Auguste Comte (1798-1857), who was greatly influenced by Saint-Simon.

Comte was the founder of sociology *(8)*, which to him was the same as philosophy. Under the influence of Saint-Simon he expected that social phenomena, just as physical phenomena, could be reduced to scientific laws. He taught that the facts of history must be explained not by providential interventions, but by referring them to conditions inherent in the successive stages of social existence. The parts of social existence are always associated with and determined by the contemporary condition of intellectual development. The history of intellectual development now is the predominating agency in the course of social evolution. The key to the history of intellectual development is the Law of the Three States *(9)*, which lays down that there are three successive phases in which the human mind explains phenomena; these phases occur in the following order: the theological, the metaphysical and the positive.

The theological stage is that in which all phenomena are explained as caused by supernatural powers, whether these powers find themselves in an unlimited number of fetishes, in a limited number of gods or in only one deity. In the metaphysical stage it is no longer supernatural powers by which phenomena are explained, but abstract notions, e.g. force or cause. In this stage man indeed has a critical attitude towards his environment but not yet the capacity to create an entirely new philosophical conception and to loosen himself completely from transcendental ideas belonging to the first stage. In the positive stage man limits himself to observation and logical thinking, if he wants to explain phenomena. An answer is no longer sought for the "why", first cause, ultimate goal or inner nature of phenomena, but only for their "how". Only the positive stage is that of real science *(10)*. The different branches of science pass through the three stages, but not during the same period of time; the least complicated branch arrives first at the positive stage, the most complicated arriving last The order is as follows: mathematics, astronomy, physics, chemistry, biology, sociology. Comte now considered his special task to be that of bringing sociology to the positive stage, and because each branch of science was based on results of the preceding, the study of social life and social evolution meant as far as he was concerned the unveiling of the last secrets which science could discover. This new period would culminate in determination of man's future by positive science. Comte himself demonstrated the direction of this apotheosis by the construction of a new religion, based on veneration of mankind - according to T.H. Huxley "Catholicism minus Christianity" - in which God is replaced by Humanity *(11)*.

There is no doubt that Comte's philosophical work has been of great importance and that he was the first to bring forward a theory of social evolution of a more enduring value.

Comte's stage-theory inspired De Greef *(12)* to arrive at an original refined hypothesis. De Greef accepted Comte's classification of sciences but added to this his own ideas on classification of social sciences. He advanced this conception in what he regarded as an order extending and developing from the lower and the simplest to the higher and more complex human activities, as put by Spencer *(13)*. These activities - not mere thoughts -, the social factors, have developed serially, the more complex depending upon the less complicated. The order of social sciences and the social factors upon which they depend, is according to De Greef, as follows:

1) Economics, or the science of social nutrition;
2) Genetics, or the science of population, socially organized;
3) Aesthetics;
4) Collective psychology: religion, metaphysics, positive philosophy;
5) Ethics;
6) Law;

7) Politics;
In each of these categories perfection can be reached by the attainment of a certain goal. These goals are successively:

1) Socialization along Syndicalist lines;
2) A purely contractual civil marriage;
3) Art embodying social aspirations in close touch with the people;
4) Extinction of all religion;
5) The responsible but perfectly free individual;
6) Complete realization of contractual relationships and restriction of the severity of criminal law;
7) Replacement of political sovereignity by Syndicalist structures of natural occupational groups.

Only when perfection has been reached in the first category can it be attained in the second, and so on. In the case of regression the opposite order is followed: political decline will precede legal decline, moral regression can only follow after legal regression, and so on until economic decline follows after the decline of civil marriage.
De Greef sees the economic factor as so predominant in respect to the others that he considers it hopeless to expect that evolution of the other factors might be succesful as long as economic reforms in accordance with Syndicalism have not been realized. The evolutionary changes will then run in the order described above.

Georg Friedrich Wilhelm Hegel (1770-1831) saw in history *(14)* a chronological arrangement of events *(15)* reflecting a logical order. To him this order is the process of the history of the world's mind; mind's substance is freedom; mind or idea is in hostile confrontation with an alien world and strives after a revolutionary transformation of this world *(16)*. This history of the world is the "intelligent, necessary course of the world's mind (*"Weltgeist"*); the world's mind is the same as God. History is therefore God's temporal development, nature being God's spatial extension or externalized mind that is unconscious of itself as mind. Man's history, on the other hand, is that of mind in the act of becoming itself conscious of itself as mind. The urge for self-knowledge induces man to ascend, when his knowledge increases, to the plane of absolute self-conscious mind, or fully actualized God. The separated moments of the world's history are the national minds *("Völkergeister")*, each of which have to accomplish their own mission and which are discharged after fulfilment. So conceived, the world's history is similar to the world's judgement. This implies that the historical development has the aim of giving man insight into his infinite value and procuring freedom for all; the historical facts can however only be understood in the way that only from later events, earlier facts can be explained. The key for unlocking history is the doctrine of dialectics. History is brought about by the conflicts between mind or idea and matter. These conflicts create changes according to the dialectic scheme of thesis, antithesis, synthesis. When the synthesis has been completed the same process may develop again on a higher level *(17)*.

In the conception of Karl Marx (1818-1883) *(18)* Hegel's image of mind in hostile confrontation with an alien world became a notion of "philosophy" in confrontation with a hostile world. To Marx the existing world was not a world in which man had become himself known as God, and the idea that such a vision still had to be realized, brought Marx to the conception that the actual world was not philosophical. To Marx this meant that man was alienated from the world; the visible manifestation of man in his state of self-alienation was to Marx the property-less proletariate; in Marx's thinking man became proletariate as philosophy's material weapon. Proletariate represents the complete loss of man and can therefore only regain itself by man's complete resurrection. Proletariate is no more a class of society but the dissolution of all classes and victims of wrong in general, not of any special wrong.

Man's resurrection now depends on the economic structure of social life and methods of production; this stratum is the lower part of social, political and cultural life; the upper part of these aspects of life is determined by the lower part. Because now in this way it is the lower part of social, political and cultural life which determines the course of history in the upper part, this theory is called economic determinism: economic progress determines social progress. This theory was called that of historical materialism by Friedrich Engels (1820-1895).

Marx saw the changes caused along the lines of economic determinism as a dialectic occurrence and therefore not as a lineate process. The types of society which relieve each other are each other's opposite; the dialectic development is however directed towards a better situation. During the existence of a certain type of society its reversal into its opposite is prepared: the quantitative changes in this period bring qualitative changes about. So the continuous increase of concentration of capitalist enterprises will ultimately result in a complete destruction of the capitalist system. The moment of such a change is that of a revolution; revolution is a natural means of evolution and the proletariat's resurrection can only be attained in this way.

The dynamic process of history runs, according to Marx, from primitive communism along the stages of feudalism, capitalism and socialism to communism. The stage of communism is the highest type of society, where man is free from the burden of labour, except for a minimal amount of work that must be done but that will be accomplished under the most agreeable conditions. For the rest human activity will consist of creative leisure and artistic expression.

It is here that we will leave the most characteristic examples of stage-theories of social evolution. A division of a certain historic development into stages can be useful but we cannot attach more value to it than it actually has, viz. that of giving a certain clarification by indicating important periods of time within the framework of a historical survey.

The interpretation of history is not only determined by time, place and special circumstances of the interpreter but also by what is known about determining factors behind historic events and developments: instead of explaining what has really happened we have only better opportunities to determine what has certainly not been the case.

As it was demonstrated by van der Pot in (Periodisering) *all endeavours to arrange historical facts in such an order that the course of future can be predicted have appeared to be at fault*. By this conclusion there remains no stage-theory of social evolution which can be accepted as a reliable description of reality.

These inferences do not of course exclude the fact that the stage-theories do contain valuable and even truthful notions. They might even comprise hypotheses which are important for the explanation of the historical development of social phenomena, but even then prediction of future developments seems rather dangerous.

The only things that we can distinguish in the course of social evolution are certain trends, as will be discussed in *(IV.B.3)*. We cannot however state whether social evolution is a continuous process or a process which occurs in shocks; but opportunities exist and there seems at present no reliable method for predicting which opportunity is destined to be realized: nevertheless the selection of one of these opportunities may to a great extent depend upon the human intellect endeavouring to guide the process, which may - as historic examples demonstrate - loose control of it.

Another problem is whether the process of social evolution is of dialectic nature. In *(I.B.2.d)* I stated my reasons for rejection of the dialectic principle as a suitable notion for the explanation of phenomena of social evolution. This rejection I maintain, independently of its use, either in an explanation of social evolution as a continuous process, following the theory of Tarde, or in the Marxist conception of revolution, or even in cybernetics *(19)*.

We have now met with endeavours to explain the process of social evolution separated from notions of evolution in biology and separated from developments in the sciences of communication and information. It is now the time to pass on to some theories where the conception of evolution is considered as embracing more than social evolution only and more than biological evolution only.

(I.C) COMMON BIOLOGICAL AND SOCIAL CONCEPTIONS OF EVOLUTION

(I.C.1) Introduction. In the preceding chapters a survey has been given of explanations of evolutionary occurrences in both the areas of biology and of human society. These explanations had the common factor that their approaches were based on the presumption that evolution in those distinguished areas has generally occurred according to different principles: if in a certain case, e.g. the notion of struggle for life, similarities exist, then this is considered as no more than a coincidence.

In this chapter some theories are treated which appear to be based on other principles: organic and human social evolution occur at least partly or even completely according to similar regularities; there is only one notion of evolution and this notion transcends the realms of social life, living nature and possibly inorganic nature.

Whatever the justness of these theories, the attempted approach itself seems the right one, since the development of cybernetics. Some of the following theories can be considered as predecessors of a cybernetic approach towards the problems of evolution; the other theories are at least important for providing insight into the problems which a theory of evolution,not limited to biology or human social life alone, has to face.

We have already met ethical considerations in the theory of Teilhard de Chardin; such considerations will be met again in the theories of Spencer and Julian Huxley. Juridical activities of the two former authors will be dealt with in *(I.D.3)* and *(I.D.2)*; to those of the latter are referred to in *(IV.E.6)*.

(I.C.2) Herder's Philosophy of History. Among those who tried to search for one law, ruling nature, both organic and inorganic, as well as human history was Johann Gottfried von Herder (1744-1803) *(1)*. Herder developed his philosophy of history in the "Ideeen zur Philosophie der Geschichte der Menschheit" (1784-1791). Human history was to Herder a pure natural history of human acts and human motives according to place and time; human history is God's passage through time as well. History is a difficult course towards progress, directed to the rule of reason and love, towards humanity. Herder saw in the course of history a twofold succession of the periods of youth, adulthood and old age: first in the ancient world of the Mediterranean and secondly in the "Northern World" of the

Germanic peoples; in these successions the old age was represented respectively by the Byzantin Empire and Herder's own time. These periods were not to be repeated in the history of the same nation; after the period of old age, which is already a period of decline, downfall is the only destiny to which a nation is doomed *(2)*.

Herder considered a coherence in both organic and inorganic nature, close to that of a cybernetic conception: nature and culture are a great pageant of forces, working in organized shapes by means of organs; not only does a coherence exist between these forces but also an ascending line, running through the points mineral, metal, plant, animal, man. To Herder these forces together are the same as God.

Herder's solution is still influenced by older conceptions in philosophy of history, but he was himself aware of the fact that human progress is related to developments in interhuman communication. In his "Ursprung der Sprache" (1770) he defends the idea that human speech does not have a heavenly or an animal origin, but a human one, viz. as a product of sound and innate reason *(3)*.

(I.C.3) Geiger's Theory of Speech and Evolution. The first 19th century scholar, who tried to explain both phenomena of social and biological evolution was Lazarus (Eliezer Solomon) Geiger (1829-1870), generally known as Lazar Geiger. He was a linguist and a philosopher; from 1861 he occupied a position as teacher at the Jewish high school (Philanthropin) of Frankfurt-on-the-Main.

Already before 1859, the year of Darwin's first publication, and therefore also before the appearance of Spencer's "First Principles" in 1862, Geiger had come to the conviction, that evolution is a fundamental principle of all nature; he arrived at this conclusion during his studies for the preparation of his chief work "Ursprung und Entwicklung der menschlichen Sprache und Vernunft", Vol. I, Stuttgart, 1868; Vol. II, Stuttgart, 1872, 2nd ed. 1899, begun in 1852, the still fragmentary second volume of which was published after his death by his brother Alfred Geiger *(1)*.

Lazar Geiger was the first to apply the conception of evolution to reason and language *(2)*. The human species must originally have been in a condition similar to that of animals, viz. without speech, religion, art and morals. But man's growing familiarity with the world and his increased sensibility to pain have by degrees sharpened his faculty of distinction and comprehension. To this development belongs the evolution of human speech from an insignificant cry ("Sprachschrei") to a meaningful language. The sound of a word now has its source in sound as perceived by the ear, but a word's meaning originates from light perceived by the eye. There has been an evolution from "Sprachschrei" to a word's meaning and from this process resulted the development of reason according to the universal law of causality. The sound of the word and its meaning have, without purpose or consciousness, varied and differed for a great period of time until the two have become quite independent of each other.

The great importance of Geiger's theory is, that it tries to explain human evolution as a development of what might be called codes of information; 20th century theories of information and communication emphasize, that human societies have a coherence, which is not only energetic, like that of a watch, but which is also achieved by information *(3)*.

Geiger's theory of evolution is indeed contrary to a literal interpretation of the Genesis-story, and therefore contrary to doctrines of orthodox Christianity, but it does not conflict with orthodox Judaism *(4)*. Lazar Geiger himself did uphold the cause of Jewish orthodoxy against the movement of reform-Judaism of which his uncle Abraham Geiger was one of the greatest leaders; in 1854 he published a pamphlet against the installation of an organ in the new synagogue in Frankfurt-on-the-Main.

(I.C.4) The Schools of Darwin and Spencer. It was on the base of the Lamarckian theory that Charles Darwin (1809-1882), Alfred Russell Wallace (1825-1917) and Herbert Spencer (1820-1903) contributed to a new conception of evolution which extends over a much greater area than biology alone and which, in spite of the processes of obsolescence to which it was necessarily subject in the light of later researches, still exerts its influence in quite a few branches of natural and moral sciences until the present day.

In 1852 the English Philosopher Herbert Spencer published "The theory of population". Here for the first time since antiquity the idea, that the struggle for life leads to a survival of the fittest *(1)* was expressed. In the same year he published "The Development Hypothesis". In this greatest work on evolution - before Darwin's "On the origin of species" - he demonstrated the reality of evolution in biology. In the year 1855 he published "The Principles of Psychology", a description of the evolution of mind. In 1857 Spencer published his "Progress, its Law and Cause". This work is based on the law of the Esthonian biologist Karl Ernst von Baer (1792-1876), who wrote that biological development passes from general to special, i.e. from homogeneous beginning towards a heterogeneous differentiation: so the line of development in mammals runs according to the progression: organism, animal, vertebrate, mammal. This development can to a certain extent be noticed both in the embryonic growth of the individual as well as in that of the species; it was the German biologist and philosopher Ernst Haeckel *(2)* (1834-1919) who formulated the latter principle in the biogenetic fundamental law.

In 1859 Charles Robert Darwin published his "On the origin of species by means of natural selection, or the preservation of favoured races in the struggle for life". This title embraces Darwin's ideas in a nutshell. Natural selection is the nucleus of Darwin's theory: The number of descendants that are born is much greater than the number that can remain alive; consequently there is a struggle for life resulting in the survival of the fittest. Originally there was only one species, or perhaps there were a few. The present species have developed from the original, because natural selection has exterminated the inefficient individual animals and plants. Only the best adapted, by chance fitted with the best instruments in the struggle for life, have continued their existence and reproduced themselves. This survival of the fittest is the cause of the birth of new species, for the adaptations become hereditary; neither Darwin nor Spencer relinquished their faith in the theory of Lamarck *(3)*. Darwin later considered, under Spencer's influence, the survival of the fittest as the driving force behind evolution. This theory has until now not only greatly influenced biology, but also all the other sciences concerning human and non-human life.

Independently of Darwin a similar theory was developed by the English biologist Alfred Russell Wallace (1825-1917). He informed Darwin about his theory in 1858 when the latter was preparing his book on the origin of species. Then on 1st September 1858 both read their ideas to the Linnean Society in London. The theory developed by Darwin in the "Origin of species", was a biogenetic theory of transformation. The first edition of this work does not even contain the word "evolution". Only in the sixth edition the notion of evolution, as described by Spencer, is introduced and combined with the theory of transformation.

The importance of the theory of transformation is not its break from the traditional vision of nature as an unchangeable order *(4)* - this we can find already in Kant, Leibniz, Maupertuis, Goethe and possibly in Saint Hilaire - but the explosion which it caused in public opinion, especially after Spencer's publication of the "First Principles" in 1862 *(5)*.

In 1858, when considering what he had written so far on evolution, Herbert Spencer was impressed by the unity and order in his theories, and suddenly the idea burst upon him that the principles of evolution might not only be applicable in the science of biology, but in any science, whether natural, social or moral. Spencer spent the rest of his life in demonstrating the truth of this vision. His principal work in this respect is "A system of synthetic philosophy" (10 vol., London, 1862-1896). It embodies the "First Principles" (1862) as a general introduction, the "Principles of Biology" (1872), the "Principles of Psychology" (1873), the Principles of Sociology" (1873-1896), and the "Principles of Ethics" (1893). Moreover Spencer published in 1887 "The factors of organic evolution", in 1858-1874 and 1891 his "Essays"; in 1904 his autobiography appeared.

Spencer's philosophy is based on the principles of positivism and mechanicism. The fundamental mechanical principle *(6)* is to him that of evolution, by which he tries to explain the growth of the whole visible cosmic order, embracing inorganic nature, life, consciousness and society.

Evolution is described briefly by Spencer as an integration of matter, attended by a dispersion of movement *(7)*; this means that evolution is a *differentiation* of the homogeneous into the heterogeneous. This idea of differentiation was adopted by Darwin in his biogenetic theory of transformation. Evolution is to Spencer identical with progress. He does not discuss the possibilities of a decline, degeneration or disintegration. For him there is only one road in history, running from low, simple or little differentiated, to high, complicated, or much differentiated.

Spencer analysed in his "Principles of Sociology" (1873-1896) social evolution as society's development from its military stage to an industrial form. Within a military state the individual is a useful member of society because he is forced to act as such by violence, but within an industrial society its members are useful of their own free will. An industrial society is therefore characterized by a more real coherence between its members, combined with a continuously proceeding differentiation by division of labour. A military society is ruled by despotism and bureaucracy, an industrial society by scientists and engineers.

A peaceful world composed of industrial nations is not to Spencer however the end of evolution. Although egoism is necessary for the development of a peaceful world based on the liberal principle of "laisser-faire, laisser aller" natural selection will gradually cause the proportion of people with an altruistic character to increase. Then the world will grow to a perfect anarchic society without any legal coercion, where all men will obey with pleasure the rules laid down in the "Code of Absolute Ethics", a kind of perfect natural law-system which will be brought about by the process of evolution. Spencer wrote about this in "The Prinicples of Ethics", (1879), Vol. I, part I, The Data of Ethics, p. 275: "one who has followed the general argument thus far, will not deny that an ideal social being may be conceived as so constituted that his spontaneous activities are congruous with the conditions imposed by social environment formed by other such beings. In many places, and in various ways, I have argued that conformably with the laws of evolution in general, and conformably with the laws of organization in particular, there has been and is, in progress an adaptation of humanity to the social state, changing it in the direction of such an ideal congruity. And the corollary before drawn and here repeated, is that the ultimate man is one in whom this process has gone so far as to produce a correspondence between all the promptings of his nature and all the requirements of his life as carried on in society. If so, it is a necessary implication that there exists an ideal code of conduct formulating the behaviour of the completely adapted man in the completely evolved society. Such a code is that here called Absolute Ethics as distinguished from Relative Ethics - a code the injunctions of which are alone to be considered as absolutely right in contrast with those that are relatively right or at least wrong; and which, as a system of ideal conduct, is to serve as a standard for our guidance in solving, as well as we can, the problems of real conduct".

Spencer was the first to apply the conception of evolution to ethical and legal principles. His ideas in the latter respect will be discussed in *(I.D.2)*.

(I.C.5) Haeckel and the German interpretations of Darwinism). The theories of darwinism found special interest in Germany. In this country the darwinian hypothesis became not only an interesting object of study for biological research but also a conception that appeared suitable for adaptation to that typical German climate of opinion of which the first and the second world war were the results.

In the preceding paragraph reference was already made to Haeckel's merits. Haeckel was not only Darwin's most prominent disciple, but he was also one of the great leaders of German *Darwinismus*, which school was more darwinian than that of Darwin and Spencer; Haeckel went so far as to extend the principle of natural selection to inorganic nature, a bold initiative which even Spencer had not dared to take. His theory of an all-embracing "Law of Substance", uniting the principle of evolution with the laws of the constancy of matter and the conservation of energy was indeed doomed to failure, but 20th century cybernetics might provide a key to the solution for which Haeckel sought. In biological respects Haeckel upheld a modified darwinism with Lamarckian features.

It was not, unlike the opinion of Dampier, Haeckel's school of *Darwinismus*, which preached the "omnipotence of selection", but the school of A. Weismann (1834-1914), that of *Neodarwinismus (1)* or *Weismannismus*. It was this latter school which provided a biologic conception that was of use to those who believed that Nietzsche's *Uebermensch* (superhuman) was of "Germanic race" *(2)*.

Friedrich Nietzsche (1844-1900) was indeed of the opinion that the *Uebermensch*, depicted in his poem *"Also sprach Zarathustra"*, could only be created along the lines of eugenic measures; he also taught that morality and theology should be restated along the lines of the theory of evolution. But Nietzsche never thought that the Germanic race was superior and he detested anti-Semitism *(3)*.

(I.C.6) Julian Huxley and "Evolutionary Humanism". The great finalist theories of evolution, those of Bergson and Teilhard de Chardin, have been treated in *(I.A.3.b.1)* and *(I.A.3.b.2)*. The latter theory especially offered to us an interesting and important example of an integrated approach towards both biological and social evolution.

The theory of neodarwinism, on the other hand, is only a biological theory. Nevertheless an important conception of human social evolution has been developed on the base of this theory. This conception, as will be demonstrated in the following pages has been developed by interaction with the growth of Teilhard de Chardin's theory but is not similar to it. Teilhard de Chardin theories with respect to biological evolution and with its implications for human society have namely some important parallels in the ideas of Sir Julian Sorell Huxley (born 1887), although to Huxley, who reformulated theories of Darwin in the light of new discoveries concerning the mechanism of heredity *(1)*, natural selection is by far the greatest driving force behind evolution. There is no doubt that they mutually influenced each other *(2)*. Both distinguish between biosphere and no-osphere; both refer pure natural selection to the area of biosphere; within no-osphere it is not a struggle for life between individuals, which prevails, but a struggle between human cultures or the social groups which are their exponents *(3)*.

This struggle will, according to both, not lead to a survival of the fittest, but to a cultural unity between the different branches of human civilization *(4)*. This means that they do not accept a certain culture or social group as paramount, but this does not prevent them from distinguishing between lower and higher cultural stages. As Julian Huxley states *(5)*: "A certain school of writers, prominent among whom is Lévy-Bruhl, claim that savages think in an essentially different way from civilised men, and would characterize their thought as pre-logical or a-logical. It is, however, generally admitted that this is an error. Their thought may be extremely logical, but often gives us the impression of illogicallity because it is founded on wrong premises. Apart from this, the chief difference between savage and civilised thought is in the completeness of logical attack, the lengths to which it is pushed, and its use to break down the barriers between different compartments of experience.

The main differences between the low stage and our own consist in the primitive man's failure to have grasped the value of scientific method, and his failure to unify the different aspects of his mental life *(6)*; otherwise the differences are mainly differences of emphasis and of premises".

In spite however of this conformity there are, due to their backgrounds, great differences between the ideas of Julian Huxley and Teilhard de Chardin. The latter was a Roman Catholic priest, the former is an atheist. Huxley, although fully recognizing the activity in the cosmos of spiritual forces *(7)*, which he brings together with the material forces in nature within one monistic conception *(8)*, does not agree with Teilhard de Chardin's theory on centripetal accumulating psychic energy. Therefore it is impossible for Huxley to share Teilhard de Chardin's vision on a future human collectivation, resulting in a super-organism *(9)*. Julian Huxley does not deny that a future world might become a world in which one new human culture, based on human freedom, prevails, but he is of the opinion *(10)* that it will remain composed of human personalities which have kept their individual capacities, for both good and evil; man always remains able to reject evolution and to choose a "Brave New World" as described by Julian Huxley's brother Aldous Huxley.

Julian Huxley has tried to integrate within his ideas on biological and human evolution all the discoveries of scientific and scholarly research, and the result is a philosophical conception which he calls "Evolutionary Humanism" *(11)*. In this conception he defends the inadequacy of the great world religions, Marxism included, to meet the spiritual needs of those who have acquired a clear insight into the discoveries of present scientific and scholarly research. Huxley now tries to demonstrate how a man who is aware of his place within the realm of evolution can satisfy his spiritual needs by scientific and scholarly knowledge and by acting in conformity with this knowledge.

Huxley describes man's place in nature, as revealed by biology, in the following way *(12)*: "He is the highest form of life produced by the evolutionary process on this planet, the latest dominant type, and the only organism capable of further major advance or progress. Whether he knows it or not, whether he wishes it or not, he is now the main agency for the further evolution of the earth and its inhabitants. In other words his destiny is to realize new possibilities for the whole terrestrial sector of the cosmic process, to be the instrument of further evolutionary progress on this planet ..... .
In particular, man is likely to fulfill his destiny more succesfully if he exploits to the full those improvements which have given him his position as latest dominant type, notably his properties of reason, imagination and conceptual thoughts, and his unique capacities of accumulating, organizing and applying experience through a transmissable set of ideas .....
Man's most sacred duty, and at the same time his most glorious opportunity, is to promote the maximum fulfilment of the evolutionary process on earth; and this includes the

fullest realization of his own inherent possibilities".

This realization can be achieved in a society where development of scientific research and the practice of various arts are encouraged.

In *(I.C.7)* I will discuss a.o. Huxley's normative description of evolution and some implications of Huxley's religion of "Evolutionary Humanism".

(I.C.7) The elements for a Normative Description of Evolution. The preceding enunciation of the evolutionary conception, as developed particularly in biology and social sciences, requires an amplification by an exposition of the actual stage of thinking about the question as to what should now really be understood by the pure notion of evolution.

In *(I.B.1.d)* we met with Hobhouse's normative description of evolution as any sort of growth, and the applications of this description to social sciences. In that paragraph the reasons were stated for rejecting the applications of this description to social science. It is here necessary to reject Hobhouse's description as such; growth cannot be considered as similar to evolution, because it may also imply a regression, as can be seen in the examples of extinct pre-historic animals like the mammoths or the giant reptiles; the social implications of this subject are treated in *(III.B.1)*. In *(I.C.4)* reference has been made to Spencer's normative description of evolution; in *(I.D.2)* it has been demonstrated why Spencer's application of this description to ethics and law was destined to fail. A fully satisfactory general description of evolution has not yet been developed. This unsatisfactory situation is not of course a deterrent to the making of new theories of evolution, for it is always possible to enumerate a number of symptoms and to distinguish these symptoms from others.

A normative description of biological evolution, which is nevertheless important because it can be used beyond the area of biology, has been given by Sir Julian Huxley *(1)*. This description is therefore especially interesting, because it gives a solution for the difficulty that the establishing of an event or phenomenon, whether it is an advance in relation to preceding events or phenomena, or not is always based on subjective appreciation. For Huxley gives an objective criterion of what he calls evolutionary progress *(2)* when describing that of biological progress *(3)* as *advance in the making for greater control over the environment and the making of greater independence of changes in the environment (4).*

The Dutch philosopher K. Kuypers *(5)* criticizes Huxley's normative description because it is difficult, in his opinion to use it as a general criterion, and because it is useless in respect to human values. It might indeed be possible to apply Huxley's description in relation to all physical sciences, but difficult in relation to for example the development of the attitude towards criminals: greater control here may imply either a less cruel attitude as well as death-penalty for less important crimes. When considering Kuyper's remarks however it should be emphazized that it was Huxley's intention to give a description to which an ethical criterion may be applied *(6)*. Huxley formulated such a criterion himself when saying *(7)* "that man's role is to discover his destiny as agent of the evolutionary process .... Ethical progress of society, and indeed human progress in all its aspects, consists not in combating the cosmic process but in wrestling with it (as Jacob wrestled with the angel), and in finding out what we can do to direct it, and this depends on our understanding of it and on our learning how to discharge our role of leadership in it".

Huxley speaks in this connection of an increasing realization of possibilities *(8)*. This "general way of thinking about man's destiny" is called by Huxley "Evolutionary Humanism".

Huxley's description embodies however special limitations: it can only be used in respect to a relationship between a living creature and its environs. So when considering advancement in means of transportation, evolution of, for example the automobile could be described as man's increasing control over the automobile and his increasing independency of changes - by wear and tear or accidents - in the automobile. If we now want to establish advance in the automobile, then man should be considered as not varying. Advance in man as an automobile-driver might on the other hand only be established when considering the automobile as not subject to changes.

Here now we meet a structural disadvantage in Huxley's description: something that varies should be referred to a non-varying environment; the varying is always contra-distinguished from the non-varying. This does not mean that it is an entirely useless description, for during a relatively short time a living creature or a group of living creatures could indeed be considered as unchanging, and so the environment's changes might be studied step by step, as in our example of the changes in the automobile.

It is however difficult to take the environs for a relatively short but sufficient space of time, as invariable for the purpose of studying the control over the environs: one cannot completely study the driver's control over the automobile when considering the automobile as not subject to wear and tear or accidents. But it is impossible to take the environment as invariable for studying independence of changes in the environment: one cannot study the automobile-driver's independence of his car's wear and tear or accidents if this car is considered as not subject to wear and tear or accidents.

There is moreover another inconvenience in the use of Huxley's description. When again taking the example of the automobile we meet with two kinds of environment in relation to the motor driver; first the automobile as a machine which he has to learn how to control, and later the automobile, now under control, amidst other automobiles in the highway traffic, which he also has to learn to control. In the first case control over the environment is acquired by the driver alone: when learning the use of his tool, man and tool start to form a unit. Huxley's description here seems only applicable as long as man and tool have not united, for after this occurrence the tool does not belong to man's environs any more but has become an extension of man himself. In the latter case control over the environment is neither acquired by the driver alone, nor by the automobile alone, nor even by the driver and his automobile taken together as a unit of man and tool, but by co-operation of all who share in the traffic as units of driver, automobile and highway. The same remarks can be made regarding independence of the environs.

In other words: control over the environment and independence of changes in the environment here seem to be acquired by the environment itself; and the living creature, taken together with its tools, seems to participate in its environment to such an extent that it does not seem incorrect to conclude that its environment includes itself.

If a notion of environment does comprise a unit of man and tool to such an extent that no separation can be made between the environment and that which the environment surrounds, then we may infer that the notion of environment has lost its meaning. Then actually this extent is a situation of integration between the living creature, together with his tool as an extension piece, and certain aspects of the world around him. This situation is that of an *entirety*, consisting of parts and of relations between these parts, which is directed towards an increasing control over *itself* and an increasing independence of changes in *itself*. Julian Huxley's description here does not appear as applicable any more, for it does *expressis verbis* establish the environment's control by a factor, i.e. a living creature, clearly distinguished from the environment.

So in the case of the automobile it is actually the relationship between man and automobile to which an advance can be established, but not to man or automobile when separated. Such a relationship embodies a situation of integration which may range from a very small amount of integration to that of being fully integrated. Whatever grade of integration might be reached, the more or less integrated components make together within this situation of integration more than their arithmetic sum *(9)*. Integration of such a relationship now means that the more the relationship is integrated, the greater will be its control over itself and independence of changes in itself.

So in the relationship between man and motor-car on one side and the highway on the other, the unit of man and automobile has to be adapted to requirements of the highway and the highway has to be adapted to the requirements of the unit of man and automobile. The integration then reached between the two components gives the relationship a greater control over itself, the more so when the requirements for safe driving are fulfilled by both of its components. The relationship has a greater independence of changes in itself; more changes in one of the two components do not mean that arrival at the destination will be later than it would have been had no such changes taken place; in other words: the relationship's stage of integration is similar to its stage of advance.

In this example it would not be just to establish that it is the driver alone who makes this relationship between himself and his car on one side and the highway on the other obtain this control and independence, for behind the highway stand the persons who are responsible for its construction and its use, as well as the rules for highway traffic, for which men are also responsible.

Drivers, motor-cars, highway, traffic rules, traffic signals, traffic regulators thus make together an operationalized system, "a device for converting incoming messages into outgoing messages" *(10)*, directed towards an optimal control over itself and independence of changes in itself. So the above-mentioned traffic accessories are related to each other in a system of action and reaction which has self-regulating properties.

The discovery of a normative description of evolution

should therefore be attempted by considering the self-regulation of a system of action and reaction composed of a unit of living beings and environs *(11)*. The subject of systems however, with self-regulating properties, belongs to cybernetics. It now appears that we cannot find a satisfactory general description of evolution without using ideas which the science of cybernetics has developed.

The goal of this study being to find principles of legal evolution, a cybernetic approach towards the problem of describing evolution would mean that legal evolution should be described with the help of cybernetic notions. Before trying to construct such a defintion, however, an investigation is necessary into some fundamental questions which arise when trying to discover whether the conception of evolution is applicable to law.

(I.D) THE ROLE OF LAW IN CONCEPTIONS OF EVOLUTION

(I.D.1) Introduction to the problems of Legal Evolution. The conception of evolution has now been discussed from biological and social points of view as well as from considerations which take this conception as a common notion of various branches of science. The moment has come now for considering the conception of evolution in the area of jurisprudence.

An investigation into possible influences of the evolutionary conception on jurisprudence leads to disappointing results. Certainly, the word evolution is not completely lacking in literature on jurisprudence but its sparing use is always limited to the actual meaning of development and never related to a philosophic interpretation of this word *(1)*. Therefore it is not in the literature on jurisprudence that we can find some data on introduction of the evolutionary conception into this branch of science, but among those theorists on evolution who took legal subjects into their considerations.

There are three of the greatest among these theorists who have developed activities in the legal direction and even in the same branch of jurisprudence, viz. that of fundamental human rights. Spencer and Teilhard de Chardin have both given us a theory of human rights within the frameworks of their theories of evolution *(2)*; Sir Julian Huxley's work in this respect is however still more unique although he did not elaborate a human rights-conception immediately based on his own theory of evolution. In the years 1946-1948 Huxley was invested with the office of Director-General of U.N.E.S.C.O. and in this position he fulfilled an important role in the framing of the Universal Declaration of Human Rights. This declaration has reached the limits of positive law in the shape of internationally recognized *ius constituendum*. Huxley's work in this respect will be mentioned in *(III.E.6)*.

It is not a curious coincidence that it has been the human rights problem which occupied these three scientists. If we take the conception of evolution as comprehension of human destiny, it stands to reason, that one should not only look at the past, but also consider the future. From the great number of tragedies from which humanity has suffered and still suffers the idea is formed that continuated human evolution is desirable and that humanity's development in future requires an efficient protection of man against man. The juridical base for such a protection, which is a protection of human evolution itself, cannot but be found in the acknowledgement that each human being has certain inviolable and unalienable rights. A human rights conception is therefore an essential part of any theory of human evolution.

Moreover, the ways in which human rights in a nation are attributed or not, the ways in which such rights, if recognized, are actually protected, are indications of human evolution. A nation may be provided with a perfect set of positive laws, but if these are not accompanied by real protection of a minimal and essential framework of fundamental human rights, then there would appear to be something wrong with human evolution. We may therefore conclude that a parallelism might exist between the practise of human rights and human evolution.

There is more however. Law itself is, like it will be argued in *(III.B.1)*, a basic instrument in the regulation of processes of human or no-ospheric evolution. This means that relative to evolution of no-osphere, legal evolution is a determinative factor. The consequences of this will be discussed in *(IV.B)*, but here it seems important to devote a few words to the ways by which law in this study is approached.

Law's human side is by far the most important; law has been created for men, not for lawyers. This does however not imply that law's strict juridical side should be neglected. As long as we ourselves realize that law regulates relations between human beings and not between juridical abstractions we should elaborate our juridical distinctions towards the greatest possible refinements and perfection, for this is in the interest of human beings for whom the law has been created.

It is for these reasons that - without neglecting the human side of legal evolution - investigations are required into legal evolution's strict juridical nature; this means research into the fundamental structures of law with integration of both the human and the strict juridical aspects. It is therefore necessary to consider what has been done in this respect.

Now in *(I.D.2)* and *(I.D.3)* the human rights theories of Spencer and Teilhard de Chardin will be treated. Hereafter, in *(II.A)*, *(II.B)* and *(II.C)*, I will discuss researches into the fundamental structures of law, especially those from the school of analytical jurisprudence. It will appear that within this school important contributions have been made for the isolation of law's fundamental structures. It will however appear as well, that the greatest merits within this school are counteracted by incomplete or even untenable considerations on basic juridical notions.

In *(II.D)*, *(II.E)* and *(II.F)* therefore a new endeavour will be made to isolate the fundamental structures of legal relations, based on developments in modern logic and on the hope that the objections against earlier attempts have been obviated. In *(III.C)* the isolated fundamental legal structures will gain their place within a cybernetic approach towards the nature of juridical relations.

(I.D.2) Fundamental Human Rights in Spencer's Theory of Evolution. It was Herbert Spencer who, in his "Principles of Ethics" (1893), was the first to introduce the theory of evolution into jurisprudence. He tried here to formulate a new moral law, based on biology. This was contrary to the ideas of Thomas Henry Huxley (1825-1895), who in the year of 1893, in his "Romanes Lecture on Evolution and Ethics" at Oxford, stated that biology could not possibly form a key to ethics, because of nature's cruelty *(1)*. Spencer now stated, that behaviour conforms to the highest morality when it causes a greater integration and a greater coherence of the individual or the group amidst a heterogeneity of ends *(2)*.

It can be argued that this opinion does not account for determination by time, place and circumstances of the causes of greater integration and coherence and of the targets and their heterogeneity. Spencer was himself aware of this objection and he tried to anticipate it by using the basic concepts of Utilitarianism. He stated that progress of justice is only possible, when the external antagonisms of the communities decrease, whilst there is an increase of the internal harmonious co-operation of their members. This development now was to Spencer merely a question of pleasure, for pleasure promotes function; living beings must, upon pain of extinction, take pleasure in actions conducive to their survival. Spencer understood by conduct the adjustment of acts to ends; good conduct is that which is conducive to the preservation of a pleasurable life in a society so adjusted that each attains his happiness without encroaching upon that of others. Justice *(3)* itself was defined by Spencer as the freedom of each man to do what he likes, as long as he does not encroach upon other men's freedom *(4)*. This formulation embodies a program of fundamental human rights *(5)* and reconciles the idea of a universal peace with that of natural selection.

The rights developed from this principle are a right to physical integrity, rights to free motion and locomotion, rights to the uses of natural media, a right of property, a right of incorporeal property, rights of gift and bequest, rights of free exchange and contact. Fundamental rights of women, of children and the so-called political rights (the right to vote) are treated as a special group. Spencer considers each person as inviolable and therefore condemns war; each person is entitled to own the enjoyment of life, freedom and striving after happiness; everybody is entitled to own the fruits of his labour as private property *(6)*.

The latter principle is quite in accordance with the idea of natural selection, because the element of competition in it gives, according to Spencer, equal changes to all men according to their talents; natural selection even requires this principle, for it would mean the end of human society, if the less gifted enjoyed the same profits as the better talented. The shape of the state, either democratic, oligarchic or aristocratic, is in this respect less important, as long as the state realizes the conditions for a "laisser-faire" economy.

Spencer's notion of evolution being that of a differentiation of the homogeneous into the heterogeneous, as for example division of labour in a factory, there seems an antagonism between this conception and that of behaviour which conforms to the highest morality when causing a greater integration and coherence of the group amidst a heterogeneity of ends. Division of function and integration towards coherence are different trends, both with opportunities for progress and regression. This does not however exclude the fact that Spencer's endeavour to formulate an ethical principle based on that of evolution was an interesting approach towards a solid and scientific foundation of morality outside the sphere of religion.

There is also an antagonism between this ethical principle and that of natural selection; it is however on both principles that Spencer's ideas on fundamental notions of law are based; this approach is sound and even wise, attempting to reconcile as it does the sometimes unrealizable requirements of morality with the sometimes unrealizable desires of human nature.

Spencer's outlook towards society's future development into a community with the features of both anarchism *(7)* and liberalism represents a similar reconciliation of the antagonism between morality and natural selection.

The reason why it is of indifference to Spencer whether a state is democratic, oligarchic or aristocratic can be explained by the idea, that, as long as economic liberalism is maintained, any state will develop to a society without any legal coercion.

Spencer's ideas on law and society were largely determined by the economic growth of England during the 19th century and it would be too easy to criticize these ideas without taking into account the dreadful poverty and other social evils during the same period in the same country. We should understand that Spencer was a child of his time and that he faithfully endeavoured to sketch the lines for the development of a world of happiness for all.

The idea of natural selection, anyhow in a restricted shape, seems indeed to play a role in human society, either because various grades of competition exist in different societies or simply because it is an article of faith among businessmen. Norbert Wiener has taught us, from his cybernetic point of view, that Darwinian selection is a way of learning of the species *(8)*. Such a conception implies that it is the species' interest and not the individual's for which natural selection is a must. If this is true, then it is not possible, as Spencer did, to entitle everybody to the ownership of the fruits of his labour just because of the idea of natural selection; the cybernetic view of natural selection, of a species' learning or accumulation of retrievable information *(9)*, implies earlier a claim of society to the fruits of the individual's labour, at least to excessive fruits beyond what is reasonably necessary for an amply sufficient provision of his personal wants.

(I.D.3) Fundamental Human Rights in Teilhard de Chardin's Theory of Evolution. The human rights-conception which Teilhard de Chardin developed *(1)* as a consequence of his ideas on futural human evolution is of a different nature to Spencer's.

As far as the human rights declaration of the year 1789 is concerned, Teilhard de Chardin was of the opinion that this declaration was only intended to assure each human being a maximum of individual *isolated* development. Teilhard de Chardin however believed that a modern human rights declaration can at present, as in the 18th century, no longer assure to the individual the greatest possible independency within the community; such a declaration now should define the conditions of the unavoidable collectivation of mankind; these conditions should be defined in such a way, that human collectivation is not destructive to the individual, but will raise the "incommunicable singularity" of the individual's being to a higher stage which is not the same as the individual's "independency".

Teilhard de Chardin now distinguished three of such conditions which should somehow be comprised in any new declaration of human rights:

1) A duty for the individual to develop himself to the greatest possible perfection or personalization. The reason for this duty is, that on the individual's perfection the perfection of all others around him is dependent.
2) A right for the individual to be placed in the milieu which is the most favourable for his full psychical and physical development. Society has to realize this right in its own interest.
3) A right of the individual not to be misformed or forged by external force, but to become a member of the super-organization as a consequence of persuasion.

The meaning of the third condition is that a person should not be convinced of a wish to become a member of the super-organization by means of brain-washing, for then he recognizes as truth what in his opinion is false; super-society should be entered only according to personal convictions and aspirations. If the collective group wants to limit individual independence, then this is only possible in conformity with the internal and free structure of the individual. Otherwise a fundamental discrepancy would be introduced into the heart of mankind's collective organism.

We have three objections against Teilhard de Chardin's human rights theory.

Firstly, this theory depends upon a conception of evolution which we cannot accept. Our reasons for this have been stated in *(IV.B.3.b)*, *(IV.B.3.c)* and *(IV.B.3.f)*.

In the second place it is doubtful whether Teilhard de Chardin's idea that new human rights declarations should express a duty for everybody to develop to the greatest possible perfection, is in accordance with the fact that human nature remains subject to a-moral or animal instincts, the control of which requires the relaxing use of an exhaust valve; a continuous withholding of these requirements may lead to psychical or physical disasters. Moreover, such a duty as suggested by Teilhard de Chardin is of moral nature because it is directed towards an internal activity. Such duties cannot be imposed by means of legal provisions because of the fact that by these only external behaviour can be regulated *(2)*.

Lastly, a right to become a member of an organization, either super - or not -, only as a consequence of persuasion without violence, is a sophism because of the fact that modern psychological techniques make it possible to influence persons in a desired direction without any violence at all. A legal protection against the influence of persuaders, both hidden and public would seem better. This means that Teilhard de Chardin should have placed internal force next to external force in his third condition.

These three objections are not detrimental to the fact that the three conditions formulated by Teilhard de Chardin are a challenge to anyone searching for a new conception of fundamental human rights.

II. Conceptions of fundamental jural concepts

(II.A) THE FUNDAMENTAL JURAL CONCEPTS AMIDST OTHER JURAL FUNDAMENTALS

We require knowledge of the structure of law as far as possible reduced to its fundamentals for investigating the principles of legal evolution. Do we have such a knowledge?

The search for law's fundamentals is not yet at an end. We can distinguish four groups of problems as part of this search:

1) The fundamental units, common denominators or basic jural concepts to which any jural construction is expected to be reducible. Such a concept is for instance a notion of duty or a notion of right.
2) The simplest possible relations between the basic jural concepts of the former group and the role of these relations within jural constructions embracing more than one such a relation.
3) The structure of the contents of norms.
4) The reason for law's binding force.

Ad 1).

The questions concerning law's basic concepts have been elaborated in particular by the Anglo-American school of analytical jurisprudence and the German School of Pandectism. The former school has been influenced by the latter; the German school focused its attention on systematization of 19th century Civil Roman Law; the Anglo-American school seeks a logical analysis of the whole legal order.

The school of analytical jurisprudence has presented an extremely important instrument for legal analysis: a system of fundamental legal concepts or common jural denominators and their basic relations among each other, conceived by Wesley Newcomb Hohfeld. In *(II.B)* a short description will be given of the developments in analytical jurisprudence and its connections with Pandectism which resulted in Hohfeld's system; in *(II.C)* Hohfeld's system will be described; some improvements relative to the exposition of Hohfeld's system will be discussed there and the results of these improvements will be illustrated by showing its applicability to the analyses of jural constructions such as an exception, a nullity, a conclusion of law, a claim, the position of a sanction relative to a duty, a natural obligation.

Ad 2).

What is the role of the basic relations between fundamental jural concepts within constructions which are greater than only one relation between such concepts? E.g. within a contract of sale we can distinguish at least two right-duty relations, which are relative to the position of the buyer who has to pay and the position of the seller who is obliged to deliver. Here the parties are bound by two connections, and legal science has developed terms to designate such connections, but these terms are only figurative notions derived from physical-technical examples in the form of literally binding a prisoner to a person with authority over him.

Law is not however of physical-technical nature, but belongs to the world of information and communication. This world only became a reality in 1948 when the science of cybernetics brought a new image of the roles played by information and communication *(1)*; in *(III.C)* the role of basic jural relations will be investigated from the point of view of cybernetics.

This role is one of the fundamentals for developing in *(IV)* a theory of juridical evolution fitting into a wider notion of evolution.

Ad 3).

The problems concerning the structure of norms are not concerned with the nature of law's basic denominators or concepts, but with the logic of their actual contents. Here the questions are not for example what is a right, or what is a duty, but what should be performed in relation to a certain right or a certain duty. Logical analysis is here concerned with questions as e.g. whether or how far a duty not to steal is logically similar to a duty not to kill. Logic of the content of norms is based on the idea that there are fundamental legal concepts - in our example the concept of duty - which are called "deontic operators" or "deontic modalities" and which determine the character of a norm (a norm is for example to the effect that something ought to be done or to the effect that something may be done), but not the norm's content, viz. that which should or may be done.

Analyses of relations between contents of norms are important in respect to simplification of existing law, making of new law and law's computerization. Such analyses are technical elaborations of fundamental jural principles; they can be promoted by developing such principles, but these analyses themselves are not essential for such a promotion. Thus there is no reason for discussing this interesting branch of deontic logic within the framework of this study. The reader is referred to Kalinowski (Logique), Klug (Logik), Raz (Concept), Ross (Directives), Schreiber (Logik d.R.), von Wright (Action).

Ad 4).

It is a well-known fact that various opinions exist on the reasons why the law should be obeyed. The principles of no-ospheric evolution comprise an ethical criterion, as it will be demonstrated in *(III.B.6.c)*. This criterion is not based on religious or philosophical presumptions, but developed by applying scientific principles common to all sciences, viz. principles of cybernetics. The ethical criterion is treated as a basic reason for law's binding force in *(IV.D)*.

(II.B) THE SCHOOL OF ANALYTICAL JURISPRUDENCE AND ITS CONNECTIONS WITH PANDECTISM

The purpose of analytical jurisprudence is to construct by means of classification of jural notions a universal framework for the legal systems in developed states. Such a classification is based on the presupposition, that law is an aggregate of logically interdependent rules. The use of such a classification has never been doubted when intended for teaching purposes. Analytical jurisprudence however was considered and is still considered by a great number of today's lawyers, as useless for the purpose of enabling lawyers to find their law. Nowadays and still more in the future, when legal practitioners will use computers for finding their law more quickly, a change will take place: there cannot be any computerization without classification.

A universal framework for bodies of rules of law was one of the preoccupations of Jeremy Bentham (1748-1832) who in 1789 published his "Introduction to Principles of Morals and Legislation". Not only through this work, but also by his correspondence with statesmen in Europe, America and even Egypt (Mehemet Ali), Bentham stimulated a movement for codification based on classification. In this way he influenced the French codifications of the early 19th century as well as the codifications in other countries which are based on the French codes.

The 19th century analytical jurists wished to create codifications analogous to the *Corpus Juris* of Justinian and the *Code Napoleon* as bodies of law which are complete, either actually or potentially, for all possible cases. They searched at least for logically interdependent percepts in order that comparative analyses could produce a universal systematic structure.

This endeavour was in accordance with the other two dominant methods in jurisprudence: not only the analytical school, but also the historical and the philosophical schools tried to organize legal science with stable materials, or at least with materials undergoing a certain development in a determined course.

The three schools of jurisprudence presupposed as the basis of their activity, certain non-juridical instruments. The analytical jurists based themselves on logic, the historical jurists on the idea of historical continuity and the philosophical jurists on a metaphysically given fundamental such as the will of God, or divine reason, or human reason. The development of these schools was affected by mutual influence.

The oldest school is the philosophical. Originating in ancient Greece it flourished in the 17th and 18th century as it flourishes now. Its main link with the analytical school is logic, because it is by means of logic that this branch tries to derive a body of legal principles from a metaphysically given fundamental. The main result in this respect which greatly influenced analytical jurisprudence was the idea of a law as a command; this idea may be found in the works of a.o. Thomas Aquinas, Donellus, Grotius and Blackstone and was elaborated by Bentham and Austin.

The historical school was a reation to the philosophical school, especially the branches which based natural law on divine or human reason. Its forerunner, Gustav Hugo (1764-1844) concluded from the comparative materials in Montesquieu's "Esprit des Lois" that law should be different among different nations because it should be adapted to their various circumstances of life. From Kant's theory of knowledge he concluded that reason is not able to create knowledge and therefore not able to create norms; reason was to Hugo a faculty to estimate certain historicallydetermined materials according to certain points of view. This criticism caused not only the ending in about 1850 of all teaching that natural law is based on reason, either human or divine, but it was also a stimulus to the development of historical jurisprudence.

This movement started in 1802, when Friedrich Carl von Savigny (1779-1861) published his *"Recht des Besitzes"*. Savigny was of the opinion that legal theory is nothing but legal history. His program had a curiously negative purpose. The medieval developments in law were to him impure additions to Justinian law, in violation of the sources and irrelevant *(1)*. Justinian law should however not only be purified, but also be reconstructed to a harmonious system without inner contradictions. This latter idea became the leading principle of *Pandektenharmonistik (2)*. The historical school searched for a modern and harmonious system of Justinian Law for practical use in Germany, where during the 19th century civil law was still Roman Law. When in about 1880 the coming modification in the *Bürgerliches Gesetzbuch* which was to replace Roman Law in 1900, was realised as inevitable, there was no further need for *usus modernus Pandectarum* and Roman Law studies became directed towards a pure historical approach.

The last great author of the historical school was

Bernhard Windscheid (1817-1892) whose *"Lehrbuch des Pandektenrechts"* (1852-1865) was the great culmination of the systematization and harmonization of a Roman Law body adapted to the requirements of 19th century legal practice. This work is considered as of similar value as Ulpian's commentary or Accursius' *Glossa ordinaria (3).*

However, an important reaction had already emerged earlier against the jurisprudence of descriptions and distinctions. Rudolf von Ihering (1818-1892) had still, in *"Der Geist des römischen Rechts auf den verschiedenen Stufen seiner Entwicklung"* (1852-1865, 3. Band 1858) pleaded for the development of a new knowledge of law by applying pure logical functions to the existing law. In this way he expected to make good the deficiencies in the modern Roman Law system. This method was bound to fail - it is impossible to create new law by classification of the actual jural notions - and Ihering became a renegade. In later writings he made *"Begriffsjurisprudenz"* an object of criticism *("Der Zweck im Recht"*, 1877-1884) and ridicule *("Scherz und Ernst in der Jurisprudenz"*, 1884). Earlier *(4)*, in 1872, in *"Der Kampf ums Recht"* he had already maintained that legal development is not a gradual and organic growth from customary law, active among a nation, to statute law, but a struggle between those who are interested in the old law and those who have an interest in new law: all law originates from conflict between purposes: the target is the creator of all law *("Der Zweck ist der Schöpfer des ganzen Rechts").*

This idea found its place in a description which influenced analytical jurisprudence. In 1888 the fourth edition of *"Geist des römischen Rechts"* appeared and in volume 3.1 Ihering developed a new description of a subjective right. Leading opinion, as upheld by Windscheid saw in a subjective right a faculty to will *("Willensmacht")* granted to the individual by the legal system. From this Ihering made an interest secured by law *("rechtlich geschütztes Interesse").*

The influence of the historical school on that of analytical jurisprudence dates however already from the time of John Austin (1790-1859), who was a pupil of Bentham and who spent the period of 1826-1828 visiting Heidelberg and Bonn to study German methods of legal teaching. There he made stimulating contact with Savigny and other representatives of the historical school. Bentham's important work was undeservedly forgotten and it was commonly supposed that the school of analytical jurisprudence began with Austin . His *"Province of Jurisprudence determined"* was first published in 1842; the most recent edition is that with an introduction by H.L.A. Hart, London, 1954. In 1862 his widow published his *"Lectures on Jurisprudence"*. Again in 1906 Professor Jethro Brown published an abbreviated edition of Austin's earlier lectures.

It was the distinctions and classifications developed by Austin that gave the school of analytical jurisprudence its start. As the main purpose of this school was the development of a classification by means of logic, it rejected all thinking on religious and philosophical criteria at the base of legal systems. A rather recent application of this attitude was Kelsen's theory of pure law.

The school's objective of classification could not be satisfactorily reached in the 19th century because of its attitude towards the notion law *(5)*. Bentham had insisted on regarding law as an aggregate of laws. This idea came down from the medieval study of the Corpus Juris, where every fragment in the Digest was a lex. A law was considered by early English analytical jurisprudence as a rule of conduct, prescribed by a law maker. Towards the end of the 19th century however law was in the U.S.A. viewed from the angle of a legal counsellor of industry and business enterprise, advising his clients what they could do without risk of official or private interference. This resulted in endeavours to describe a law as a prediction (Mr. Justice Holmes) or the basis of prediction (Mr. Justice Cardozo). In England and on the European Continent however analytical jurisprudence attempted to define law from the standpoint of the client seeking advice. This development sought to define a law as a threat of official action, in any case involving the sanction in the theory of command. Thus analytical jurisprudence had reverted to almost the same basic idea as that of Bentham, who also included the threat of sanction in his theory of command, and who described a law from the standpoint of the law maker and the subject simultaneously.

We are of the opinion that such concepts of sanction are fundamentally wrong and in *(II.F.1)*, *(II.F.5)* and *(II.F.6)* it will be demonstrated why.

(II.B.1) The growth of an instrument for Classification. Bentham's work on classification of jural concepts being directed to the notion of "Command", it was Austin who incorporated the term "Right" into his analyses. He justly saw that there are differences between a right against someone who should perform what he is obliged to and a right in the sense of a freedom from obligations. Austin

suggested separating the latter group from rights and calling them "Liberties" (Hohfeld would say "Privileges"); a right thus became to Austin a "faculty" residing in a determinate person by virtue of a given rule of law which avails against and answers to a duty lying on some other person.

In 1862 Windscheid *(1)* made a distinction between two kinds of *"subjektives Recht"*: a right in the Austinian sense and a *"können"*; the latter notion embraces Hohfeld's notions "Privilege" and "Power" *(2)*. Since then the division between different kinds of *"subjektives Recht"* became a matter of discussion among Pandectist writers *(3)*. This discussion influenced Sir John Salmond, who in 1902 distinguished between rights in the generic sense - any benefit conferred by the law - and rights *stricto sensu* - any legally protected interest in the sense of Ihering *(4)* correlative to a duty. The rights in the generic sense included according to Salmond: the rights in the stricter sense, liberties in the sense of Austin, powers (abilities to alter legal relations) and immunities (i.e. immunity against exercise of a power). These legal advantages were distinguished from the legal burdens: duties, disabilities (absence of power), liabilities. Salmond understood by liability both absence of a right *stricto sensu* and exposure to exercise of a power. In 1903 Seckel introduced the notion of *Gestaltungsrecht*, a concept similar to that of power framed by Salmond in the year before *(5)*.

The concepts, developed by Salmond, were adapted by Hohfeld with some modifications. "Liberty" was designated "Privilege"; "Liability" became restricted to its second meaning only; "Liability's" first meaning was formulated by Hohfeld as that of "No Right"; absence of "Liability" became "Immunity".

The eight jural concepts, now isolated, were considered by Hohfeld as fundamental and elaborated in a system which we will now discuss.

(II.C) INTRODUCTION TO HOHFELD'S SYSTEM OF FUNDAMENTAL JURAL CONCEPTS

Wesley Newcomb Hohfeld (1880-1918) was until 1914 professor at Stanford and from 1914 until his premature death in 1918 he was in charge of the courses on trusts and conflict of laws at Yale.

In 1913 Hohfeld published (in 23 Yale L.J.) his system of fundamental jural concepts, which was built on the notions developed in analytical jurisprudence and Pandectism, as they had been brought together by Salmond, as we have seen in *(II.B.1)*. The logical structure of his system was derived by Hohfeld from the logic of Hegel.

Hohfeld applied his system in his lectures and during the short period that it was given to him to teach at Yale he enjoyed the honour of seeing his method approved by several of his colleagues. After his death the colleagues continued to teach by means of Hohfeld's system. Hohfeld still had the satisfaction of receiving letters from former students, expressing their gratitude for the benefits which his discipline in thought and expression had given to them in their profession.

Hohfeld's instrument has been and still is of great influence. It became a methodological tool for law teaching at Yale; it lies at the base of the great private American codification, the "Restatement of the Law"; it was used by the economist John R. Commons ("The Legal Foundations of Capitalism" and "Institutional Economics"); in 1954 it was introduced into anthropology by E. Adamson Hoebel *(1)*.

The system of common denominators conceived by Hohfeld, although succesful, has also been subject to criticism, the greater part of which however was due to misunderstanding *(2)*. There are however some points where criticism seems justified.

The first of these is Hohfeld's terminology. Hohfeld gave names to his concepts which already had established meanings in law, but he deviated in his normative descriptions from these meanings. Other names have been suggested and tried out *(3)*. For purposes of clarity I shall keep in this book to the terms which Hohfeld conceived himself.

The second point is that Hohfeld thought it possible by means of his system "to discern common principles of justice and policy underlying the various jural problems involved" *(4)*. If Hohfeld indeed meant by these cryptic words that he claimed ethical value for his logical construction, then he certainly went too far *(5)*.

The third point, not treated as far as I can see in the main commentaries on Hohfeld's system, is that Hohfeld's logic is Hegelian *(6)*. Hegelian logic is in its essence triadic, i.e. based on three modalities of the nature thesis, antithesis and synthesis. If Hohfeld had chosen Aristotelian logic, or at least a logical system developed with Aristotelian principles, like volitional logic, he would have had the possibility of working with four modalities instead of three. It will be demonstrated in *(II.D)* and *(II.E)* that the application of respectively Aristotelian logic and volitional logic to Hohfeld's system of four basic jural relations will give better opportunities for using it as an instrument for analysis.

First however I will expose in *(II.C.1)* Hohfeld's system in accordance with his own conceptions and thereafter I will give some examples of its opportunities for application in *(II.C.2)*.

(II.C.1) Description of Hohfeld's System. Hohfeld's system is based on the idea, that all legal relations are between persons; legal relations between persons and things are in this conception impossible. Further, every legal relation is bilateral and always reducible to either one or more of four legal relations which are fundamental. These four fundamental relations are reducible to eight fundamental jural concepts; these eight concepts are the denominators for the position of either one of both parties in a fundamental jural relation; similarly they are the common denominators to which any person's position within any jural construction is reducible. Hohfeld believed that all legal problems could be stated in these eight terms *(1)*, basing himself on Hegel's triadic logic *(2)*.

Hohfeld arranged his eight conceptions in the following scheme:

Jural Opposites	*right*	*privilege*	*power*	*immunity*
	no right	*duty*	*disability*	*liability*
Jural Correlatives	*right*	*privilege*	*power*	*immunity*
	duty	*no right*	*liability*	*disability*

Fig. 1

Hohfeld did not state explicitly what should be understood by the notion "Jural Opposites", but from the way in which he treated these relationships it follows that he considered them as what in Aristotelian logic are relations of contradiction or negation. Hohfeld meant that, relative to the same performance between the same persons one cannot similarly have a Right and a No Right (absence of a Right) or a Privilege (absence of a Duty) and a Duty, etc.

The "Jural Correlatives" make the four fundamental legal relations; other relations between these eight fundamental concepts, except these four, are impossible.

We will now formulate the four fundamental relations. The order of the relations and the order of the concepts deviates from the order in Hohfeld's scheme, because our arrangement makes it possible to consider these relations as almost similar to the A-, E-, I- and O-propositions of traditional logic. This consideration will only occur in *(II.D.2)*, but it is useful to keep to standard units in formulation and Hohfeld's intentions are in no way affected by this. Hohfeld's four fundamental relations can thus be formulated as follows:

(A) *Right-Duty:* *A* has a legal expectation that *B* shall do *F* to *A*, and *B* must do *F* to *A*.

(E) *Power-Liability:* *A* may voluntary create a new legal relation affecting *B* with respect to performance *F*, and *B* will become subject to a new legal relation with respect to performance *F*, as soon as *A* has created this new relation by a voluntary act.

(I) *Disability-Immunity:* *A* cannot create by his own act a legal relation affecting *B* with respect to performance *F*, and *B* is not subject to *A*'s attempt to create such a new legal relation.

(O) *No Right-Privilege:* *A* has no legal expectation that *B* shall do *F* to *A*, and *B* is not obliged to do *F* to *A*, but is free to do *F* to *A* or not.

Notice that the relations which exist in their turn between Power-Liability and Right-Duty and between Disability-Immunity and No Right-Privilege are time-related. The Power-Liability relation can be read as: "Not one of the three other relations now, but possibly later if a power is exercised". The Disability-Immunity relation reads then: "Neither one of the three other relations now, nor later by exercise of a Power" *(3)*.

If in these formulations the word "legal" is replaced by "moral", then it is possible to apply Hohfeld's system as a means of classification for moral relationships. Hohfeld believed that juridical and moral relationships are of similar fundamental structure *(4)*.

So far as Hohfeld's terms are concerned, a few remarks are necessary in respect of his scheme:

Jural Opposites	*right*	*privilege*	*power*	*immunity*
	no right	*duty*	*disability*	*liability*
Jural Correlatives	*right*	*privilege*	*power*	*immunity*
	duty	*no right*	*liability*	*disability*

Fig.2

The "Jural Opposites" are pairs of notions which are each other's contradiction or negation. Contradiction or negation is however only a species of a genus "opposition". Other opportunities, offered by traditional Aristotelian logic are contrariety and subcontrariety; see *(II.D.1)*.

Hohfeld's relations of opposition do indeed exist between his fundamental jural concepts, but of these concepts only those placed in pairs of "Jural Correlatives" are of practical jural importance. We will therefore now consider further the relations between the pairs of "Jural Correlatives". So e.g. relations of negation exist between the Right-Duty and No Right-Privilege relation and between the relations Power-Liability and Disability-Immunity.

The notion of Right is used as follows from the formulation,*stricto sensu*. The terms Power, Privilege and Immunity express notions which can be covered by the term Right in a wide sense. The term Privilege is used in a wide sense and has the meaning of a liberty to do or not to do, both when its "opposite" is a Duty to do or a Duty not to do, *(5)*. Of the term No Right it will be demonstrated in *(II.D.6)* that it has not only the meaning of absence of a Right but as well that of presence of a necessity to respect. The concept Power is similar to that of *Gestaltungsrecht* and will be treated in *(II.E.6.a)*. The notion Liability can also be described as a risk to become subjected to a new legal relation or as an exposure to the possibility of such a subjection.

Hohfeld described his concept of Right as synonymous with the term "claim" in the sense of a claim secured by law *(6)*. A Duty was described by Hohfeld as "that which one ought or ought not to do" *(7)*. Duty and Right being considered as correlatives, a Hohfeldian Duty is an obligation of which the performance is secured by law. Such a notion of Duty is always accompanied by threat of a sanction. In

(II.F.1) the reasons will be stated why this conception should be rejected. This rejection however has no influence on the applicability of the examples of Hohfeldian relations which will follow now.

(II.C.2) Examples of application of Hohfeld's System. Hohfeld's system of fundamental jural concepts is applicable in all areas of law, and it is therefore impossible to give here an exposition of all its opportunities *(1)*. I can but give here a few simple examples of the ways by which it can be used to lay down the fundamental structure of legal constructions. Some more complicated examples will be given in *(II.D.7)* and in the subdivisions of *(II.F)*.

Hohfeld denied the possibility of legal relations between a man and a thing, and considered all legal relations only possible between persons.

Property, rights *in rem* and other absolute rights should in Hohfeldian terms be described as collections of fan-shaped jural relations, relative to a certain estate, thing or right *in rem*, between one party on one side and all other natural and legal persons in the world on the other side.

A right *in rem* was therefore termed by Hohfeld a "multital right": residing in one person it affects a very large number of people. Hohfeld called a right *in personam* a "paucital right", because, residing in one person, it affects only a few other parties *(2)*. The same applies to property and other absolute rights.

If A has a property, right *in rem* or another absolute right the following types of Hohfeldian relations exist *(3)*:

1) A collection of No Right-Privilege relations in which it is A's Privilege to do or not to do with his property or right *in rem* what he wants while B, C, D and all other possible persons have a No Right that A does what they want in this respect.
2) A collection of Right-Duty relations relative to any person's obligation to refrain from intervention in A's enjoyment of his property, right *in rem* or other absolute right.
3) A collection of Disability-Immunity relations in which A is immune from all the machinations of those who plan to impose upon him in respect of the property concerned or right *in rem* or other absolute right the burden of a new legal relation in the shape of a Duty, Liability, Disability or No Right.
4) Incidental Power-Liability relations with prospective buyers, or persons who want to obtain a right *in rem*

buyers, or persons who want to obtain a right *in rem* relative to the concerned property, right *in rem* or other absolute right. In the case where A makes an offer to B, he has a Liability for entering into a new jural relationship with B as soon as B exercises his Power to such an effect. If B makes an offer to A it is A who has the Power to create a new legal relationship between himself and B; B has a Liability to this effect.

If in these cases a Power is exercised having the effect of a new legal relationship between A and B, e.g. when A sells property, then at least two Right-Duty relations originate between them, viz. relative to delivery of the goods by A to B and to payment by B to A. In addition, the figure of the representative also belcngs to the species Power-Liability relation. He has a Power to create a legal relation to which the represented is subject, the represented having before the creation of this relation a Liability in respect of the representative, that he will fulfil his possible future Duty to the partner with whom the representative might create a new legal relation.

A Power-Liability relation is also that between a State and its subject, the State having a Power to impose taxes, the subject having a Liability for a possible obligation to pay taxes, which the State will impose upon him in future.

Disability-Immunity relations also exist between State and subject; the subject's fundamental rights may provide him with Immunity from Duties which a State has a Disability to impose, such as a Duty to marry a certain person. Such a fundamental right embodies moreover a relation in which the subject has a Privilege to marry or not to marry whom he likes, the state having a No Right in this respect.

In penal law we meet the Disability-Immunity relation in several well-known instances. The accused has an Immunity from treatment as a guilty person so long as his guilt has not been legally proven. The prosecution, representing the legal community, has a Disability in this respect.

If a person has been found guilty, then he enters into a Power-Liability relation in which his Liability to punishment may be converted by the Power of the judge into a Duty to pay a fine or to suffer imprisonment, while the state obtains a Right to execution.

A Disability-Immunity relation is further expressed in the fundamental penal law principle *"nullum crimen, nulla poena, sine praevia legi poenali"*.

(II.D) ARISTOTELIAN LOGIC APPLIED TO HOHFELD'S SYSTEM

Some logical connections between Hohfeld's fundamental jural relations, which are treated in traditional logic, are not treated by Hohfeld, although his system is intended to be consistent with logic. Hohfeld's fundamental jural relations are four in number and the number of contradictory pairs of jural relations is two; in these respects it contains all the necessary basic data for establishing that some interrelationships exist which Hohfeld did not mention. The result of this may be an arrangement of the four basic jural relations which, compared with Hohfeld's system, is more appropriate in legal analyses, legal education and law's computerization. We can do this analogous to the well-known Aristotelian square of opposition. It is therefore necessary to describe this square now.

(II.D.1) The Notion "Square of Opposition". A "square of opposition" *(1)* is a diagram representing logical relations between forms of opposite statements:

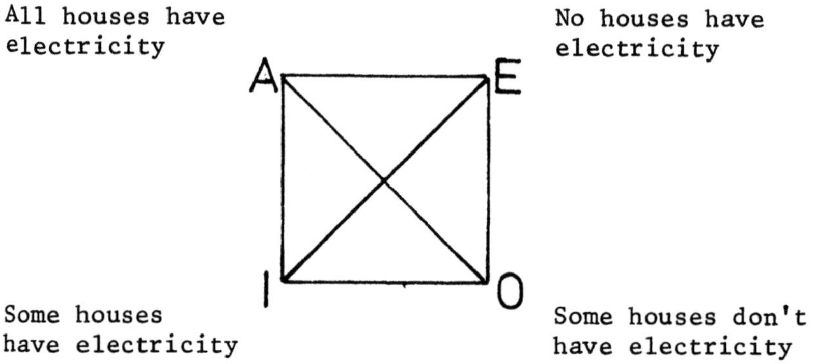

Fig. 3

The letters A, E, I and O traditionally represent the forms of statements or propositions: A is universal affirmative, E is universal negative, I is particular affirmative, O is particular negative. The affirmative propositions are given by the first two vowels in the Latin word "A f f I r m o" and the negative ones by the vowels in "n E g O".

The following relationships exist between A-, E-, I- and O-propositions:

1) A and E are *contraries*: these *can't* both be true and *can* both be false

2) A and O, as well as E and I, are *contradictions*:
these *can't* both be true
and *can't* both be false.

The contradiction of a statement is also called its *negation*.

3) I and O are *subcontraries*:
these *can* both be true
and *can't* both be false.

4) A and I, as well as E and O, stand to each other in the relation of a *superimplication*:
The truth of A implies the truth of I, but the truth of I does not imply the truth of A; equally the falseness of A implies the falseness of I, I's falseness not being implied by the falseness of A; A super-implies I and I subimplies A. The same reasoning applies to E and O. So if A is true, then I is true, hence E is false and therefore O is false.
Notice that if I is false, A is false, because if A is true, O is false and O's falseness is incompatible with the false-ness of its subcontrary I; if however I is true, then A is false if O is true, and if O is false then A is true.

We can now formulate the A-proposition as "All houses are of this nature, that all houses have electricity". The E-proposition may then read "All houses are of this nature, that no house has electricity". We can moreover substitute in the I- and O-propositions "some" by "at least one". These propositions read then: (I) "At least one house has electricity" and (O) "At least one house has no electricity".

The term "at least one" can in its turn be substituted by "one" and the term "all" by any number we want and therefore also by "one". We can now make four propositions with only one house as subject:

(A) The house is of this nature, that it is a house with electricity.
(E) The house is of this nature, that it is a house without electricity.
(I) The house is of this nature, that it is not a house without electricity.
(O) The house is of this nature, that it is not a house with electricity.

We can represent these four propositions in a square of oppcstion as follows:

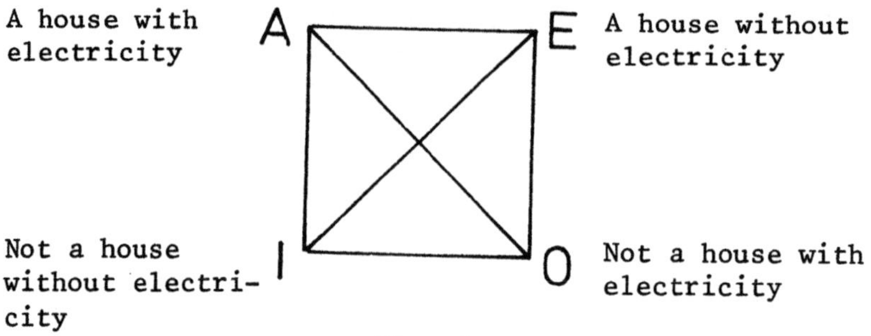

Fig. 4

This is only permitted if the propositions for which the four predicates (a house with electricity, etc.) stand have a similar subject (here: "the house is of this nature, that it is"). In the next paragraph we will represent the four Hohfeldian relations in a similar square of opposition as shortened predicates. The common subject will then be: "The legal relation with respect to performance F between A and B is .....".

(II.D.2) Logical connections between Hohfeld's four fundamental relations. In the four relations described in *(II.C.1)* we find eight concepts (Right,Duty, Power, etc.) which Hohfeld considered as fundamental. In the description here above these eight concepts are arranged in pairs of two (Right-Duty, Power-Liability etc.) consisting of each other's mirror-image: A's Right with respect to performance (F) to him by B is B's Duty and B's Duty with respect to his performance (F) to A is A's Right; similar mirror-images are represented in the other three jural relations.

B's performance F to A can be either an act or a forbearance. If B can perform F to A, it does not follow, that A can perform F to B; some consequences of this will be discussed in *(II.D.5)*.

It is possible, to consider these four Hohfeldian relations as related among each other like the A, E, I and O propositions in traditional logic. We introduce therefore the following propositions, based on the descriptions of the contents of these four relations here above:

(A) All legal relations between A and B with respect to B's performance F to A are Right-Duty relations.

(E) All legal relations between A and B with respect to B's performance F to A are Power-Liability relations.

(I) At least one legal relation between A and B with respect to B's performance F to A is a Disability-Immunity relation.

(O) At least one legal relation between A and B with respect to B's performance F to A is a No Right-Privilege relation.

We can substitute now in these propositions "All legal relations" and "At least one legal relation" by "The legal relation", because in any of these four propositions only either one of the four fundamental legal relations can apply to performance F of B to A.

The four propositions read now:

(A) The legal relation between A and B with respect to B's performance F to A is a Right-Duty relation.

(E) The legal relation between A and B with respect to B's performance F to A is a Power-Liability relation.

(I) The legal relation between A and B with respect to B's performance F to A is a Disability-Immunity relation.

(O) The legal relation between A and B with respect to B's performance F to A is a No Right-Privilege relation.

We can now form a square of opposition in which the names of the relations stand for the latter propositions:

RIGHT-DUTY

POWER-LIABILITY

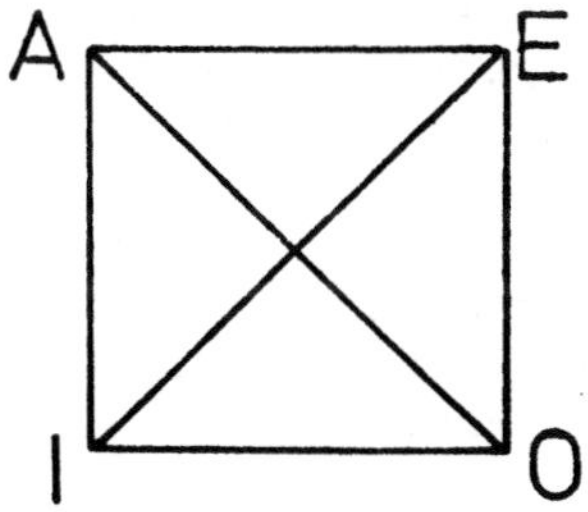

DISABILITY-IMMUNITY

NO RIGHT-PRIVILEGE

Fig. 5

In this square of opposition we meet four stages in the development of fundamental legal relations between A and B with respect to performance F by B to A.

The first stage is the occurrence of both the subcontrary Disability-Immunity and No Right-Privilege relations during the same span of time; the Right-Duty relation and the Power-Liability relation do of course not exist then: A has no Power (i.e. has a Disability) to create a legal relation affecting B and B has no Liability (i.e. has an Immunity) with respect to A's possible attempt to create such a legal relation; A has moreover no Right (i.e. has a No Right) that B shall do F to A, and B has no Duty (i.e. has a Privilege) in this respect and is free to do F to A or not.

The second stage is that which originates as soon as the Disability-Immunity relation between A and B of the first stage has been transformed into its negation, i.e. into a Power-Liability relation. Then it is possible to A, if he wants, to create a new legal relation affecting B, and B's position is, that he will become subject to such a new relation as soon as A exercises his Power in this respect. This does however mean, that the No Right-Privilege relation between A and B of the first stage still exists and during the second stage is superimplied by the relation Power-Liability.

The third stage is that in which A has exercised his Power by transforming the No Right-Privilege relation between him and B into a Right-Duty relation. As soon as this occurs A loses his Power to create this Right-Duty relation, because this relation has now been created; B has lost his Liability to enter into a Duty against A, because he has this Duty now. This means moreover, that between A and B now a legal relation has been revived, expressing the negation of the Power-Liability relation, viz. the relation Disability-Immunity, now superimplied by the relation Right-Duty.

The fourth stage is that which originates as soon as B has fulfilled his Duty to perform F to A or has definitely lost this Duty in another way. B's Duty is by such an occurrence transformed into its negation, a Privilege, and A's Right is then similarly transformed into a No Right.

The relation Disability-Immunity, revived already in the third stage, continues its existence together with the now revived No Right-Privilege relation in a subcontrary relationship.

These two relations are often of a nature similar to those in the first stage: if it is possible to repeat that B performs F to A, then a similar cycle can start. If this is not possible, then the two subcontrary relations are expression of the principle *"ne bis in idem"*.

We will consider now as example the situation in an imaginary State in which no law exists which permits the State to collect taxes on riding a bicycle. The State's gevernment (A) has a No Right that a subject B shall pay money for riding a bicycle, and B has a Privilege to pay and not to pay for riding a bicycle; he is free to go or not to go to the tax-collector or another magistrate designated for such cases and to pay by free will for riding a bicycle, e.g. because he has moral objections against causing the State damage by the wear and tear caused by his bicycle riding to the State's road surfaces. The State's government (A) has however no Power (i.e. a Disability) to impose upon B a Duty to pay tax for riding his bicycle and B has no Liability (an Immunity) if the State's government attempts to impose such a Duty upon him illegally.

If now Parliament passes a bill by which the State's government (A) becomes entitled (obtains a Power) to impose for a limited period a tax for riding a bicycle, then government (A) and its subject (B) are still in the same No Right-Privilege relation as long as the tax has not legally been imposed. However, B has now a Liability to pay the tax as soon as the State's government (A) makes use of its Power, given to it by Bill of Parliament, to declare that all bicycle-riders should pay a certain amount of money.

As soon as government A has exercised this Power it enters now with B into a Right-Duty relation: B has now a Duty to pay the tax and the government has a Right to receive it. Moreover, B has now an Immunity against imposement of the concerned tax and A has a Disability in this respect (ne bis in idem).

The Disability-Immunity relation continues its existence after dissolution of the Right-Duty relation, i.e. by B's payment or by any other possible end which law may provide for B's Duty and the government's Right. After dissolution of the Right-Duty relation the State's government and its subject B are in the same No Right-Privilege relation. If later the government wants to impose a similar tax again, then Parliament has to pass a new bill by which the government becomes endowed with a Power to impose a similar tax again for a limited period.

(II.D.2.a) Are Hohfeld's Concepts Primitives? Hohfeld believed that his eight fundamental jural concepts are neither reducible to each other, nor to other notions. In other words, he considered them as logical primitives.

Was Hohfeld wrong in this respect? The four fundamental jural relations can all be reduced to only one of them, viz. the relation Right-Duty. The relation No Right-Privilege is the negation of Right-Duty. The relation Power-Liability can be formulated as "Not a Right-Duty relation now but possibly later by exercise of the Power", which is similar to "A negation of a Right-Duty relation (No Right-Privilege) now, but possibly later not by exercise of the Power". The relation Disability-Immunity is the negation of Power-Liability.

It is very doubtful whether we are allowed to regard separated Right and Duty as primitives. Cybernetically *(1)* a legal advantage and therefore also a Right can be described as A's pattern of expectations relative to B's desired pattern of behaviour. A legal burden and therefore also a Duty is cybernetically B's desired pattern of behaviour relative to A's pattern of expectations.

A's pattern of expectations is therefore related to B's pattern of desired behaviour as the matrix of the expected contents, or in other words: Right and Duty are each other's mirror-image.

It appears therefore more correct to consider the relation Right-Duty as a primitive.

(II.D.3) Two Squares of Opposition instead of one. Hohfeld developed eight concepts which he brought together in four fundamental relationships. We placed these four relations in one square of opposition.

It is also possible to place the eight concepts in two squares of opposition if we form propositions relative to the legal position of person A with respect to B's performance F to A and relative to the legal position of person B with respect to performance F to A. These squares are then as follows:

RIGHT

POWER

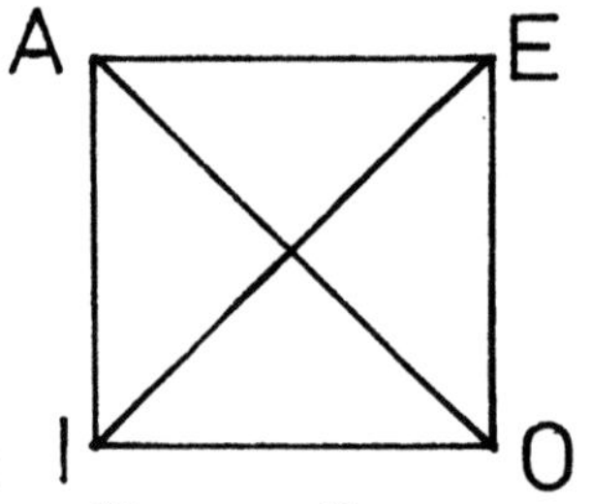

DISABILITY

NO RIGHT

(Person A)
Fig. 6

DUTY

LIABILITY

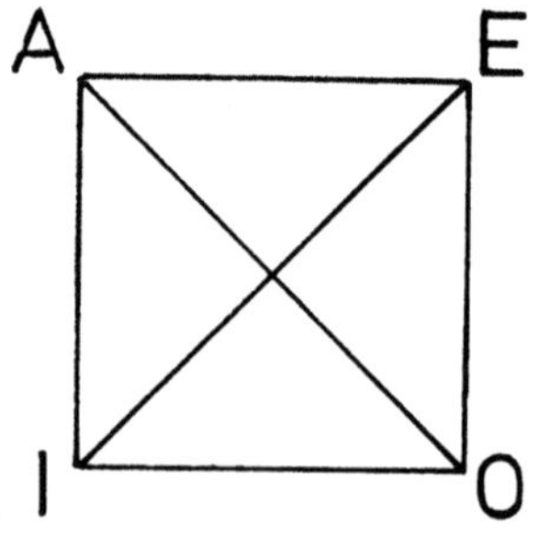

IMMUNITY

PRIVILEGE

(Person B)
Fig. 7

B's Duty stands now for the A proposition: B's legal position with respect to performance F to A is that he must do F to A. A's Right stands now for the A proposition: A's legal position with respect to performance F by B is that he has a legal expectation that B shall do F to him.

Similar reasonings are applicable to the other six concepts. The square relative to the position of person B will appear of interest to us in *(II.E.6)*, the other square in *(II.E.6.a)*.

(II.D.4) Two levels of the Law in one Square of Opposition. The Hohfeldian relations in the square of opposition here above represent two different levels of the law, the primary and the secundary rules: " ... while primary rules are concerned with the actions that individuals must do or must not do, these secundary rules are all concerned with the primary rules themselves. They specify the ways in which the primary rules are ascertained, introduced, eliminated, varied and the fact of their violation conclusively determined" *(1)*. They may also be called norms of conduct and norms of competence.

The primary rules or norms of conduct are expressed in the relations Right-Duty and No Right-Privilege, while the relations Power-Liability and Disability-Immunity represent the secondary rules or norms of competence. "Moreover .... any norm of competence may be transcribed as a norm of conduct, whereas the converse does not hold" *(2)*. Such transcriptions are given in *(II.E.5.a)*, *(II.E.5.b)* and *(II.E.6.a)*.

(II.D.5) Four Modalities or eight? Alf Ross *(1)* has distinguished, along the lines inspired by Hohfeld, four modalities of conduct and four modalities of competence. Four of these eight modalities correspond to the two modalities of conduct of B to A and the two modalities of competence of A to B in my square of opposition, the latter four represent modalities related to a similar conduct, but now of A to B, and to a similar competence, but now of B to A. Such a reversal of the places of A and B is logically correct because it is based on the premise that A and B are able to exhibit similar conduct and to have similar competences. This premise is however not in accordance with the reality of law and human life, where we cannot change wantonly parties A and B: they act or have competences in certain qualities: if A is a landlord and B a tenant we can say that tenant B should pay a rent to landlord A, but not that landlord A should pay this rent to

tenant B. The only correct premise seems, that B can do F to A, but that A cannot do F to B. If we base ourselves on this premise, then we can do with four modalities instead of eight.

(II.D.6) Hohfeld's Concepts Privielge and No Right. To Hohfeld was the concept Duty the jural opposite - we would say now negation - of the concept Privilege.

In the conception treated here above all eight Hohfeldian concepts are related to a performance F by B to A, which performance can be either an act or a forbearance. By a Duty we mean therefore always a duty to do F (command) or a duty not to do F (prohibition).

Negation of such a Duty seems therefore always either negation of a command or a negation of a prohibition. It is however also possible to understand negation of such a Duty as negation of a command and a prohibition. We can e.g. describe a Duty to do F as a command and not a prohibition. Negation of this Duty can be formulated as not a command and not a prohibition. Negation of a Duty not to do F can be similarly expressed as not a command and not a prohibition *(1)*.

The concept Privilege can therefore be understood in two senses: negation of a Duty to do F or negation of a Duty not to do F, and negation of both a Duty to do F and a Duty not to do F.
Unfortunately there is in Hohfeld's own statements some obscurity on the question of how to describe Privilege

Hohfeld took Privilege in the former and narrow sense in the following statement: "..... if A has not contracted with B to perform certain work for the latter, A's privilege of *not* doing so is the very negation of a duty of doing so"*(2)*.

Hohfeld however cannot but have had in mind the latter and broad sense of Privilege when he stated: "..... it is the privilege of a trader in a free country, in all matters not contrary to law, to regulate his own mode of carrying them on according to his discretion and choice". The closest synonym of legal "Privilege" seems to be legal "liberty" or legal "freedom..." *(3)*.

The distinction between these two notions of "Privilege" has been formalized by Manfred Moritz *(4)*. Only the second and broad sense of Privilege seems to be considered by Moritz as completely fitting into Hohfeld's system, the first meaning not only expressing the factual situation incompletely, but also deviating from traditional and factual juridical language *(5)*. The second meaning of

Privilege seems to me for similar reasons the only opportunity *(6)*.

This interpretation of Privilege should reflect itself in this concept's mirror-image, namely the concept No Right. Somebody invested with a No Right is not entitled to encroach upon the other party's Privilege but is required to respect the other's liberty or freedom in relation to the object of his Privilege. In other words: a No Right is in our opinion not only similar to absence of a Right but also to presence of a necessity to respect, to bear, to endure acts or forbearances to which the other has a Privilege.

Such a necessity to respect is not similar to a Duty to respect: the other party has not a Right to be respected but a Privilege to do or not to do certain acts; the first party is not obliged to respect the other but has no other legal opportunity *(7)*.

(II.D.7) Exceptions and Nullities in Squares of Opposition by means of Hohfeldian Concepts. The square of opposition in which Hohfeld's four fundamental jural relations are represented as A-, I-, E-, and O-propositions in traditional logic is not the only one which is useful for understanding relations between such relations.

It is possible to develop special squares of opposition for understanding special problems. Two examples of this now follow.

A legal opportunity not to fulfil a Duty may be due to three different causes: the Duty can be void; the Duty can be annihilable; the Duty can subsist but be made ineffective. If a Duty is declared void it is supposed never to have existed; in case of annihilation the Duty exists until the moment of annihilation; annihilation is reached in court by a succesful appeal to an *exceptio peremptoria*; ineffectiveness springs from a succesful appeal to an *exceptio dilatoria* or an *exceptio declinatoria*.

These positions of voidness, annihibility and ineffective subsistence can be represented in the following square of opposition:

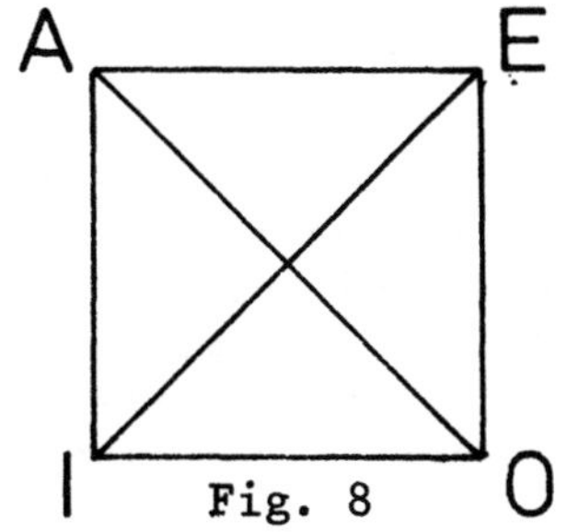

Fig. 8

The Right I-Duty I relation is the relation in which a claimant sues a defendant; the Duty II-Right II relation is put forward by the defendant as a demurrer which should make the first relation ineffective; this demurrer may be either an *exceptio dilatoria* or an *exceptio declinatoria*. The demurrer in question (Duty II-Right II) superimplies the Right I-Duty I relation because it cannot exist if this relation (Right I-Duty I) does not, and it might or might not exist if the latter relation does. If the bringing forward of such a demurrer is unsuccesful, then the simultaneous existence of the Privilege II-No Right II relation with the Right I-Duty I relation represents this unsuccesful occurrence. A succesful use of such a demurrer is represented by the simultaneous ex stence of both a Right I-Duty I relation and a relation Duty II-Right II.

An appeal on the grounds of voidness can be made by invoking the No Right I-Privilege I relation. If such an appeal is succesful then the Right I-Duty I relation is supposed never to have existed. An appeal to annihibility, by means of an *exceptio peremptoria*, is included in this device only in so far as its ultimate result is concerned, viz. nullification of the Right I-Duty I relation after a certain period of existence. This result is superimplied by the demurrer itself, as can be seen in the following square of opposition:

RIGHT I - DUTY I

DUTY III - RIGHT III

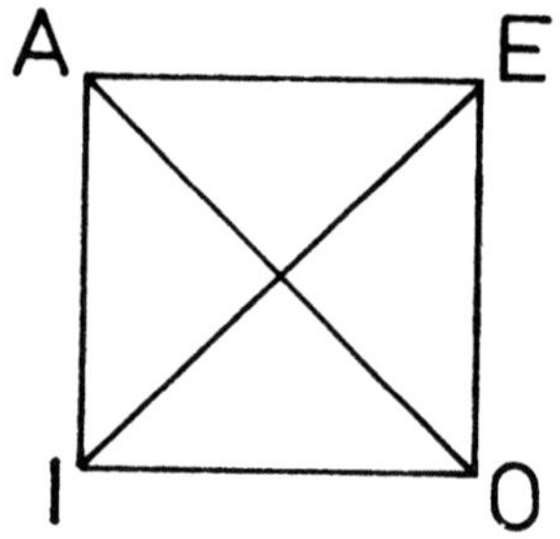

PRIVILEGE III -
NO RIGHT III

NO RIGHT I -
PRIVILEGE I

Fig. 9

In this square the demurrer (Duty III-Right III) is placed as a contrariety to the Right I-Duty I relation. If the demurrer is successful then the subsistence of the Right I-Duty I relation becomes impossible and this relation is transformed by the process of annihilation into a No Right I- Privilege I relation. In other words the *exceptio peremptoria* superimplies the denial of a Right and a Right superimplies this demurrer's denial (Privilege III-No Right III).

Notice that in each of these two squares of opposition two kinds of performances play a role between A and B, in contrast to the situation in a square where the A-, I-, E-, and O-propositions are all represented with respect to performance F. In these last two squares only contradictory propositions refer to relations concerning identical performances; the contrary and subcontrary propositions however express jural relations between A and B of which the performances are different. The formulation of propositions in these squares therefore requires some modification in the terms used, for example that which follows.

In both these squares of opposition the jural relations are provided with a Roman numeral corresponding to a certain performance. So in the Right I-Duty I relation the numeral I refers to performance I, the Privilege II-No Right II relation refers to performance II, etc.

In our latter square of opposition we might now formulate the A-proposition as: 'All legal relations between A and B are *Right I-Duty I relations*'. This means that these relations are Right-Duty relations *with respect to performance I*. Similar references to the performance will be understood to be included in the other propositions.

The E-proposition then reads: 'All legal relations between A and B are *Duty III-Right III relations*'. The I-proposition can be: 'At least one legal relation between A and B is a *Privilege III-No Right III relation*' and the O-proposition may be: 'At least one legal relation between A and B is a *No Right I-Privilege I relation*'. Similar propositions can be formulated with respect to the former square of opposition.

(II.E) VOLITIONAL LOGIC APPLIED TO HOHFELD'S SYSTEM

(II.E.1) Bentham's Volitional Logic or Logic of the Will. H.L.A. Hart has recently published an interesting paper under the title "Bentham's 'Of Laws in General'" *(1)*. This paper is a clear exposition of the main principles which Jeremy Bentham in 'Of Laws in General' *(2)* laid down. Bentham described a law as "an assemblage of signs declarative of a volition, conceived or adopted by the sovereign in a state, concerning the conduct to be adopted in a certain case by a certain person or class of persons who in the case in question are, or are supposed to be, subject to his power". This notion of law is not similar to that of a statute; a statute can be part of a law, part of different laws, a multiple of laws, or any combination of these things.

In this description a law is an expression of the will of a legislator. Bentham was of the opinion that this will can appear in four aspects or phases: Command, Prohibition, Non-Prohibition (Permission to act) and Non-Command (Permission to forbear). He upheld that these four "aspects of the will" stand to each other in logical relationships similar to those between the A, E, I and O propositions of traditional logic.

If this is correct, then it is possible to represent the "aspects of the will" in a square of opposition as follows:

COMMAND PROHIBITION

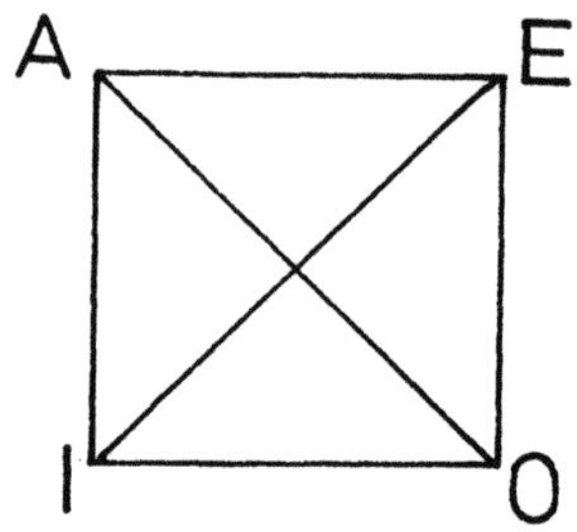

NON-PROHIBITION (PERMISSION TO ACT) NON-COMMAND (PERMISSION TO FORBEAR)

Fig. 10

When considering this theory, questions arise about the distinctions made by Bentham. Is it really necessary to distinguish between two "Permissions", or between

"Command" and "Prohibition"? Are we certain that the "aspects of the will" which Bentham isolated, are the only ones? Can we still accept Bentham's theory in the light of 20th Century thinking?

An answer to these questions is put forward in the next subdivisions. The development of such an answer appears possible by means, in particular, of Hohfeld's theory of fundamental legal concepts. It will therefore be useful to compare Bentham's theory with Hohfeld's.

(II.E.2) Bentham's Classification compared with that of Hohfeld.

(II.E.2.a) Two "Permissions", or one? "The volitional proposition, according to Bentham, expresses a state of the will of the speaker, whereas an intellectual proposition expresses a state of his understanding" *(1)*.

The relationship of subcontrariety which Bentham draws between Non-Prohibition (Permission to act) and Non-Command (Permission to forbear) suggests the possibility of expressing both permissions simultaneously in one volitional proposition. This would mean that by one expression of a state of the will two incompatible ways of conduct would be permitted with respect to one and the same act situation *(2)* or one and the same content of a norm *(3)*.

Such a simultaneous existence of two incompatible permissions only seems possible in the case that we would take - *quod non*, because as will be demonstrated, this is not correct - an aspect of the will for a static phenomenon: as soon as the will has been expressed it is a law and a law is by tradition deprived of all dynamic nature.

It is undeniable, however, that the very act of expressing a will is not static but dynamic. Such an act is a unique event: during a short interval of time a direction of the will is pointed out. The will's direction is "the conduct to be adopted in a certain case". Pointing out in one statement two incompatible ways of conduct with respect to the same act situation means that a will with two directions is expressed, and this is impossible. The very act of expressing a will is therefore suitable for the expression of either a permission to act, or a permission to forbear, but not both.

We will now consider whether these two notions of "Permission" can stand in a relation of subcontrariety after their expression, which expression can of course occur only at separated moments.

(II.E.2.b) One Static Proposition, or Innumerable Dynamic? It is fully understandable that Bentham conceived two notions of permission with the property of subcontraries that they can exist simultaneously. This is in accordance with the traditional point of view that a law is of static nature. However, developments in 20th Century philosophy make us wonder whether we can still accept that an expression of the will, a volitional proposition, a law, is fundamentally static, except at the moment of its creation.

Both the notions of "matter" and "mind" have lost their meaning as the fundamental objective constituents in the physical and psychological areas respectively; in both these worlds it is now "events" which are considered as the ultimate basic units *(1)*. Although "physical" events and "psychological" events cannot be considered as completely identical - there is for example a difference of temporal span - neither "matter" nor "mind" are now considered to consist of solid units: "matter" is not composed of solid pieces, or even particles, moving about in space and persisting in time; "mind" is not composed of solid ideas, not even by mathematical points persisting in time, nor by any other basic concept of static nature *(2)*.

This conception has consequences in relation to the traditional distinction between static and dynamic nature. Any object and any idea which in former days was considered to be static is now thought to be constituted by a collection of innumerable elementary events of microcosmic duration. An event is therefore fundamentally dynamic and we should consider anything composed by events as a dynamic multiple.

This applies to any mental construction and thus we cannot but take a volitional proposition, a law, as a multiple of dynamic will-expressions. In other words: "aspects of the will" are multiples of innumerable will-expressions which are all of dynamic nature because they are elementary events. "Permission to act" and "permission to forbear" are notions consisting of innumerable "permissions to act" and "permissions to forbear" of microcosmic duration and dynamic character.

In *(II.E.2.a)* we stated the reasons why a dynamic permission to act and a dynamic permission to forbear cannot be given by one expression of the will. Because now - as we saw above - all such notions of permission should be considered as dynamic multiples, it appears impossible that one volitional proposition contains, in respect of the same act situation, both these notions of permission. The two permissions cannot be considered, as Bentham did, to be each other's subcontrary.

(II.E.3) How to Permit Alternative Conduct. We have seen now that a sovereign cannot give at the same moment a permission to act and a permission to forbear, although he is able to give such permissions at separate moments, but that nevertheless these two permissions cannot "occur" *(1)* during the same span of time, neither during a microcosmic moment nor during a longer period. Nevertheless, there are cases where a sovereign would like to be able to permit his subjects to do a certain thing or not. In such cases the subjects are in need of an opportunity of free choice between performing an act or forbearing from it. Such a free choice is not given in Bentham's two "Permissions". They indeed embody a free choice, but this is a choice respectively between acting and obeying a prohibition and forbearing and obeying a command.

If a sovereign wishes to permit a free choice between acting and forbearing he requires another type of permission. Such a permission should be appropriate to the expression in one statement that two alternative ways of conduct are permitted. This means that the direction of the sovereign's will should be that a subject is free either to act or to forbear. Such a permission is a permission either to act or to forbear.

This notion "permission either to act or to forbear" is a device to indicate that someone, relative to a certain performance, no matter whether this is an act or forbearance, has neither a duty to carry out this performance, nor a duty not to do so. This meaning is similar to that of Hohfeld's fundamental concept Privilege *(2)*.

Notice that a permission on either to act or to forbear can indeed be expressed by a sovereign, but that it is more than an "aspect of the will" alone: it applies as well to any act situation in respect of which the sovereign expressed no will at all. *Everything* is permitted, unless there is a contradictionary "ought".

(II.E.4) Two "Commands", or One? Bentham formed the notion of "prohibition" by describing it as a "Command" to forbear, limiting the use of "Command" to ways of conduct which are acts. A way of conduct is to Bentham part of an "aspect of the will": "Command" and "Permission to act" are distinguished from "Prohibition" and "Permission to forbear" by the ways of conduct to which they are relative, and not by the act situation.

We have seen why such a distinction at present

appears to fail as far as the two notions of permission are concerned. A solution to this problem was developed by substituting both permissions with one notion: a "Permission either to act or to forbear".

This notion of "permission either to act or to forbear" negates either a "Command" or a "Prohibition", no matter which of the two is opposed to it.The notion of negation is used here according to Bentham's intention "not to negate the act but the decided aspect".

A notion now has fundamentally only one negation. "Command" and "Prohibition" are therefore negated in what they have in common: the notion of "Ought", or "Duty", or "Command" in a broad sense.

Such a notion of "Ought" is of course relative to a certain way of conduct and certainly the sovereign will state whether this way of conduct should be acting or forbearing. But acting and forbearing are ways of conduct with respect to a certain act situation and they have no bearing on the question of whether a way of conduct is an "Ought" or a "May". The notions to act and to forbear are therefore not essentially related to the nature of the will which is expressed; there is no reason to use them for drawing distinctions between "aspects of the will". So far as the imperative aspect of the will is concerned we can do with one notion of "Ought". We may call this notion "Ought", or "Should", or "Duty", or "Command" in a broad sense .

The relation of negation between this notion of "Ought" and "Permission either to act or to forbear" corresponds to that between Duty and Privilege in Hohfeld's system.

(II.E.5) Two other "Aspects of the Will". We have found now that instead of Bentham's four "aspects of the will" we can do with two notions: "command in a broad sense" and "permission in a broad sense". These two notions cover the situations for which Bentham took four.

One may ask now whether Bentham did not overlook other situations in which a sovereign stated his will in a certain determined form which also might be called an "aspect of the will". Two forms of will-expression will be discussed now, which frequently occur but which are neither command nor permission in the broader sense which has been given to these notions here above.

(II.E.5.a) Not the Risk of a Legal Burden now, but possibly later. The first of these additional expressions of the will is a declaration that the performance of an

act or forbearance, which actually is not a legal burden, may become a legal burden in the future. Such a will-expression is for example, a statement in a State's constitution that obligations to pay certain kinds of taxes can be imposed by special statutes. The subjects are then in fact under no obligation to pay such a tax, but they run the risk that they may be obliged to pay it in future as soon as the legislator has made a law to that effect.

This construction is similar to that of Hohfeld's fundamental concept of Liability, which concept is relative to the legal burdens in Hohfeld's system, viz. Duty, Disability, No Right and (another) Liability.

(II.E.5.b) Not the Risk of Legal Burden now, and not later. The second of these additional will-expressions is a declaration that the performance of a certain act or forbearance, which actually is not a legal burden, will not become a legal burden in future. Such a will-expression is, for example, a statement in a State's constitution *(1)* that no statute can be passed forcing somebody within the State's jurisdiction to belong to a certain religion.

This construction is similar to that which Hohfeld attributed to his fundamental concept of Immunity.

(II.E.5.c) A Relation of Negation. The newly found "aspects of the will", the concepts Liability and Immunity, were called by Hohfeld "jural opposites". Hohfeld meant by this qualification that these notions mutually exclude each other; we would say now that Liability and Immunity are each other's negations. This contradictionary relation fits into Bentham's system: it is used here "not to negate the act, but the decided aspect".

(II.E.6) The logical Relations between "Aspects of the Will". We have found that the four newly developed "aspects of the will" make two pairs of contradictories, viz. the concepts of Ought and Permission and the concepts of Liability and Immunity.

There are, however, more logical relations between these four notions. Ought and Liability can be considered as contraries: they cannot be willed simultaneously and a sovereign's will can be expressed in a volitional proposition (Immunity or Permission or both) which does not affect both.

Immunity and permission are subcontraries: they can be willed simultaneously in relation to the same act situation - the expressed ways of conduct are compatible -

but it is impossible, even for a sovereign, to exclude both.

This is due to the fact that Ought and Liability respectively superimply an Immunity and a Permission: as soon as an Ought is imposed upon a subject he has an Immunity against such an Ought in future; so long as a Liability is imposed upon someone he still has a permission to do or not to do anything which he would be obliged to do as soon as his Liability was transformed into an Ought.

The logical relations between the four newly found "aspects of the will" can now be represented in a square of opposition of the following shape:

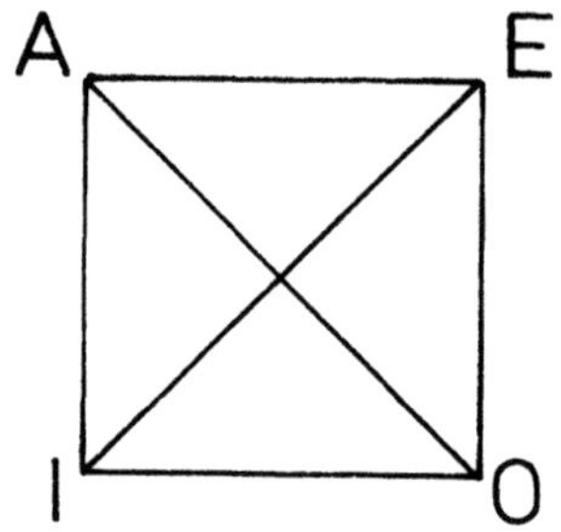

Fig. 11

(II.E.6.a) "Power" and a Sovereign's Power. We have found as first additional will-expression of the sovereign a concept, similar to Hohfeld's Liability and expressing that the performance of an act or forbearance, which is actually not a legal burden, may become a legal burden in the future. The concept "Power", in Hohfeld's system Liability's correlative, may therefore be understood in this sense that the performance of an act or forbearance, which is actually not a legal advantage, may become a legal advantage in future. This legal advantage may be a Right, an Immunity, a Privilege or another Power

A Power is, in other words, a competence to create, to change or to annihilate legal relations. Its nature is therefore identical to that of *Gestaltungsrecht (1)*, even if the exercised Power is used in order to annihilate a Right, an Immunity, a Privilege or a Power. If we speak of the Power of a sovereign or of somebody else we therefore mean that he has not a certain legal advantage now, but may create it by his will-expression in future.

A similar reasoning can be followed relative to the negations of Power and Liability, the concepts Disability and Immunity. Even an Almighty sovereign has Disabilities: he is not able to create legal advantages for himself in future, if these advantages exist already now.

The subject of an Almighty sovereign has similarly an Immunity against attempts of the sovereign to create legal burdens in future, if these have been created already. Disability-Immunity relations appear of course also together with a No Right-Privilege relation where a sovereign has no Right and no Power, e.g. in territorial areas or personal circles outside his jurisdiction.

(II.E.7) "Right" and "Duty" in Hohfeld and in Bentham. The logical relations between the newly found "aspects of the will" correspond to the logical relations between Hohfeld's four fundamental jural relations, but are not identical to these: the newly found "aspects of the will" are identical to Hohfeldian concepts, but not to the jural relations which these concepts form with their Hohfeldian "correlative".

Bentham's system of "aspects of the will" emphasises in its volitional propositions only one side of the speaker's will: the conduct to be adopted by the one who is addressed. If a sovereign imposes a duty upon his subjects to pay a certain tax to him, then this relates only to what the subjects should do and nothing is expressed regarding the position of the sovereign whose apparent intention is to collect the taxes *(1)*.

In Hohfeld's system the sovereign has a legal expectation that the taxes are paid to him, a Right. This system neither emphasises the notion of Right nor the notion of Duty; it emphasises that there is a jural relation in which one person has a Duty and another person a Right.

That Bentham did not introduce a notion of right into his system - the word itself was not shunned by him - is ultimately due to his Utilitarism. This philosophy is based on the idea that all emotions are reducible to either pleasure or pain. Any act is intended to give somebody pleasure in the form of a favour. A sovereign's will-expression now provides for a favour by means of imposing a burden, a pain, upon a subject charged by a duty. This pain is not the duty but the threat of a sanction; the notion duty itself is an "aspect of the will". It is now in Bentham's system always certain that a duty is accompanied by threat of a sanction, but it is not certain that the intended pleasure will occur.

A pleasure is also intended when a permission to act is given or a permission to forbear. In these cases the pleasure consists of the absence of a "Command" or a "Prohibition", or generally a duty.

These two notions of intended pleasure are indeed of a different nature, but both are called right in legal theory and practice. There is no objection to this as long as one realises that there is a fundamental distinction. Hohfeld limited the use of Right to the meaning of the converse of a Duty and he made his notion of Privilege correspond to that of a Duty's negation; Bentham incorporated only one kind of the intended pleasures, viz. his two "Permissions", into his system. In Hohfeld's system the notion of Privilege has as its converse that of No Right, in Bentham's system it is not clear whether he, who permits has any legal position at all.

Hohfeld's system can be formalized by means of the notion "Right-Duty relation", Bentham's system only by means of the concept "Duty" *(2)*.

(II.F) A SYNTHESIS BETWEEN THE THEORIES OF BENTHAM AND OF HOHFELD

It is not true to say that it depends on the will of the sovereign whether one may have two kinds of right or only one kind of right, or none at all. From Bentham's and Hohfeld's theories a conception may be developed which is a device for indicating a person's legal position. From Bentham one may take his theory of the will as a sovereign's imperative, not because it would be the best possible answer to the questions to which it attempts to reply, but because it can easily be substituted by other conceptions concerning the reasons why a certain conduct should be, or may be, adopted in a certain case. From Hohfeld one may take his theory of four fundamental jural relations because this theory has some advantages over Bentham's theory on "aspects of the will".

The Hohfeldian system fits, as we have seen, into Bentham's: Bentham's aspects of the will can be reduced to Hohfeldian fundamental concepts. Hohfeld, however, treated the two sides of fundamental jural relations, whereas Bentham treated only one side of such relations. Hohfeld considered moreover time-related notions of which Bentham was not conscious *(1)*. Combined together the theories can indicate moreover the logical juridical position of fundamental notions such as "Rule of Law", "Conclusion of Law", "Claim", "Sanction" and "Natural Obligation".

(II.F.1) Problems concerning the notions Threat of a Sanction and Claim. Both Bentham and Hohfeld considered that a Duty is always accompanied by threat of a sanction.

Threat of a sanction is threat of a subsidiary Duty should the original Duty not become fulfilled. If a Duty is indeed always accompanied by threat of a santion, then a sanction is also in its turn accompanied by threat of a sanction, and the same with this last sanction, and so on. This is not in accordance with jural reality. The nature of a Duty is that something ought to be done or ought not to be done and it is not that a sanction will be applied if something does not occur in the way it should be done or not done.

We will therefore consider a Duty as not being automatically accompanied by a santion. In legal science such Duties are the effects of a natural obligation or of a *lex imperfecta (1)*.

A Duty which is not accompanied by threat of a sanction is correlated to a Right which is not similar to a claim because there is no *actio*.

This consideration of Right and Duty gives us an opportunity to describe in *(II.F.5)* and *(II.F.6)* the structure of Claims and Duties with threat of a sanction, as structures of fundamental jural concepts; such a description is impossible in Hohfeld's original conception, because there such Duties and Claims are already fundamental jural concepts.

(II.F.2) What does a Sovereign will? A sovereign's will-expression is, according to Bentham, to the effect that one of his subjects should or may adopt a certain conduct towards the sovereign himself or towards another subject.

In the first case the sovereign can, for example, express his will in the following ways:

1) "I impose on A a Duty to do F to me".
2) "I give myself a Right that A does F to me".
3) "I create a Right-Duty relation between myself and A with respect to performance F, in which I have the Right and A the Duty".

Whichever of the three the sovereign uses, the effect is always that of the third expression. There is not, as in Bentham's theory, only a conduct to be adopted by the one who has a Duty, but also by the one who has this "intended pleasure", this "legal expectation", that the Duty will be performed. This conduct is related to the reception of the performance; the one who has a Right may have a Duty to receive the performance; he has legal remedies, some of which will be discussed later. A sovereign therefore does not immediately create by means of his will-expressions a rule of conduct for his subjects, but mediately, by means of the creation of a legal relation between his subjects and himself, and by this he mediately creates for himself as well, a certain rule of conduct.

What has been said here applies also to relations which the sovereign creates amongst his subjects. Thus three forms of will-expression are possible, e.g.:

1) "I impose on B a Duty to do F to A".
2) "I give A a Right that B does F to A".
3) "I create a Right-Duty relation between A and B with respect to performance F, in which A has the Right and B has the Duty".

Here also the sovereign's will, whichever of the three formulations he might use, is to the effect of the third expression.

The examples used here concern the Right-Duty relation.

They also apply to the other three relations of Hohfeldian origin.

When a legal relation is created by a sovereign between subjects amongst each other, legal relations - that is to say at least two - originate as well between the sovereign and any of the involved parties. These relations can be exposed as follows:

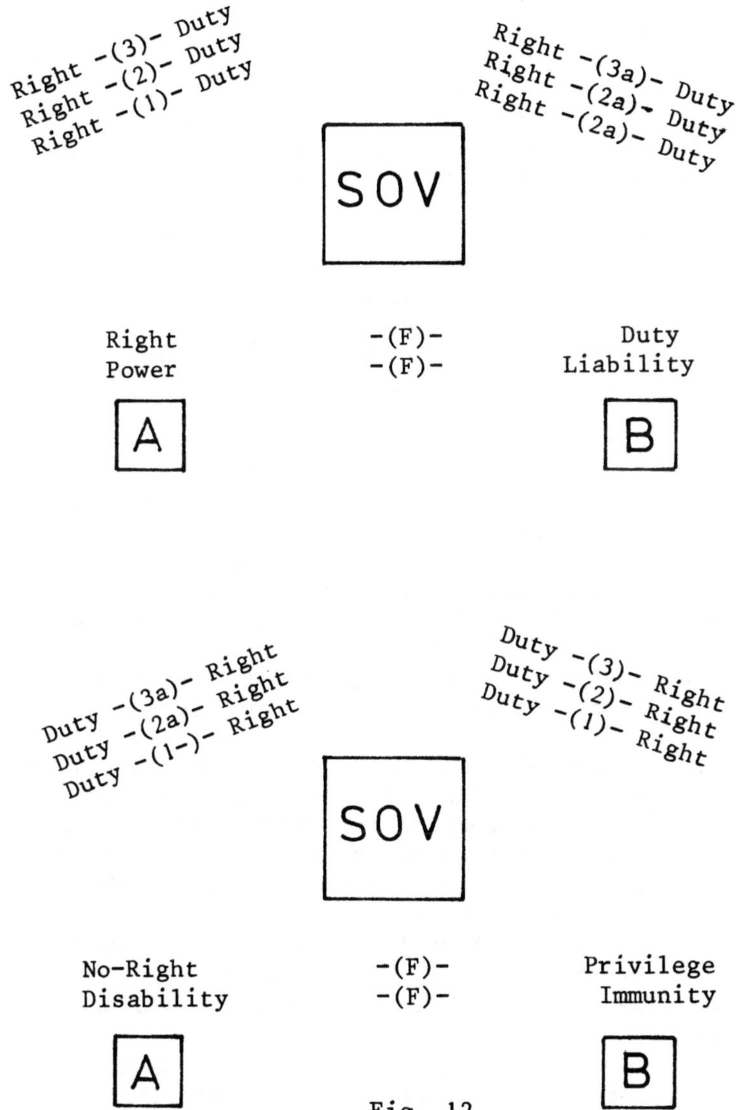

Fig. 12

The letter F means that a certain relation is relative to performance (F). The numbered relations concern Rights and Duties between subject and sovereign relative to: obeyance to the Rule of Law (1) and (1a), conclusions of Law (2 and 2a), claims (3) and sanctions (3a).

(II.F.3) Obeyance to the "Rule of Law". The relations (1) concern a Duty of the sovereign to respect that one subject makes use of his Right, Power, Privilege or Immunity against another subject; the former subject has a Right to such a respect from the sovereign.

The relations (1a) concern a Duty of one subject to the sovereign to perform (F) to another subject in accordance with the Duty, Liability, No Right or Disability which he has to this other subject; the sovereign has a Right to the former subject that he shall do (F) to the latter.

It is obvious from the Right-Duty relations 1 and 1a, that both a subject and a sovereign are tied by legal relations which are of a higher order than the will of the sovereign. We only signalize these relations here as deposits of a transcendental principle - that of the "Rule of Law" or "Lex est Rex" - and we will see in *(IV.B.3.h)* how far "Lex" may indeed be "Rex".

(II.F.4) Conclusions of Law. The Right-Duty relations (2) concern act situations in which a subject can ask the sovereign (or a court in his name) to give him a formal declaration as to whether a certain jural relation exists between himself and another subject, or not. The sovereign (or his court) should give such a Conclusion of Law.

The Right-Duty relations (2a) concern a Right of the sovereign (or a court) to give such a declaration on request, and a Duty by the non-requesting party to respect that such a declaration is given to his opponent.

(II.F.5) A Subject's Claim in Court. The Right-Duty relations (3) concern a Right of a subject to ask the sovereign to force his opponent to perform (F) to him. This is implied in a Claim against the opponent, and the sovereign, or his court, has a Duty to provide for such a compulsion; the nature of a Claim is either Right (F) or Power (F) or Privilege (F) or Immunity (F), each accompanied by Right (3) *(1)*. Note that Right (3) is A's right against the sovereign or his court, but A's *actio* against his opponent B.

If there is no such Right-Duty relation (3) then no one can claim before the sovereign or in court that his opponent performs according to a Duty, Liability, No Right or Disability.

(II.F.6) A Sovereign's Right to Enforce Sanctions. The Right-Duty relations (3a) concern the cases in which a sovereign is entitled to use force against a subject who does not perform according to his Duty, Liability, No Right or Disability towards another subject. Such is the sovereign's Right to use armed force in order to support the execution of judicial decisions. Duty (3a) is the sanction accompanying Duty (F).

(II.F.7) Natural Obligations and other "Natural" Relationships. Bentham's system left no room for the natural obligation because it emphasised too strongly the role of the sanction as a necessary accessory to a duty.

So far as Hohfeld's system is involved, there is no absolute clarity as to how far it is applicable to natural obligations; Hohfeld himself did not touch on the problem in his writings; it is only certain that his notion of Right was identical to a Claim.

By distinguishing a separated Right of a subject A against a sovereign to claim in court with respect to a performance of subject B, a formalized criterion is given here for establishing whether a jural relationship - not only an obligation - is "natural", or not.

If there is no Right -(3)- Duty relation, then a Right -(F)- Duty relation between A and B is called a "Natural Obligation". In such cases there is also no Right -(3a)- Duty relation.

If Right -(3)- Duty relations are absent with respect to the other three Hohfeldian relations, then there is also no reason for not calling such relations "natural" as well. In all these cases there is a relation of Hohfeldian nature, but claiming in court that someone acts according to his Duty, Liability, No Right or Disability is then impossible. The court is then able, however, if asked, to give a Conclusion of Law.

III. Conceptions of cybernetics

(III.A) INTRODUCTION TO CYBERNETICS

(III.A.1) Philosophical Conceptions behind Cybernetics. The conception of cybernetics is applicable in the biological, the physical, the social and the legal sciences. This enunciation is not limitative; it is sufficient to demonstrate that it breaks through traditional barriers between areas of human thinking.

The reason for this break-through can be found in 20th century conceptions concerning the notions matter and mind.

The Cartesian idea of a dualism within reality between mind and matter seems at present obsolete. This is not only due to the 19th century division of matter in mass and energy. Modern science has brought about new insights into the structure of atoms and each day new discoveries are published on its particles. The real nature of space and time are still in the early stages of disclosure. New insights into the nature of psychic phenomena are also still developing. Physical and psychical phenomena are not described any more by exclusively deterministic terms. It has not been possible to establish a logical connection between the field theory of relativity and the quantum theory; the modern physicist must work with both the wave theory and the particle theory, which are contradictory. Extra-sensory perception, less limited to distances in space, also breaks through barriers of time, according to principles not yet adequately met by modern physics *(1)*.

The only thing that seems certain, is that all our knowledge of the phenomena is achieved by the installation of a structure, and that a causal structure is only one of the possibilities.

But also a dualism between a real and a non-real world seems out of time. We can become certain that our knowledge of singular phenomena is similar to that of other men, by making them describe in detail the same phenomena; if such a description permits a discussion we have sufficient certainty that our knowledge of these phenomena is operationally identical to that of others.

In psychology it has been the notion of image that

appeared to be a suitable working-hypothesis *(2)*. That it may lie at the base of any science, either natural or moral might be inferred from its application by Norbert Wiener (1894-1964), the father of cybernetics. He distinguished between *pictorial* image and *operative* image *(3)*: "The operative images, which perform the functions of their original may, or may not bear a pictorial likeness to it. Whether they do or not, they may replace the original in its action, and this is a much deeper similarity *(4)*. Instead of pictorial and operative images as used by Wiener, we can actually speak more accurately of operationalisation of objects or systems.

So we might e.g. consider the promulgation of a law-rule as a system's operationalisation.

It was Wiener's intention that the cybernetic principles developed by him would be of universal value and therefore applicable in both natural and moral sciences. This also now applies to Wiener's normative description of a machine *(4)*. Wiener says: "From one standpoint, we may consider a machine as a prime mover, a source of energy. This is not the standpoint which we shall take in this book. For us, a machine is a device for converting incoming messages into outgoing messages. A message, from this point of view, is a sequence of quantities that represent signals in the message. Such quantities may be electrical currents or potentials, *but are not confined to these, and may indeed be of a very different nature (5)*. Moreover the component signals may be distributed continuously or discretely in time. A machine transforms a number of such input messages into a number of output messages, each output message at any moment depending on the input messages up to this moment. As the engineer would say in his jargon, a machine is a multiple-input, multiple-output transducer" *(6)*. There is no reason for not applying this conception of a machine's operationalisation to operationalisation of a State's legal system and of other juridical or social machinery.

The above sketched conception of operationalisation makes a practical working-hypothesis in which neither a dualism within reality, nor a dualism between reality and something else, has any epemistological relevance *(7)*. This hypothesis provides us with a key to the solution of mysteries which neither vitalism *(8)* nor neovitalism could explain and already Wiener himself produced new insights into phenomena of evolution *(9)*.

It is now the moment to discuss the relatedness of cybernetics with the theories of information and communication.

(III.A.2) Cybernetics and the Theories of Information and Communication. Cybernetics is an offshoot of the theory of information. This theory is based on the fact that during any perception, measurement or communication, man is reached by a signal which bears information concerning the outside world. This signal is the physical embodiment of a message; the physical embodiment may occur either in the shape of a wave, a trembling or a current, as for example by the phenomena of light, sound, or electricity, or in the form of a mass which bears information, as for example a letter, a record or a tape. The former shape of embodiment is a means for the transportation of information, which is called communication; the second shape is a means for storage of information, which is called a memory.

The theory of information is now intended for indicating the quantity of information in relation to the communication and storage of messages.

After researches in America by Harry Nyquist and by R.V.L. Hartley in the years between 1917 and 1928 *(1)* it was the Russian scientist A.N. Kolmogoroff and the American scientists Norbert Wiener and Claude Shannon, who mostly contributed to the theory of information. Claude Shannon, a pupil of Wiener, succeeded in developing a mathematical system for the establishment of the relation between efficient use of information and the redundance of words and expressions in human languages.

The efficient transportation of signals is analysed in another offshoot of the theory of information, viz. the theory of communication. The problems which the theories of information and communication have to face are so interwoven, that often the name of one or both is used for indicating the other or both of them; the scientists who contributed to the theory of communication were the same as those who elaborated the theory of information. The theory of communication originates from researches into problems concerning electrical communication *(2)*, but is of value however for any method of communication. The principal problems which the theory of communication has to face are those concerning the adjustment of information, generally by means of encoding, to the capacity of the channel along which the information will be transported. Transportation of information now is always subject to interferences, called fading, which corrupt the meaning of the message. Well-known examples of fading are atmospherics during radio- or TV-broadcasts.

It was also Claude Shannon who succeeded in developing a mathematical method for encoding a signal in such a way, that the information is received without damage by the corruptive activity of fading *(3)*. He arrived at the surprising result, that the best encoding of a signal should occur with the help of control-signals, in such a way, that the encoded signal has statistical properties similar to those of the fading in the channel of communication.

The problems concerned with the transportation of information in self-regulating systems as biologic organisms and human societies caused the development of the science of cybernetics.

(III.A.3) The Notion of Cybernetics. The term "cybernetics" originated *(1)* from Plato. By κυβερνητικα Plato did not only understand the control of ships, but control in general, and so for example the control of states as well. In the year of 1834 the notion of cybernetics was used again by the great French scientist André Marie Ampère (1775-1836), in the classification of all human knowledge, which he started towards the end of his life and in which he tried to formulate his own philosophic opinions. The term cybernetics was used by Ampère for indicating particularly the art of governing a state. Only over a hundred years later the American mathematican Norbert Wiener founded the science of cybernetics, in co-operation with the Mexican physiologist Arturo Rosenblueth. Their co-operation resulted in Wiener's book "Cybernetics: or Control and Communication in the Animal and the Machine" (Cambridge, Mass., 1948 -1).

The principal authors on cybernetics are besides the American scientist Norbert Wiener: The English scientist W.R. Ashby, the Soviet scientists I.A. Poletajew, W.D. Moissejew, S. Rowenski - in co-operation with A. Ujemov and J. Ujemowa - and the Eastern-German philosopher Georg Klaus *(2)*.

To Wiener cybernetics was the science of communicating messages, the control and self-regulation in man, animal and machine. Klaus described cybernetics as the theory of the coherence of possible dynamic self-regulating systems and systems which participate in them *(3)*; Klaus postulates differently from Wiener *(4)* that cybernetics is the science of the possible ways of behaviour of possible structures and thus not of wantonly chosen structures, but of dynamic structures, which means structures which are built within processes dependent on time.

The study of cybernetics thus equally covers coherences, processes of control and regulation, relations of structures and functions, which are actually realized either in technical science, or in nature or nowhere, and does not differ in this respect from any scientific theory or discipline.

(III.A.4) Cybernetic Conceptions

(III.A.4.a) Servomechanism. Self-regulating systems differ in this way from systems regulated by external forces, in that their coherence is not only assured by internal energetic activities, but as well by means of information; there are even self-regulating systems in which the coherence is principally or almost exclusively assured by means of information, as for example societies of men or animals. If within a human society the coherence is assured by military or police measures, then this coherence is not yet exclusively based on the use of information, but on the use of mass and energy as well; a perfect anarchic society, as foreseen by Herbert Spencer or Karl Marx, however does indeed have a coherence, only assured by information. Such self-regulating systems are machines in the sense as Wiener described them; they are also called servomechanisms *(1)*.

A servomechanism may be described as a machine which has to strive under changing conditions to achieve certain aims at the hand of continuous information *(2)*. The information is received in the machine's instruments for perception - as for example an antenna, a telephone, a push-button, an eye, an ear, sensory-organs *(3)*. Hereafter it is transported in the machine's channels of communication, either electric wires, nerves, or the postal delivery service, until it reaches the machine's memory, where the information is stored. This place may be either a tape, a card-index, a catalogue, a notice-book, or be lodged in an animal or a human brain. It is now in the machine's brain that the information, stored in the memory, may be digested, according to certain criteria in relation to the machine's desired pattern of behaviour. We may distinguish, although not entirely separate from each other, a desired pattern for internal behaviour in this respect and one for external behaviour. The internal pattern is always directed to the aim of the machine's self-regulation and may further be directed to the purposes of self-preservation, of growth, of self-reproduction. The pattern of desired external behaviour concerns the purposes to which the machine is directed in relation to the world outside it, as e.g. the control of an aeroplane, the attainment of a certain place by a human being by means of walking, or government legislation or jurisdiction in a State.

In order to perform according to desired patterns of behaviour the machine is, as long as it exercizes this function, in need of information concerning deviations from its own desired patterns of behaviour or from the desired patterns of behaviour of the objects which it controls; such deviations are due to interferences of machine or controlled objects with their environment.

Patterns of controlled objects may moreover be considered as one and the same with the machine's patterns of behaviour, if we consider the machine and the object which it controls as one entirety, as e.g. computer and aeroplane, or brain and spinal marrow on one side and organic body on the other side, or magistrate and state.

After arrangement of the received information, according to criteria concerning the machine's desired pattern of behaviour, information indicating that a deviation is occurring from the desired pattern of behaviour is selected. This information is now carried back from the machine's brain, along its channels of communication, to the instruments with the help of which it exercizes its function, as e.g. the rudder of a ship, the feet of a walking man, the police-force in a State. The information which now is carried back reaches the instruments in such a way, that they commence acts with the tendency to decrease the deviation. These acts may be either movements with the help of mass and energy, like those of a ship's rudder, of the truncheons of the police, or purely informative, like a magistrate's appeal for national solidarity, or both energetic and informative, like commands of policemen with the warning that violence will be used in the event of disobedience. From the moment that the information, which has been carried back, causes events to occur which have a tendency to decrease the deviation, it changes the expected input of later information received by the machine. For if such events would not have been caused, the information received later would have been different. So if in our examples the ship's rudder would not have been moved and the ship brought to another position, later information might have concerned a shipwreck; if the police-force would not have been brought in after information concerning riots, a revolution might have occurred.

This method of carrying back information is called *negative feedback*; the notion of "negative" is used because this feedback is directed towards decrease - and not increase - of a deviation from a desired pattern of behaviour.

Negative feedback is a means of assuring and increasing

coherence within and among living organisms or between living organisms and dead nature *(4)*. We possess knowledge of a scale of increasingly complicated and therefore higher arranged cybernetic systems by which it is possible, extrapolating all the time, to imagine a limit of total disorder and consequently the absence of any feedback at all *(5)*.

(III.A.4.b) Theories of Game. The relations between a self-regulating system and factors outside it which in some way try to influence the system - among these relationships those between separated self-regulating systems should also be counted - can be considered as relationships of games between different partners. To any act in the game of the first partner the other partner answers with a contra-act. It was the Hungarian-American mathematician John von Neumann (1903-1957) who developed a mathematical theory of games, applicable in any situation where men are struggling, either in playing chequers, chess or poker as well as in military conflicts, struggles of hostile populations in the animal world or in economic competition. Together with Oskar Morgenstern he applied his theory of game to economic situations *(1)*.

Neumann's theory of game is based on the supposition, that the players are not only familiar with the rules of the game, but also have knowledge of any situation which might occur in the play and know exactly what in any situation would be the best solution for winning the game.

This feature of von Neumann's theory was rejected by Wiener *(2)* as not being relevant to game-playing machines. Wiener describes the way in which such machines existing *(3)* at present do not function according to the pattern of the Neumann game theory, but are "much more closely analogous to the procedure of the ordinary human game player": both game-playing machine and game-playing man learn by experience, being only familiar at the game's beginning with the rules of the game. On the possible applications of his game-conception - the "learning game" - Wiener said *(4)*: "The chief criterion as to whether a line of human effort can be embodied in a game is whether there is some objectively recognizable criterion of the merit of the performance of this effort. Otherwise the game assumes the formlessness of the croquet game in Alice in Wonderland, where ... the umpire (was) the Queen of Hearts, who kept changing the rules and sending the players to the Headsman to be beheaded. Under these circumstances, to win has no meaning, and a successful policy cannot be carried out with success.

However, given an objective criterion of success, the learning game may certainly be played, and is much closer to the way in which we learn to play games than in the image of a game given in the von Neumann theory. Unquestionably the technique of the learning game is certain to be employed in many fields of the human effort which have not been subjected to it. Nevertheless ..... the determination of a sharp test for good performance raises many problems concerning learning games".

That human behaviour can be described as a game was in particular demonstrated by the Dutch historian Johan Huizinga (1872-1945). In his work "*Homo Ludens*" (1938) he investigates the problem, as to how far human civilisation is a game *(5)*. It is a thorough analysis of the role of game as a fundamental structural feature in past and actual human societies *(6)*. Huizinga's conception of game fits in more with that of Wiener than with that of Neumann, for Huizinga sees only a possibility of playing, if there is no absolute determinism *(7)*.

Civilisation is a notion which neither Wiener nor Neumann treated in their works. We have formulated a description of civilisation in *(IV.B.3.c)* and in our last note to *(I.B.2.b)* we discussed the relatedness of civilisation to societies.

The data collected in "*Homo Ludens*" might be of great value for the analysis of cybernetic principles in communities of men. Huizinga's notion of game is limited to a conscious playing, with a certain self-restraint, as a condition for civilisation's existence: those who break the rules of the game break civilisation: war is not a game *(8)*. This conception is in accordance with that of the role of games as a means to assure and increase a coherence between the players or a player and an object of playing.

Neumann's theory has its own merits in the theory of communication. Communication can be considered as a game, which is played, according to certain rules, with encoded information: the rules of the play and the encoding provide the players with a common strategy, and they would know exactly what to do, if there would not be a third factor, viz. that of unknown parameters, which are the origin of fading. With their common strategy the players now not only play a game among each other, but also with fading. The occurrence of fading can only be neutralized, if the players apply Claude Shannon's theory, that the encoded signal should have statistical properties similar to those of the fading in the channel of communication. In other words: communication is also a game, which the communicating parties play with nature.

The game conceptions in the theories of information and communication hold that coherences between a self-regulating system and other objects, which may, but should not, be other self-regulating systems, may either be developed by means of learning games or emerge at once by means of Neumann games. Such coherences, from which at least one self-regulating system is a part, may be considered as self-regulating systems in their turn. We will see now how this is possible.

(III.A.4.c) Game-playing Servomechanisms, especially in the area of Law. A machine which controls another object, may be considered as playing a game with the object of control. The controlling machine forwards information to the object of control, containing a message which is an instruction for behaviour by the controlled object. The controlling machine receives information concerning the controlled object's behaviour by means of perception. If the controlling machine perceives that this object's behaviour is not according to the instructed pattern then it may forward a corrective signal, which is a message with the tendency to decrease the deviation in the controlled object's behaviour. If this negative feedback has an effective result, then we are allowed to say that the controlling machine makes a score in the game; if the negative feedback is unsuccessful then it is the controlled object which makes a score. Such a play is for example that between computer and aeroplane; if the computer looses this play then its loss might well be similar to a total loss in the sense of insurance-law.

Controlling machine and controlled object thus make one entirety, with a common pattern of behaviour. The coherence between the parts of this entirety is realized by means of a game between these parts. If the controlling machine is a learning machine it may learn better to perform acts of negative feedback by means of the information which it receives by perception, and so in the course of time the coherence between the parts of the entirety will increase. A motorist and his car, an author and his typewriter, someone with bad eyesight and his spectacles, they all make different entireties, of which the parts may increase their coherence.

If somebody now owns a car, makes use of a typewriter and wears spectacles, then he can be considered as a system which controls distinguished objects. Controlled objects and controlling system may now be considered from different aspects. It is possible to defend that all the controlled objects make together with the controlling system one great entirety. It is also possible to consider separately the relations between any controlled object and the system which it controls; then we may take the controlling system as divided into different qualities and per quality sharing in different entireties with different objects of control. In this latter case direct relationships need not exist at all between these entireties, as in our example of the entireties which embody respectively the motor-car and the typewriter. But there may be indirect relevant relations between such entireties. If for example control over the spectacles is lost it might be impossible to continue the control over the motor-car or the typewriter. So far now as the car's use is concerned there may be a legal prescription, forbidding a person to drive a car if he does not wear his spectacles. Such a legal rule belongs both to the desired pattern of behaviour for the entirety of man and motor-car and to the entirety of man and spectacles. If the controlling system - man - loses its spectacles when driving, man is expected to transmit instructions to his car causing it to stop safely. The car and the spectacles being the driver's property, we see here, how a law-rule may embody a desired pattern of behaviour for an entirety, self-regulating system, composed by man and property. Equally we may consider any entirety composed of man and any good or right which he has under him as an owner, possessor, detentor or by other qualification, as a self-regulating system, a servomechanism.

We are now able to see as well, that an entirety of controlling system and controlled object may be controlled again in its turn. In the example of the motor-car driver who loses his spectacles it is the police-force and the judicial power behind it which may be considered as the controlling system, which has the capacity to give instructions to the entirety of man and motor-car for behaviour according to the rules of law, if this entirety deviates from the desired pattern of behaviour contained in legal rules.

So two servomechanisms, of which one strives to control the other, play a game; the controlled servomechanism has relative to the controlling one, a desired pattern of behaviour; the controlling servomechanism has relative to the controlled one, a pattern of expectations and negative feedback opportunities in order to correct deviations from the other servomechanism's desired pattern of behaviour and to make this behaviour as much as possible in accordance with its (the controlling servomechanism's) pattern of expectations. The game played is necessarily a learning game; the pattern of expectations in the controlling servomechanism is identical to the desired pattern of behaviour in the controlled one but its behaviour itself may deviate from these patterns within the limits posed by negative feedback.

It is possible to consider two game-playing servomechanisms, of which one strives to control the other, as one servomechanism. Such a servomechanism has a desired pattern of behaviour identical to that in the controlled one and the pattern of expectations in the controlling servomechanism. This servomechanism is therefore working towards a certain aim: behaviour by the controlled servomechanism according to the expectations of the controlling one, or winning the game by the latter.

I will illustrate this by a few examples from the world of law.

It is the principal's pattern of behaviour which determines that of the agent: the agent's behaviour ought to be in accordance with the pattern of which he has been informed by the principal, and if not, then the principal can employ a mechanism of negative feedback in the shape of legal remedy. Principal and agent can thus be considered as making one servomechanism, with a pattern of behaviour directed towards the aim that the agent will fulfil the mandate.

This is equally the case in any other unilateral obligation. So creditor and debtor, have, so far as their relationship to a certain debt is concerned, a common pattern of respectively expectations and desired behaviour, for the creditor has the capacity to determine the debtor's behaviour with the help of negative feedback in the shape of legal remedy and his decisions on this determination are dependent upon his own pattern of behaviour. So also debtor and creditor can together be considered as one servomechanism, with a desired pattern of behaviour, determined by the laws and the contract from which their obligations originated. While debtor and creditor play a game the servomechanism is directed towards the end, that the creditor will win, or that the debt will be paid.

We will now consider the case, that two servomechanisms mutually control each other. Here the servomechanisms play a game, in which they mutually give each other instruction for the correction of deviations in each other's desired pattern of behaviour. So each system's own behaviour determines the negative feedback with the help of which it tries to correct undesired deviations from the desired pattern of behaviour of the other system. Also here the two systems may be considered as making one servomechanism, with a common purpose and a common pattern of behaviour. Such servomechanisms are those in which the systems by which they are composed play a game within the framework of a mutual obligation. Here it is not, as in the previous examples, a situation in which a person is subordinated to another person, but one in which two persons are mutually subordinated to each other.

A servomechanism of this kind is e.g. that composed of a buyer and a seller: it is directed to making the buyer a proprietor of the goods and the realization of the price by the seller. This servomechanism is ordained to terminate when the aim has been reached, i.e. when seller and buyer have both fulfilled their obligations, or, if the fulfilment did not occur before, when their obligations became superannuated or the contract ended in other ways regulated by law or the contract itself.

A servomechanism of the same class is that composed by a partnership. The partners have mutual obligations towards each other to co-operate together for a common purpose; their common desired patterns of behaviour are determined by this common purpose and are similar to their obligations of co-operation. They mutually control each other and have the power to correct each other's deviations from the common desired pattern of behaviour. We find a similar situation in a servomechanism which is composed of two individuals who are married to each other; this servomechanism is popularly called a couple.

By treating, with the help of juridical examples, control of cybernetic machines by cybernetic machines, we arrived at a rough description of some juridical servomechanisms. These juridical servomechanisms are characterized by among others the fact that they contain men among their components, but only in a certain quality. They are servomechanisms in a similar way as a servomechanism composed by an automobile and its driver: whether a bad motorist is an emancipated woman or not, is not relevant.

The juridical servomechanisms which I treated here are operationalized systems and they have therefore an existence which can become known by us; they exist in relations between man among each other and may be relative to corporeal or incorporeal things; their structure will be considered in *(III.C)*. Before treating this specialised branch of cybernetics as an introduction to the principles of legal evolution we have to consider now the relations between cybernetics and evolution in general.

(III.B) A CYBERNETIC CONCEPTION OF EVOLUTION.

In *(I.C.7)* we concluded that the discovery of a general description of evolution should be furthered by considering the self-regulation of a system of action and reaction composed by a unit and its environment.

The self-regulation of such a system of action and reaction now can only provide for the coherence *(1)* of the elements from which it is composed when this system's structure is based on control over itself and independence of changes in itself. If the system has no control over itself and no independence of changes in itself, then it is not self-regulating. A system which provides for control over itself and independence of changes in itself is according to the principles of cybernetics a servomechanism, i.e. an operationalised system which has to strive under changing conditions to achieve certain aims at the hand of continuous information.

We will investigate now how we can describe evolution of such systems. Evolution being in any case an increase in quality it is the science of information which has related this idea of evolution to the use of information as we will now see.

(III.B.1) Evolution, Information, Disorder and Law.

The laws of thermodynamics state that within a closed system energy remains constant in quantity as time passes, but that there is a decrease in the system's quality.

Within a system of living beings and environment it is the living being who tries to collect information from his environs. This may result in an increase in disorder on the side of the environment. This can be seen e.g. in a book. While the reader increases in quality by the information which he absorbs, it is not only the book as a bearer of information which decreases in quality, but also the information itself contained in it: this information is increasingly subject to fading. Similarly this is the case with information on records, tapes or movie-pictures: each time they are played there is an increase in fading. Moreover, any storage of information is already a cause of decreases in its quality, even if the information - bearers are kept in the safest corners of archives, libraries or museums. Any object bears information about itself and its environment in past and present and these data can be extracted from it by direct perception or by indirect perception with the help of instruments. Any collection of information results in an increase of the collector's quality, but, so far as information is collected from a physical object there is a decrease in quality or increase in disorder on the object's side: information collected later from a physical object will be subject to more fading than information collected earlier.

This latter may however not be the case with information collected from a living being.

Living beings resist - in contrast with physical objects *(1)* - to increases in disorder or decreases in quality *(2)*; they strive after increasement in quality or greater order *(3)*. This does not only result in biological specialisation, but also in creations of specialised nature such as technical products or works of art.

A *closed* system of living beings and physical environment can fundamentally not decrease its disorder: there always remains a decrease of the system's quality.

The reason of this is that the increase in quality of a living being may be almost as great as the increase in disorder of its environment, but never greater. Within a closed system of living beings and environment this increase in quality is realized at the cost of the environment which increases in disorder. Biological and social evolution can in such a system only continue as long as the environment's quality is sufficient. Evolution of the system as a whole is however impossible because its quality cannot increase *(4)*.

This conclusion applies however only to absolutely closed systems and does not include the possibility that a living being cannot rearrange his environment anew in such a way that new information is at his disposal. Then a decrease occurs in the environment's disorder and the quality of the system becomes greater. Of course such a rearrangement appropriates information from the living being, who undergoes an increase in disorder, but this increase in disorder may be less than the greater quality obtained in the environment and therefore obtained in the system as a whole.

A living being can rearrange his environs by means of negative feedback. This is due to the fact that negative feedback originated in living nature as a defensive method against the disorder which intrudes upon it from every angle *(5)*.

It is not even necessary for the rearrangement to be brought about by the living being: it may be due to causes in the environment itself. A thunderbolt may set an impenetrable jungle on fire and so create a fertile agricultural area or open the road to the discovery of important minerals. A system of living beings and environment can therefore increase in quality as long as the environment is not absolutely stable. The environment's stability depends on the activity of living beings or properties of the environment itself, or both.

Present day's struggle against environmental pollution and the exhaustion of natural resources is a search for rearrangements in the environment. If this is waged in such a way that it leads to important limitations in industrial development then its results may lead to disastrous increases in disorder. If nothing is done, the results may be equally serious. Rearrangement of the environs should therefore be guided in such a way, that new useful information becomes available. This can only occur however, if mankind disposes of information on the ways to find this new information. This means that funds should be devoted as much as possible to research and education for research, and not only research into the immediate scientific and social problems of environmental pollution and exhaustion, but also into problems apparently not related to these questions: the side effects of a research may be of much greater importance than its direct results.

A first step in this direction are the inventarisations and predictions published in "The Limits To Growth - A Report for the Club of Rome Project on the Predicament of Mankind" (New York, 1972) *(6)*. If the conclusions in this report - the world's demographic and economic growth should decrease - are correct*(7)*, then this report may give a stimulating impulse to a struggle against threatening disorder everywhere in the world.

We have here a clear example, that growth by itself is not evolution; in systems of living beings and environment, where environs can be rearranged anew evolution is a decrease in disorder of the system, due to the rearrangement. If the environs cannot be rearranged anew, then such a system is not subject to evolution, but to increases in disorder. In both cases the struggles occur against threatening disorder according to similar principles.

It will be clear that knowledge of these principles is extremely important to mankind. Processes of evolution, which are struggles against disorder, are fundamentally related to the existence of the world and therefore to the existence of the individual. An insight into the structure of these processes may also have consequences with respect to our ideas on the structure and the fundamental principles of law and morals. It is by morals and laws that among human beings order is created and maintained, and disorder prevented *(8)*. We detract nothing from the value of morals by establishing that in modern societies this role is for the greater part fulfilled by law *(9)*. Law is moreover the main device by which order is created and maintained between human societies. Further, it is by means of law that human interferences into nature and the human environment may be controlled. It seems therefore correct to conclude that law is mankind's basic device in its struggle against the eternal threats of disorder in no-osphere.

(III.B.2) Evolution of systems of living beings and environs. In *(III.A.4.a)* and *(III.A.4.c)* we saw that servomechanisms can have various desired patterns of behaviour. Some of these patterns now may be related to learning processes and have therefore, if they are followed, the effect of a greater coherence between the parts of which a servomechanism is composed. Such patterns are directed towards the objective that the servomechanism shall obtain a certain fixed measure of control over itself and independence of changes within itself.

This also applies to systems of living beings and environment. If in such systems the desired increases in control over itself and independence of changes in itself indeed occur, then we can speak of advance or evolution of the system. Notice that this conception of advance is relative to systems of particular living beings and their particular environment.

(III.B.3) Evolution and the notion "Game-bound Unit" or Qualitative Servomechanism. There are some particularities with respect to our notion of evolution which include advance of systems of particular living beings and their particular environment.

The main issue here is that a living being can form differentiated servomechanisms with differentiated parts of its environments. A man and a motor car constitute a servomechanism which can be distinguished, although not absolutely separated, from the same man and his typewriter. The same is true if the particular environment is a servomechanism in its turn. A man and his wife can be considered as a servomechanism which is different to that composed of the same man and his secretary. In all these cases there is a person who is bound, for a relatively long time or for a relatively short time, in a particular servomechanical unit. Within these differentiated units different games are played consisting of attempts to correct or prevent deviations from desired patterns of behaviour. It is by means of special games that such systems have a coherence and may be subjected to advance or evolution in the sense described here above.

Here we see that this evolution is in point of fact evolution of various elementary servomechanical units composed of a living being, acting in various qualities, and of various elementary parts of its environs corresponding with certain qualities of the living being. These units are therefore the smallest possible absolute units which can be subject to evolution. They are absolute because they cannot be divided into smaller units which can be subject to evolution. As absolute units however they are part of at least one relative unit, i.e. a unit which can be distinguished between absolute units. Such a relative unit is e.g. a system of living beings and environs in which an individual and all parts of its environment with which it plays games, is considered as one entirety.

From a pure cybernetical point of view there is no fundamental distinction between organic and inorganic servomechanisms. What has been said now about evolution of systems of living beings and environment therefore applies to any servomechanical system, composed of a servomechanism, either organic or not, and its environs. It is moreover a matter of indifference, whether the environment is in whole or in part a servomechanism itself. All these servomechanical systems of servomechanisms and environment can be classified in absolute and relative units. It is by means of games that these units have a coherence and may strive for advance in the sense described in *(III.B.2)*. It is for this reason that we name these units "game-bound units" or qualitative servomechanisms.

The game-bound units have been identified here as absolute game-bound units, which are the smallest possible game-bound units, and relative game-bound units. These will be normatively described now as composed of absolute game-bound units in which the games are played by either the same servomechanism and different particular environs, or by two servomechanisms which have a particular environment relative to each other. Relative game-bound units may therefore be, but are not necessarily, complex entireties of a game-playing servomechanism and its environment.

Among game-bound units we can therefore distinguish between the following forms:

1) Absolute game-bound units. These are composed of a servomechanism and a special part of its environment with which one special game is played. If different games are played with the same part of the environment, then there are different absolute game-bound units. A special part of a servomechanism's environment may be another servomechanism. An absolute game-bound unit's desired pattern of behaviour is a set of rules relative to one game.
2) Relative game-bound units. These are composed of absolute game-bound units and can be distinguished by:
   a) relative game-bound units in which a servomechanism plays differentiated games with the same part of its environment;
   b) relative game-bound units in which a servomechanism plays - differentiated - games with various parts of its environment;
   c) relative game-bound units in which a servomechanism plays games with the whole of its environment.
3) Complex entireties of absolute or relative game-bound units. In these it is several servomechanisms, playing one or more games with their environs or at least one special part of it, which also play games among each other.

Another particularity of game-bound units is that the environment may also include information, because this can be contained in the environment of any servomechanism and be the object of a game. Within game-bound units it is ultimately always information which a game-playing servomechanism strives to digest. This information concerns either the environment or the servomechanism itself. The environment can only interact with the servomechanism by means of information. The information from the environment or from the servomechanism itself may even concern the servomechanism's desired pattern of behaviour: if information is received to the effect that a desired pattern of behaviour becomes changed or substituted by another pattern, then a change occurs in the rules of the game and therefore in the course of the game.

An important characteristic of game-bound units is further, that within the framework of a greater game-bound unit replacement and succession is possible of the smaller game-bound units of which it is composed, just as in any construction the parts may be changed, while the construction as a whole remains in its essence the same.

(III.B.4) Evolution as Evolution of Game-bound Units. Evolution of game-bound units is always evolution of absolute game-bound units. If this evolution of absolute game-bound units has the effect that relative units obtain a greater control over themselves and independence of changes within themselves, then we can establish evolution of relative game-bound units. It is not necessary that such an effect occurs; evolution of an absolute unit may happen at the cost of another absolute unit within the framework of the same relative game-bound unit and this may lead to retrogression in the relative unit. The same is true in respect to any complex game-bound unit in relation to the less complex game-bound units of which it is composed. Evolution of a complex game-bound unit is therefore always reducible to evolution of at least one of the less complex units of which it is composed and ultimately reducible to evolution of at least one absolute game-bound unit. Evolution however of a less complex unit only may, but does not necessarily lead to evolution of a greater unit of which it forms a part.

It is on the basis of these principles that we can give the following normative description of evolution: *Evolution is an increase in control over itself and an increase in independence of changes within itself of a servomechanical unit, composed of a servomechanism and that part of its environment with which it plays a game, or of a complex of such units.*

Or, in other words, *evolution is an increase in control over itself and an increasing independence of changes in itself of a game-bound unit or of complexes of game-bound units.*

This description is applicable in biosphere and in no-osphere; it can be used to establish evolution in human values because the notion of environment includes that of information; it is moreover the base for the description of legal evolution which will be formulated in *(IV.A.4)*.

(III.B.5) Evolution in Biosphere. It is usual to speak of evolution of species in relation to biosphere. A species can be considered as part of a complex game-bound unit with at the base absolute game-bound units of an individual and his environment. The absolute units may form relative units, composed of individuals and their environment, or other relative units, as for example collections or groups of identical plants and their environs and such relative units can form together a still greater game-bound unit, a species and its environs. *Biological*

evolution is an increase in coherence of a game-bound unit composed of a species and its environment.

Within a species transmission of genetic information occurs by intermingling of the individuals, and selection of the appropriate genetic information occurs by natural selection. We have seen that Norbert Wiener sees Darwinian selection as a learning process of a species *(1)*.

This process may only occur however, if within a species, intermingling is possible in such a way, that in each successive generation additional individuals are affected by the new genetic information until all new individuals of the species have received it. It may be however that groups originating from a species are isolated from each other; in this case isolated game-bound units follow their own path of evolution. Changes in the environs and changes in the games between species and environs are also of great importance. This can be seen in the domestication of animals and plants. Evolution in the case of domestication can only be established by ascertaining whether game-bound units of species and environs have a greater control over themselves and independence of changes in themselves before or after a process of domestication. The period of changes in the environment and the games played with it should of course be related to the period of changes in the species. The environs are in any case the actual geo-physical conditions under which a species lives, biological phenomena and in many cases phenomena of human origin.

The learning process within a game-bound unit of a species and its environs from which evolution of such a game-bound unit may result, can also be seen as a selection between the game-bound units of which the entirety of species and environment is composed. Notice that these game-bound units are not only determined by the genetic information in the individual of the species, but that the environs also play important roles in the selection. Notice moreover that the game-bound units between which selection takes place may be relative and absolute and concern any kind of game in which individuals of a species are related to their environment. The game-bound units with the greatest coherences have the best chances in the process of selection and this leads to survival of these game-bound units composed of individual and environment, which have the greatest coherence because they are composed of smaller essential game-bound units with the greatest possible coherence.

The principles of selection among game-bound units act in biosphere in the same manner as in no-osphere and will be discussed in *(III.B.6.a)*.

(III.B.6) Evolution in No-osphere. The principles treated in relation to evolution in biosphere lay at the base of evolution in no-osphere. *No-ospheric evolution is evolution of the game-bound unit of mankind and its environs*; this kind of evolution is human evolution and therefore its phenomena demonstrate the influences of the fact that human beings, compared to non-human beings, constitute with their environs game-bound units having considerably greater control over themselves and independence of changes within themselves.

The environment of human beings has a greater element of information than the environment of non-human beings; moreover it is at least for human beings possible to transform assimilated information into new information.

In considering game-bound units in no-osphere not only those composed of man and environs should be taken into account, but also game-bound units of man-controlled organic and inorganic servomechanisms and their environment. They are of a lower order than game-bound units in which a human being plays a game because they are controlled by men, i.e. because they are in greater game-bound units the environs and playmates of a human being.

(III.B.6.a) The principles of Selection in No-osphere. In *(III.B.5)* we considered evolution in biology as evolution of a game-bound unit composed of a species and its environment, caused by a selection among game-bound units comprised in such an entirety. Evolution in no-osphere does not differ fundamentally from that in biosphere, but the relations among the game-bound units involved are still far more complicated than in biosphere. There is however a fundamental distinction between the nature of the game-bound units in biosphere and no-osphere and this distinction influences the results of selection.

Selection in no-osphere is a selection among game-bound units in which the pattern of desired behaviour are determined by human values. In *(III.B.6.c)* human values will be distinguished in ethical, aesthetical and technological values, the values of the highest order being, in my opinion, the ethical.

Selection among no-ospheric game-bound units may lead to no-ospheric evolution, i.e. to a greater coherence of the game-bound unit composed of mankind and its environs, but a similar increase in coherence is not necessarily the case with those game-bound units which operate in the process of selection. These game-bound units may be the mediate or immediate cause of no-ospheric evolution:

1) by a decrease in coherence;
2) by their dissolution;
3) by their creation;
4) by an increase in coherence.

This selection among game-bound units can be considered as a learning process. The game-bound units which decrease in coherence or become dissolved are succeeded by newly created game-bound units or by already existing ones which are of greater coherence. Those game-bound units which are the best fitted to promote greater coherences of no-osphere are those in which information concerning human values is realized in their control over themselves and independence of changes within themselves. The learning process is a process of the game-bound unit of mankind and its environs. Within the framework of this game-bound unit this learning is a learning of mankind as a whole and the organic and inorganic servomechanisms which it controls.

The ultimate result of this selection among game-bound units is greater coherence of no-osphere by means of a more appropriate realization of human values. We will consider the role of these values in *(III.B.6.e)* and *(IV.B.2.a)*.

(III.B.6.b) The effects of Selection in No-osphere. We have seen that selection among game-bound units is the immediate or mediate cause of no-ospheric evolution.

Selection acts immediately if by its result the game-bound unit composed of mankind and its environment directly increases in coherence. Selection acts mediately by means of cumulative effects and side-effects.

A greater coherence in a game-bound unit is always the result of selection among game-bound units. Such a greater coherence may lead to still greater coherences of other game-bound units by affecting game-bound units with which it forms greater entireties: such greater systems may, but will not necessarily, increase in coherence in their turn, and so on, until the greatest possible game-bound unit is affected, which is in no-osphere that composed of mankind and its environs.

These cumulative effects may however not occur if such an advance takes place at the cost of other game-bound units which contribute to the coherence of greater systems or even no-osphere. Also this is a queation of selection. E.g. introduction of monogamy in polygamic organised agrarian societies where the wives cultivate the land, may lead to a shortage of food. Possible greater coherence in matrimonial game-bound units is counteracted by a decrease in coherence between the game-bound units composed of the husbands and their real estate.

Side effects of a selection among game-bound units are increases in coherence of game-bound units not involved in the selection, which are of comparable order to the selected game-bound units within the framework of a greater entirety or within the framework of comparable entireties. Such effects will be discussed in *(III.B.6.d)* where it will be seen that these effects are the result of imitation or inspiration by examples of games in selected game-bound units.

(III.B.6.c) Selection and Information on Human Values. The main difference between biospheric and no-ospheric evolution is the notion of selection. Human evolution can indeed be considered as a process of learning, but the selection by which this occurs is no longer a pure "natural" proceeding. This is due to the fact that in the environs of human beings information is included in human values. This information has been accumulated and digested in the course of history and concerns desired patterns for behaviour of men relative to other men or other parts of human environment. Although it is not ruled out that some of these patterns are innate, as for example that a mother should protect her children, it seems certain that most of these result from processes of learning. This can be seen in the fact that various religious or philosophical conceptions may lead, although this is not necessarily so, to similar desired patterns for human behaviour.

The transmission of genetic information is influenced by the fact that human individuals make game-bound units in which desired patterns for behaviour are determined by human values, or that human thinkers make game-bound units together with information on human values in which this information is digested and transformed into possibly new information. This influence can occur consciously or unconsciously. The latter we see for example in a society's choice for or against polygamy: in a polygamic society we see transmission of more identical genetic information than in a monogamic society. Influence of the former kind, of consciously influenced transmission of genetic information is e.g. that of birth-control practice, of artificial insemination or of eugenic measures.

(III.B.6.d) Human Values as stimulating forces in No-ospheric Evolution. It is not only the idea of selection which in no-osphere is different to that in biosphere because of the disposal of information on human values *(1)*. Information on human values determines desired patterns of behaviour in no-ospheric game-bound units, as we have seen. If this desired behaviour according to human values can be realized by negative feedback opportunities, then this realization of human values, like any realization of desired behaviour in a servomechanism has the effect that the concerned game-bound unit obtains a greater coherence, a greater control over itself and independence of changes within itself. This may be of evolutionary effect relative to the game-bound units of higher order to which it belongs and can therefore ultimately determine evolution in the whole no-ospheric area. There may moreover be indirect effects, by means of information, concerning the behaviour followed and this may be an example or inspiration in other similar cases. These effects are side effects, which may cause evolution of other game-bound units with desired patterns of behaviour relative to human values, both composed of the same individual as well as of others; also these side effects may determine evolution in the whole realm of no-osphere. This can be seen in the effects of the examples and inspiration given by mankind's great saints, thinkers, inventors and artists.

Moreover, we have already seen that new information on human values can be generated within game-bound units composed of philosopher or inventor and information. This new information in its turn may stimulate evolution in no-osphere by development of new desired patterns of behaviour in game-bound units.

(III.B.6.e) An Ethical Criterion based upon the Principles of Evolution. We have seen that our general description of evolution is applicable to evolution of man and its environment if desired patterns of behaviour and appropriate negative feedback are to the effect that human values are realized.We will consider now, whether an ethical criterion may be derived from this applicability.

An ethical criterion is a criterion for human values and concerns human behaviour. Ethical values are not the only human values but they are at the base of any human social life and therefore at the base of any other human value *(1)*. Next to ethical values are technological *(2)* and aesthetical values *(3)*. These three kinds of values, often interwoven, determine the conditions of human life.

Criteria for human values are generally subjective and in their turn determined by religious or philosophic convictions. They are therefore often based on facts which one should presumably believe implicitly without any actual possibility of checking by scientific methods, especially so far as religious criteria are concerned. Sometimes they are indeed also based on results of science or on facts which in principle are suitable for checking by science, especially so far as they are related to philosophic criteria.

It is of course an unsatisfactory situation, that criteria for human values are derived by different men from different religious or philosophic sources, although in practice criteria for human values based on those of a religious or a philosophic system with great numbers of followers in different cultural areas may demonstrate a large number of similarities in many respects. Of course this can be explained by the fact, that a religion or a philosophy cannot extend itself over different cultural areas, if it does not provide suitable answers to universal human needs.

It might now seem possible to formulate a catalogue of human values, which these religious and philosophic systems all commonly consider as paramount, and to develop in this way objective criteria for human values, by which evolution in human values might be established.

If such criteria could indeed be developed, even taking into account that they are dependent on conditions of place and time, then there is still one thing which they lack: one cannot establish whether they are indeed criteria, which together are adequate for application in any human situation; it might appear that such objectivated common criteria only cover but a part of the possible human situations, and that they do not even coincide with actual or future criteria developed through scientific research.

In *(I.D.2)* we discussed Spencer's endeavour to formulate an ethical criterion based upon his concept of evolution. Also neodarwinism has brought forward an interesting approach towards an objective criterion for human values in which the human values are dominated by a fundamental ethical principle. Sir Julian Huxley has tried to formulate, in addition to his normative description of biological progress, a description of ethical progress *(4)*, being at the same time a description of human progress. Huxley's criterion declares that it is man's destiny to discover, by means of an increasing realization of possibilities, how to control and how to direct evolution.

It is indeed possible to construct on the basis of this conception a number of prescriptions for human behaviour and Huxley himself has used it as a foundation for his "Evolutionary Humanism". Whatever the merits might be of Huxley's ethical criterion, there is one objection to it: it is still based on an element of faith, viz. faith in thepossibilities of man *(5)* and an *a priori* belief in evolution. Indeed it should be acknowledged that Huxley has stated scientific reasons for his faith, but this does not change the fact that faith is a different kind of knowledge to that based on scientific data and theories, although these give to the researcher a certain faith as well; a criterion based on faith however cannot be accepted as an objective criterion, since faith is an entirely subjective insight.

We have already seen in *(III.B.6.c)* that information on human values determines, by means of selection among game-bound units, desired patterns of behaviour in game-bound units and may determine negative feedback opportunities by which behaviour according to these desired patterns of behaviour can increasingly become a more probable occurrence. Such a realization of behaviour according to human values leads, like any other result of learning in a servomechanism, to a greater coherence of a game-bound unit.

We have also seen in *(III.B.6.b)* that a greater coherence in a selected game-bound unit may lead to greater coherences of greater entireties of game-bound units and even no-osphere, by means of cumulative effects. This also applies to game-bound units where the desired patterns of behaviour are concerned with human values.

We have seen as well in *(III.B.6.d)* jo *(III.B.6.b)* that evolution of a game-bound unit by behaviour according to human values may lead to side effects: such a behaviour can be an example or inspiration within other no-ospheric game-bound units and in their turn cause cumulative effects in greater ones. These side effects may promote the velocity of evolution of the system of mankind and environs.

It is on the basis of these principles, that behaviour in accordance with human values may ultimately result in evolution in the game-bound unit composed of mankind and environs. If it is ultimately impossible that human behaviour could have this effect, with the presumed values correctly applied, then the values followed are wrong. The whole complex of human values requires therefore a criterion relative to the desiredness of application of basic principles for human behaviour.

All relations in which man is involved can be imagined as game-bound units, i.e. self-regulating systems in which games of differentiated types are played which have a tendency to increase the system's coherence. These processes are *fundamental*: if games with this tendency are no longer played then there is no game-bound unit left, because of the continuous threat of disintegration of the system, or at least continuous struggle against threatening decrease in coherence, or disorder. Striving for such increases in coherence is therefore also essential for the existence of no-osphere, i.e. the game-bound unit composed of mankind as a whole and its environs.

Human behaviour should thus of necessity be so organised that it may ultimately lead to greater coherence or evolution of no-osphere and it should certainly not be potentially harmful to no-ospheric evolution by causing increases in disorder.

In other words: *man should act consciously in such a way that a greater control over itself and independence of changes in itself might result, by cumulative or side effects, in the game-bound unit of mankind and environment.* His acts should therefore have the potential to lead cumulatively to greater coherences in successive cumulating game-bound units in which he is an accessory with his environment, and they should moreover be potential examples for imitation or inspiration to other men.

This criterion of ethical nature can determine all human behaviour and is therefore also applicable in respect to values outside the area of ethics. We will name this ethical criterion the criterion of evolution's interest; it's nature is that of information with which any human being can form an absolute game-bound unit. The desired pattern of behaviour in this game-bound unit can be formulated in the sense, that man is expected to apply this criterion as a desired pattern of behaviour in all other game-bound units in which he is a game-player. Man is indeed free to apply or not to apply this criterion, but if he does not, retrogression or dissolution of game-bound units is the result. Ultimately no-osphere, the game-bound unit of mankind as a whole and its environs, may be destroyed. If man strives to apply this criterion perhaps no paradise will follow but the effect of greater coherences will give satisfaction to man's creative needs, and this will lead to greater coherence, to evolution within the human individual himself: man does not only play games with his external environs, but also with the world within him.

Application of this criterion is not easy, both because of man's inclination to egocentricity, and because of the necessity of assembling appropriate information for a selection of appropriate behaviour.

It is now possible to attribute the qualification "good" to every event or phenomenon that has a tendency to promote no-ospheric evolution; the qualification "evil" may now be attributed to every event or phenomenon in contradistinction to such a promotion. Of course "good" and "evil" in this conception are only two poles, between which large numbers of notions extend which in this respect are either neutral or mixed; in the latter situation the ethical criterion may nevertheless serve as a reliable guide.

For instance, so far as the attitude towards criminals is concerned, treatment directed to their return in society, compared with life-long imprisonment, denotes ethical progress. As free men they might contribute more to society's evolution than as prisoners; such a contribution might occur directly, but in any case it could occur indirectly, because this treatment may express the value of each individual for evolution, even if the treatment is unsuccessful.

Our interpretation of evolution and its application to an ethical criterion for ethical progress embody together a conception which is based on scientific data and concerning which an attempt has been made to link it up with both the historical development of the most important theories of evolution and present day's ideas on man. The ethical criterion developed here is a general criterion for all human behaviour. It is therefore also a fundamental principle with the capacity of determining the area of law *(6)*. Before investigating, however, the relations between law and the criterion of evolution's interest, we should know law's place in no-osphere and the relations between no-ospheric evolution and legal evolution. We now propese to devote the following pages to these subjects.

(III.C) A CYBERNETIC CONCEPTION OF LEGAL CONSTRUCTIONS

(III.C.1) Introduction. Law belongs to no-osphere and legal evolution belongs therefore to the area of no-ospheric evolution. We have seen in *(III.B.2)* that no-ospheric evolution is evolution of servomechanisms. It is possible that legal evolution also permits of a description as evolution of servomechanisms.

All writers on cybernetics agree that the world of law can be analysed from a cybernetic point of view. The argument for this is that in legal systems negative feedback is used, like in other systems originating in or from living nature, as a defensive method against encroaching disorder.

That so little analysis is done in this respect is first of all due to the fact that lawyers are used to work with jural criteria and distinctions which have been developed over the centuries and even millennia while new generations of lawyers add their contributions to this development. This leads to the accepted fact that legal terminology is the only appropriate instrument for the description of jural problems.

In point of fact there are tremendous problems relative to legal education and legal computerization which call for solutions. Due to the rapid increase in the number of law students and the slower increase in the number of law teachers, an increased efficiency in legal education is required. Due to an increasing need of legal counselling and legal decision making, legal practice requires more efficient methods to store and to retrieve jural information and is in need of appropriate instruments for the digestion of information and the generation of new jural information.

We have seen how analytical jurisprudence may provide for an appropriate instrument for classification of jural notions. We will see in *(III.C.2)* how this instrument, the Hohfeldian system of fundamental jural concepts, can be described by means of notions derived from cybernetics. This is not enough however. We should know how the Hohfeldian system can be placed within a framework of images of servomechanisms and therefore we should be familiar with the nature of jural servomechanisms.

The science of cybernetics does not yet however provide for descriptions of servomechanisms in law. It therefore appears necessary to develop a conception in this respect, which will be formulated in the following pages.

(III.C.2) The Cybernetic structure of Hohfeld's Four Fundamental Relations. We have seen in *(II.D.2.a) th*at the four legal advantages of Hohfeld's system can be considered as patterns of expectations and the four legal burdens as desired patterns of behaviour; we found that these two patterns are related to each other as mirror-images.
In other words: the concepts Right, Power, Privilege and Immunity each indicate a type or class of a pattern of an expectation; the concepts Duty, Liability, No Right and Disability each indicate a type or class of a program or desired pattern for a behaviour.

The four Hohfeldian relations express therefore that there is a correspondence between the type or class of someone's pattern of an expectation and the type or class of another's program for a behaviour, and they express moreover that this pattern of expectations and this program for a behaviour have similar contents; these contents are the contents of a norm.

A person in whom a program for a behaviour is invested has factual opportunities to deviate in his behaviour from his program when it is operative and realisable but not realized. These factual opportunities may go to the length of not realizing the program at all. Opportunities for deviation from a program of behaviour can be termed positive feedback opportunities.

A person in whom a pattern of expectations is invested has factual opportunities by which he can try to correct deviations in the execution of someone's corresponding program of behaviour. These opportunities can be termed negative feedback opportunities.

The negative feedback opportunities are:

1) Opportunities to demand the other person unofficially to behave according to his program of behaviour.
2) "Self help" opportunities in order to realize a pattern of expectations or to correct deviations from a desired pattern of behaviour, like e.g. the *Lex XII Tabularum* (8, 12) provides the victim of *furtum* with a legal opportunity to kill a *fur manifestus*.
3) Opportunities to demand from a court or another authority a statement that a program of behaviour is or will become operative.
4) Opportunities to demand in court a correction of deviations from an operative program of behaviour.

The negative feedback opportunities are possible

reactions to the use of positive feedback opportunities, viz. opportunities to deviate from a program for behaviour.

Patterns of an expectation and programs for a behaviour exist both in the world of morals as well as in the world of law *(1)*. In both areas they can be accompanied by the first group of opportunities for negative feedback. The second, like the third and fourth group of negative feedback opportunities are only possible within the framework of a legal system: the second group is typical of archaic law and hardly exists now in modern legal systems, except for the Law of Nations (blockade, armed intervention, *bellum justum*). The third group are to the effect of conclusions of law and are the Right-(2)-Duty relations between subject and sovereign which have been treated in *(II.F.4)*; the fourth group are the Right-(3)-Duty relations between subject and sovereign, treated in *(II.F.5)*; they are to the effect that any of the four classes of patterns of expectations is a claim against a deviator from a program of behaviour to ensure that he behaves according to his program. We will now see in *(III.C.3)* how this cybernetic structure of Hohfeldian relations fits into our notion of game-bound unit.

(III.C.2.a) The role of bona fides within the Cybernetic structure of Hohfeld's Relations. Good faith or *bona fides* was in Roman Law originally considered as the base of all legal relationships for which there was no foundation in written law. The fundamental idea was that all men, either Romans or non-Romans, ought to keep their promises; *bona fides* was therefore protected by the gods.

In classical Roman Law it became the criterion by which the judge could supplement or diminish the obligations of parties in *iudicia bonae fidei*. The judge was not limited to the formal description of the case, like in what Justinian Law later called *iudicia stricti iuris*, but could at his own discretion include all concrete circumstances in his considerations.

In Justinian Law *bona fides* became similar to *aequitas* or equity in the sense of fairness. This notion is connected to the image of controversial legal attributes weighed on a balance.

The idea of *bona fides* is connected with that of freedom of contract, or, in Hohfeldian terms, a Privilege to create Right-Duty relations without restriction as to form or contents. The reception of Roman Law in Europe brought a slow application of the notion *bona fides* in its

Justinian sense as related to *bonae fidei iudicia (1)*. These modern interpretations of *bona fides* as *aequitas* were however counteracted by the influence of Canon Law. Since the 14th century it had become the opinion of the leading canonists that informal agreements impose legal duties *(ex nudo pacto actio oritur)*, because of the fact that someone who does not keep his promise was considered as perpetrator of the sin of lying. This meant an interpretation of *bona fides* in the original Roman sense and since the end of the 16th and the beginning of the 17th century this became as well a norm in secular law, at least for causal pacts*(2)*.

Moreover, already before the Roman Law reception a long tradition had existed in Western-Europe that a man should keep his promises. Fidelity had been the base of the relations among members of the ancient Germanic clans and, strengthened by an oath, among Germanic blood friends *(3)*.

In ancient Germanic law a debtor could swear an oath of fidelity to his creditor in which he promised to fulfil a certain performance. A mutual oath of fidelity lay at the base of the relations between the lords of the land and their subjects.

Bona fides in the classical Roman sense of a touchstone for the judge was incorporated in the German Civil Code of 1900 and it has been subject to a fruitful application *(4)*. The German translation of *bona fides, Treu und Glauben* is of special interest to us. In the words *Treu* (fidelity) and *Glauben* (faith) *(5)* we find the expression of a double nature of *bona fides*.

Treu is behaviour according to a given promise or according to an earlier demonstrated behaviour; *Glauben* is confidence that shall be enacted in accordance with a promise or an attitude *(6)*.

We have seen in *(III.C.2)* that a Right can be considered as a pattern of expectations and a Duty as a pattern of desired behaviour. We may now consider *Treu* as behaviour to a promised or earlier demonstrated pattern of behaviour; *Glauben* may be understood as confidence that action will be in accordance with a pattern of expectations formulated in a promise or demonstrated in an attitude. Therefore *Treu* may be considered in the Law of Obligations as behaviour according to a pattern of desired behaviour formulated in a Duty and *Glauben* as confidence that action will be according to a pattern of expectations formulated in a Right.

This does not only apply to the Law of Obligations. In classical Roman Civil Law usucapion was, under certain conditions, possible of goods obtained from a non-owner *(7)*. Among these conditions was the requirement that the obtainer of the concerned good was *bona fide*, or, more correct, was not *mala fide*, at the moment of transfer. Canon Law extended this requirement to the whole period of usucapion *(mala fides superveniens nocet)*. *Bona fides* is here *Glauben* that action will be according to a Right that the other shall only transfer goods which are his property; the other's *Treu* is his behaviour according to his corresponding Duty towards the first person to transfer only goods of his own. Usucapion now was possible if the obtainer has disbelief that the goods belonged to somebody else, i.e. if there was in him no absence of a *Glauben*.

There seems no objection against extending the conception of *Treu* and *Glauben* to other patterns of behaviour and expectations than those formulated in Right-Duty relations. The conception also applies to the relations Power-Liability, Disability -Immunity and No Right-Privilege.

Also there is *Treu* behaviour according to a promise of earlier demonstrated behaviour and *Glauben* its complementary correlative. In all the four Hohfeldian relationships however *Treu* and *Glauben* are only relevant if there is a Duty to practise *Treu* and a Right that will be acted according to the contents of a corresponding *Glauben*; *bona fides* has always been provided, as we have seen, with a legal or a moral fundamental.

(III.C.3) The Concept Law-bound Unit. We saw in *(III.B.3)* that absolute game-bound units are units composed of a servomechanism and a certain part of its environment relative to a particular game and therefore only relative to a particular desired pattern of behaviour.

Among the absolute game-bound units are structures in which a servomechanism is attributed with a pattern of expectations relative to another servomechanism with a desired pattern of behaviour which is a mirror image of the pattern of expectations in the first. If these two servomechanisms are each composed of at least one human being, if the servomechanism with the pattern of expectations has relative to the other at least one fixed negative feedback opportunity in order to attempt the realization of the other's desired behaviour and if the expected or desired behaviour concerns one particular act or forbearance, then we find an absolute game-bound unit in which the pattern of expectations is either one of Hohfeld's fundamental concepts Right, Power, Immunity or Privilege and in which the desired pattern of behaviour is either a

Duty, Liability, Disability or No Right.

Absolute game-bound units of this structure belong to the world of law or of morality. They belong to the area of morality if there is only a negative feedback opportunity in the form of an unofficial request, or if there is no negative feedback opportunity at all. They belong to the area of law if negative feedback opportunities are organized along fixed patterns of possible behaviour, e.g. by regulated opportunities to request a magistrate or a court or another authority for a conclusion of law or an enforceable decision, or by regulated "self-help" opportunities *(1)*.

Also the absolute game-bound units in the areas of law and morality can form relative game-bound units. These complexes of game-bound units can comprise only a few or all legal or moral relationships in which two or more individuals are involved.

The game-bound units in the area of law are termed by us *"law-bound units"* and we will distinguish, analogous to our division among game-bound units, between absolute and relative law-bound units.

So far as the game-bound units in the moral area are concerned, we leave it to the specialists on morals to give them an appropriate name *(2)*. They are distinguished from the law-bound units by the fact that they have no negative feedback opportunities which in their turn can be described as game-bound units with fixed game-rules (fixed patterns of expectations and desired behaviour), either written or unwritten. To morals may, but should not necessarily, apply only the first group of negative feedback opportunities treated in *(III.C.2)*.

(III.C.3.a) Basic structures of Law-bound Units. Absolute law-bound units can be represented as follows:

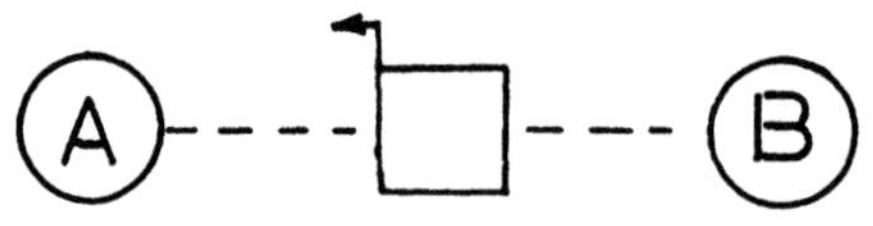

Fig. 13

or

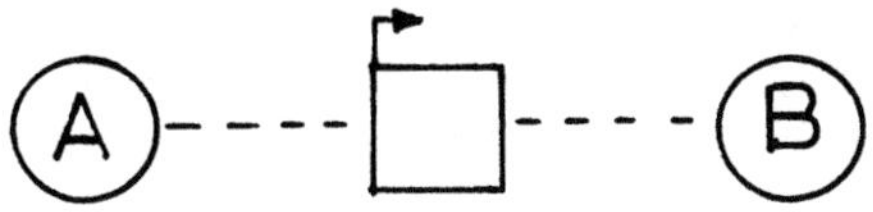

Fig. 14

In Fig. 13 and 14 absolute law-bound units are represented, in which there exists one Right-Duty relation. In Fig. 13 A has a Right and B a Duty, while in fig. 14 A has a Duty and B a Right. Notice that the square in the middle of the drawings represents the square of opposition of Fig. 5 in *(II.D.2)*, exposing Hohfeld's four fundamental relations. The other possible absolute law-bound units between A and B are these:

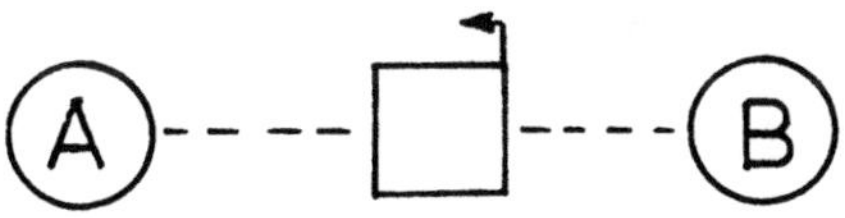

Fig. 15

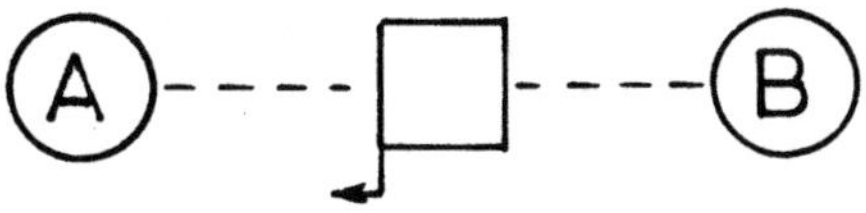

Fig. 16

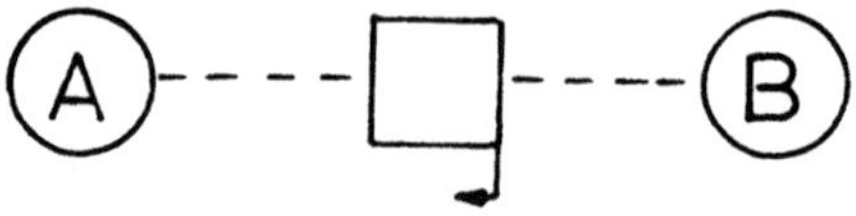

Fig. 17

Fig. 15, 16 and 17 represent absolute law-bound units which contain successively the relations Power-Liability, Disability-Immunity and No Right-Privilege. These law-bound units are represented analogous to fig. 14. The figures 14, 15 and 16 can however without changing their meaning, also be expressed as follows:

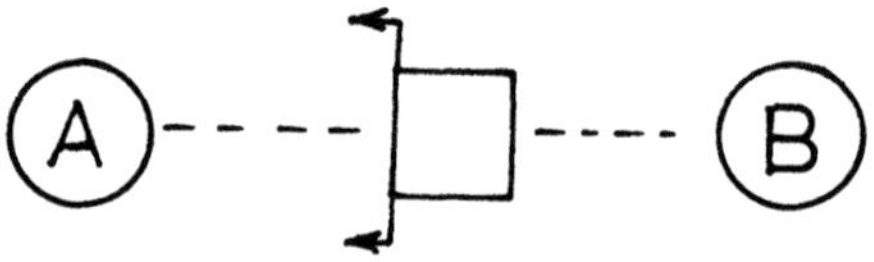

Fig. 18

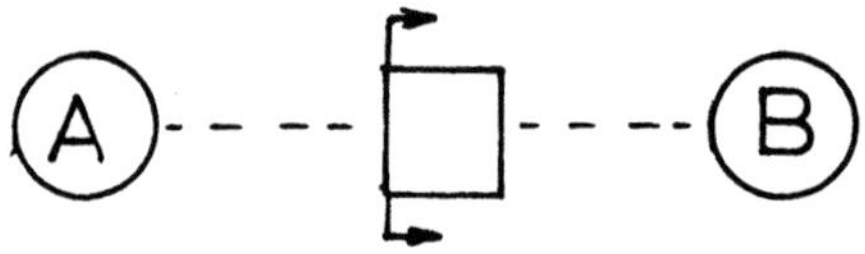

Fig. 19

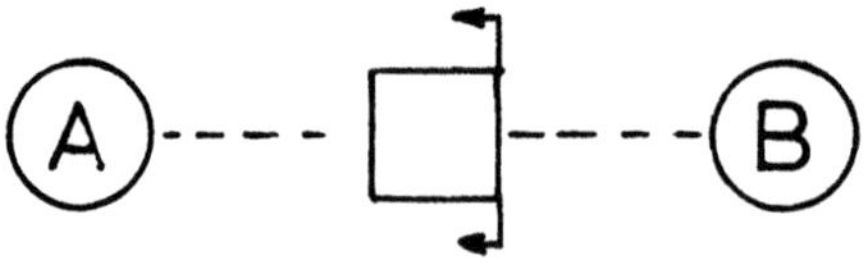

Fig. 20

In fig. 18, 19 and 20 those relations, which are always superimplied, are introduced into the figures. In the greater part of the following figures we leave these relations out because of reasons of simplification; we will meet them again in fig. 35 ff. where absolute rights are represented.

Law-bound units with subcontrary relations can be represented as follows:

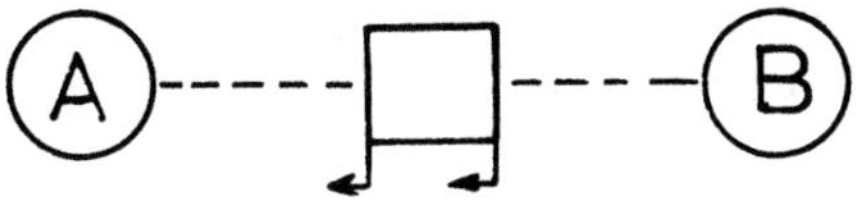

Fig. 21

The figures 18, 19, 20 and 21 are not absolute law-bound units, but the smallest possible relative or complex law-bound units. Their patterns of expectations or desired behaviour concern the same act situation.

Similar act situations do not obtain in e.g. a mutual obligation. A law-bound unit, formed by the parties in a mutual obligation can be represented as follows:

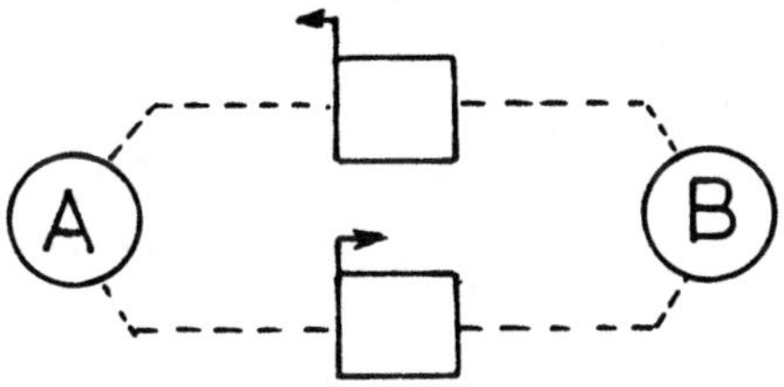

Fig. 22

or

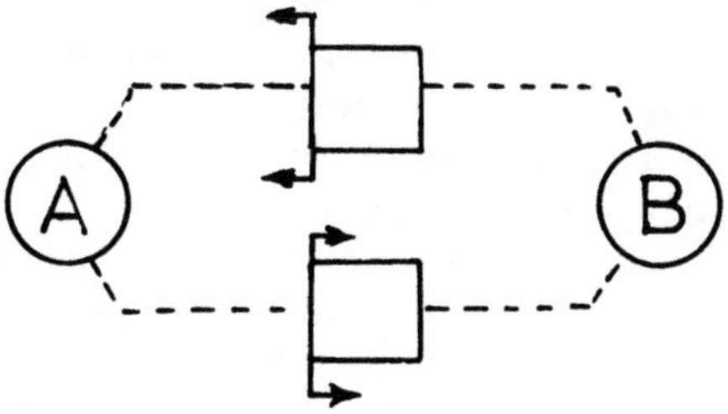

Fig. 23

Fig. 23 is more correct than fig. 22, but there is no objection to omit superimplied relations as long as their existence is not forgotten.

The examples given so far do not only apply to law, but also to morality. Law is distinguished from morality in that negative feedback is only possible along certain fixed patterns.

If the negative feedback opportunity concerns certain regulated "self help" activity, e.g. a Right of a State A against another State B that State B endured a blockade by A if B does not fulfill its obligations towards B or the international community, then we have a simple figure:

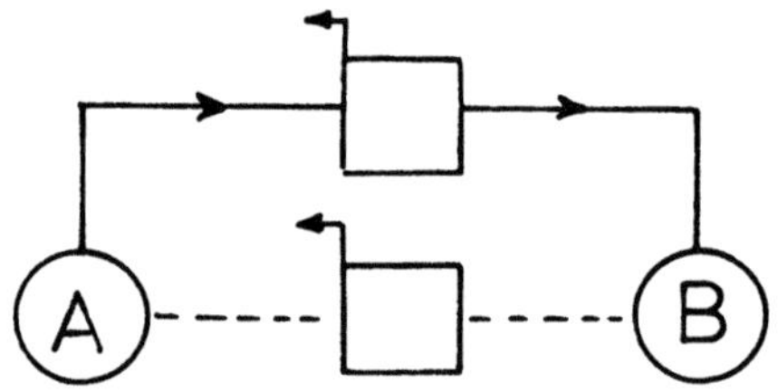

Fig. 24

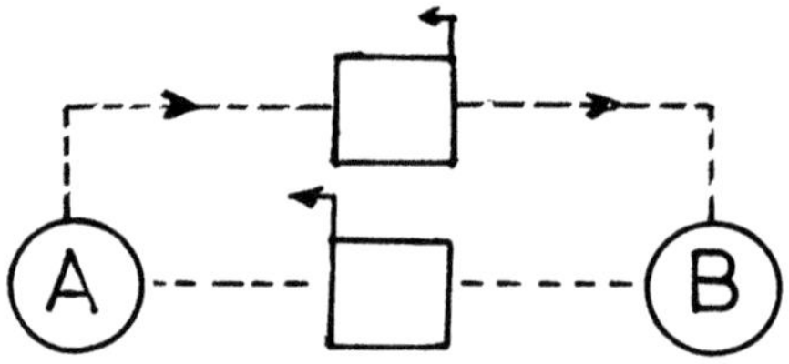

Fig. 25

Fig. 24 indicates the situation wherein a state of blockade is in operation according to international law; fig. 25 indicates the situation where State B runs a risk of a blockade being imposed upon it by State A, should it not fulfil certain obligations.

By a broken line we indicate the possibility of using a negative feedback opportunity; an unbroken line means that use has been made of this possibility.

If there are negative feedback opportunities by means of a legal authority, a court, an arbitrator, then we may find the following structures *(1)*:

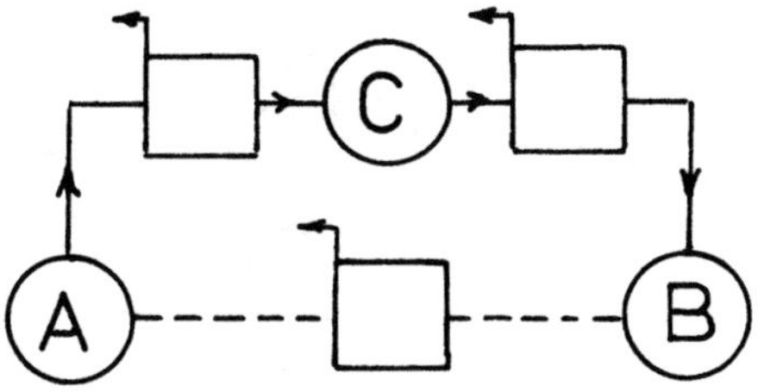

Fig. 26

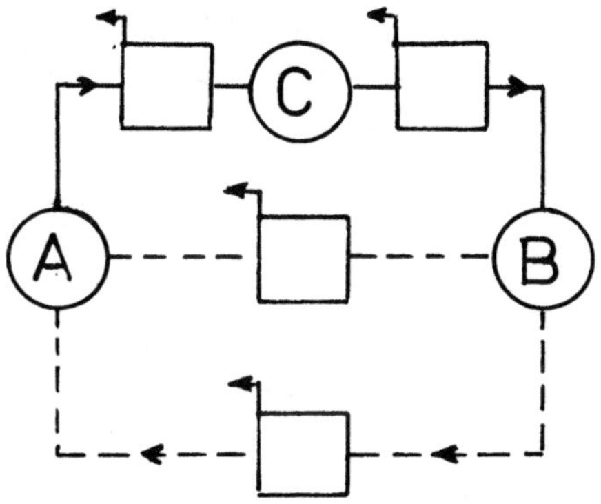

Fig. 27

Fig. 26 represents a situation, in which a conclusion of law is given; fig. 27 represents a situation where an exta Duty, e.g. a penal sum, is imposed.

A law-bound unit comprising a mutual obligation with mutual negative feedback opportunities can be represented as follows:

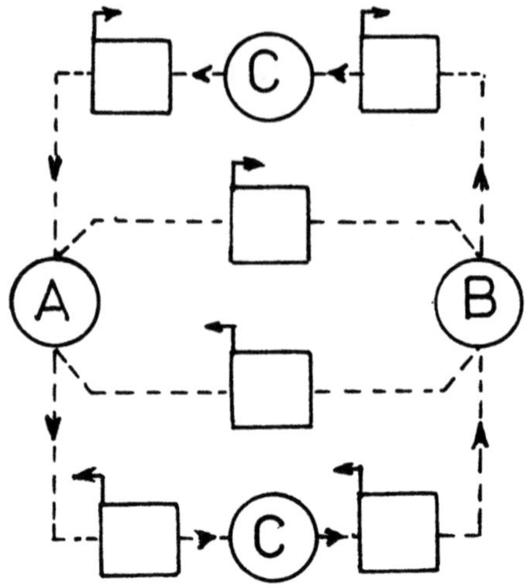

Fig. 28

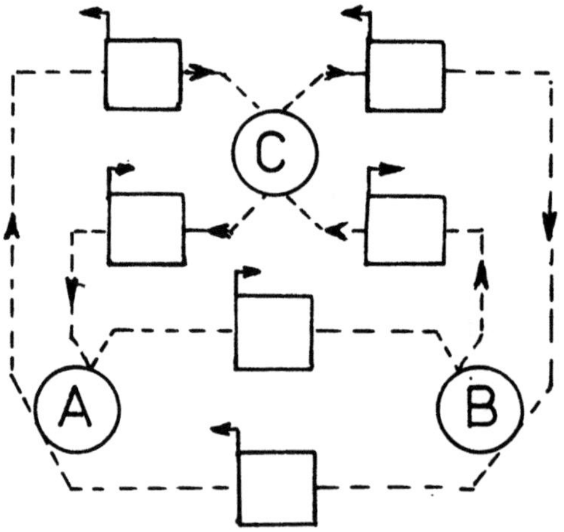

Fig. 29

Both figures 28 and 29 represent the same kind of law-bound unit. It is not only for reasons of clarity that fig. 28 seems more suitable than fig. 29: if in fig. 28 one of the two C's is replaced by D, then it is possible to indicate that A's obligation falls under the jurisdiction of a different legal suthority to B's. This - generally hypothetical - case can be represented as follows:

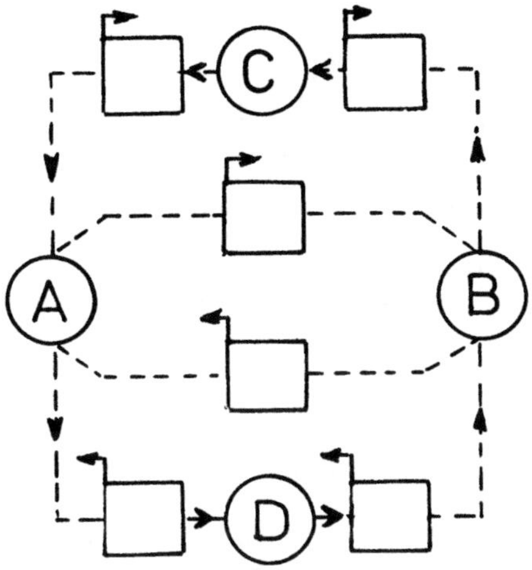

Fig. 30

In the figures 28, 29 and 30 we see now somewhat complex law-bound units. The number of absolute law-bound units, to which they are reducible, is twelve in any of these examples; six of them are represented, the other six are superimplied by these.

Notice that in the figures treated here the various squares of opposition in a law-bound unit are all related to distinguishable performances, e.g. a Duty to deliver, a Duty of a judge to give a judgement if legally asked, a sanction etc. It is possible to express these distinctions and to indicate at the same time whether and relative to which law-bound unit another law-bound unit is part of a negative feedback opportunity. We may use for this a decimal system relative to performances F1 or F2 etc. The situation of fig. 28 (mutual obligation) can then be expressed as follows:

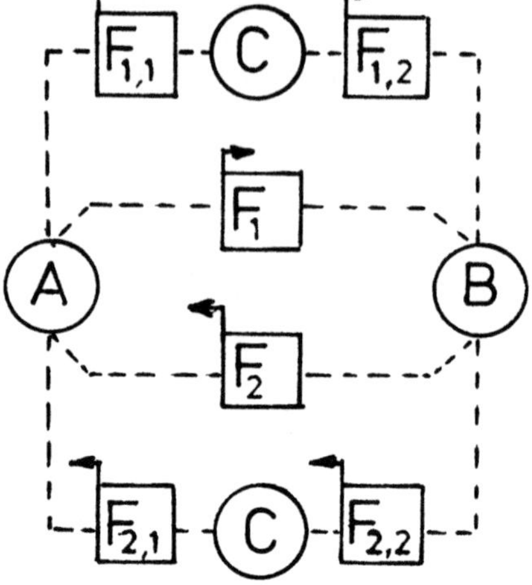

Fig. 31

Instead of F1, F2, F1.1, F1.2 etc. one may of course use other more suitable signs, to represent the contents of norms. The reasons why such alternative signs are not treated in this study have been stated in *(II.A)*.

Law-bound units are servomechanical structures. We have considered now their internal structure, viz. as relations of games between the servomechanisms which are part of them. A law-bound unit may also be a game player itself with a servomechanism outside it. Juridically: a law-bound unit can be a subject of law. This is the case with legal persons. We may represent such a situation as follows:

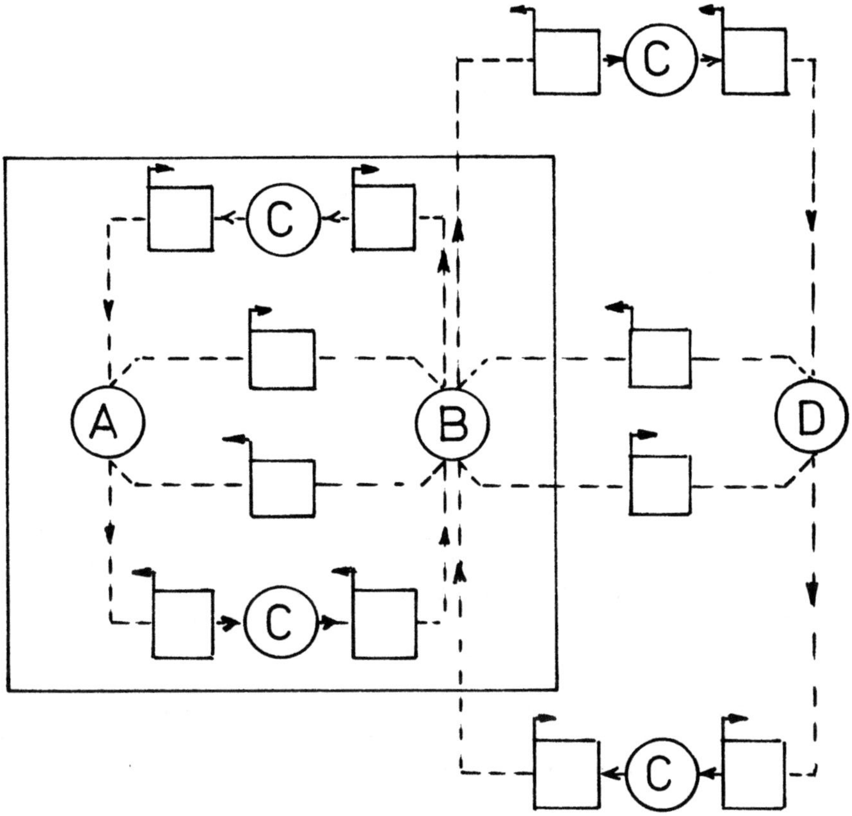

Fig. 32

A and B form together an organization with legal personality. Internally they have mutual obligations, reinforced with negative feedback opportunities via court C. Externally it is the law-bound unit, formed by their organization, which has a capacity to enter into mutual obligations with D, and these obligations are reinforced in an equivalent manner via the same court C. In this figure it is B, which represents the legal person. We see here clearly, that there are no feedback relations between D and B as a private person, but only between D and the legal person represented by B.

Applications of the theory of law-bound units to legal

persons will be treated in *(III.C.4.a)*ff.

Law-bound units in which someone represents a private person are different from those in which a legal person is represented. They can be exposed e.g. as follows:

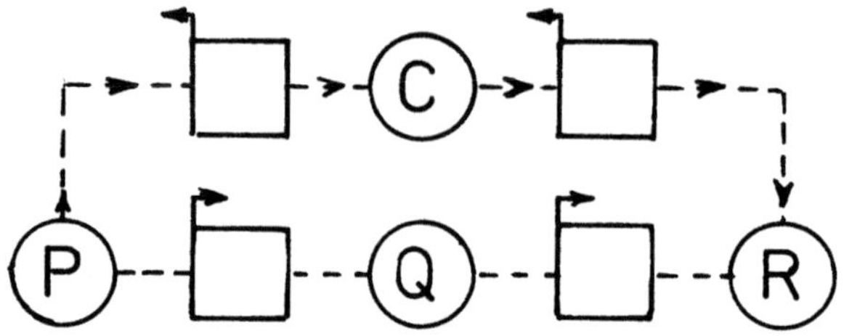

Fig. 33

In fig. 21 it is P who has a Duty to represent Q. In his capacity as representative he can create a Right-Duty relation between Q and R. In this figure it is P who has negative feedback opportunities against R and not Q. Such is the case in guardianship, in *mandatum* or in *negotiorum gestio*.

In cases of representation it is the represented Q who may obtain a feedback control relative to the third party R. This can be seen in the following figure:

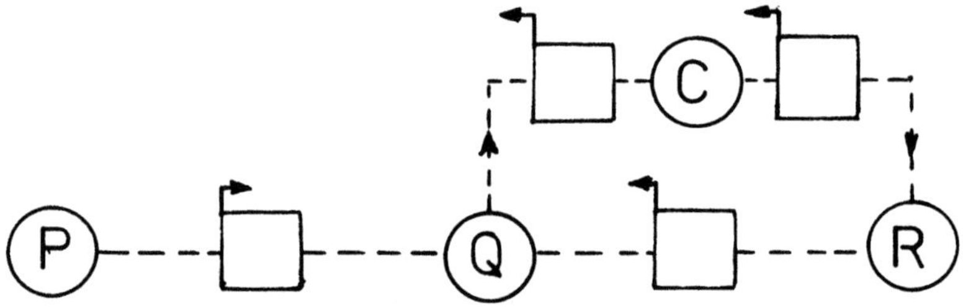

Fig. 34

There are of course, both in figures 33 and 34, also negative feedback opportunities with respect to the relation between Q and P. The reader can draw these himself if desired.

Lastly we will discuss the basic structure of law-bound units relative to property, rights *in rem* and other absolute rights.

If A is an owner, has a right *in rem* or an absolute right, then his position against B in a law-bound unit is as follows:

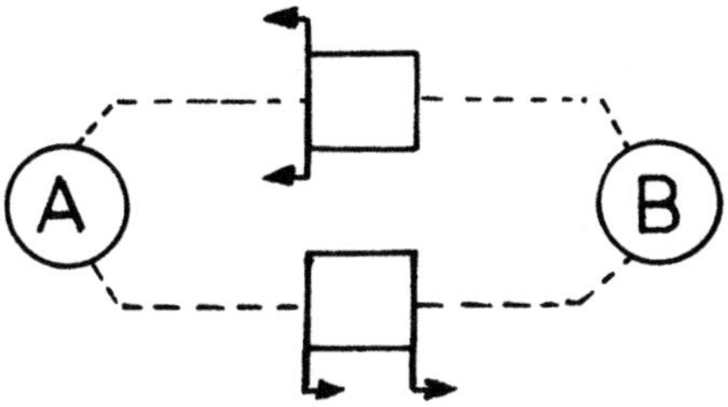

Fig. 35

Here we find the first three relations discussed in *(II.C.2)* as well as the superimplied relation Disability-Immunity, which was not discovered by Hohfeld *(2)*, but will be treated in the next lines. Fig. 35 can also be represented in a simpler way:

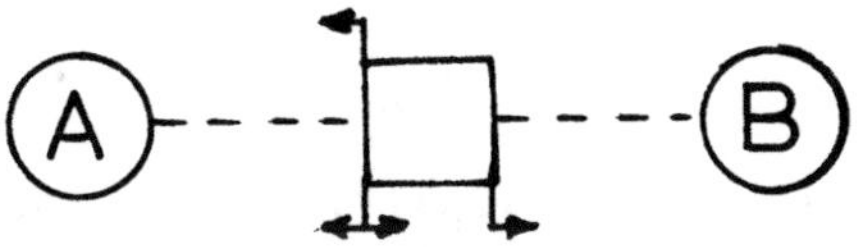

Fig. 36

A's relations with persons other than B are fundamentally of similar structure. A's property, right *in rem* or absolute right is now a pattern of expectations in a law-bound unit of the following basic structure:

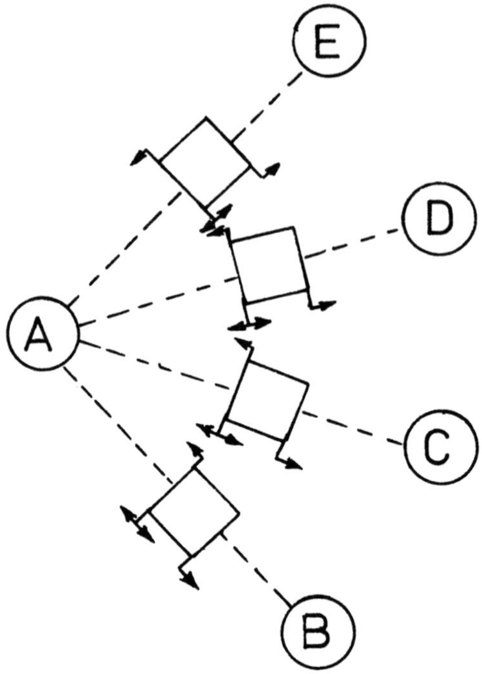

Fig. 37

Fig. 37 should now be amplified with the negative feedback opportunities of the involved parties as represented in fig. 38.

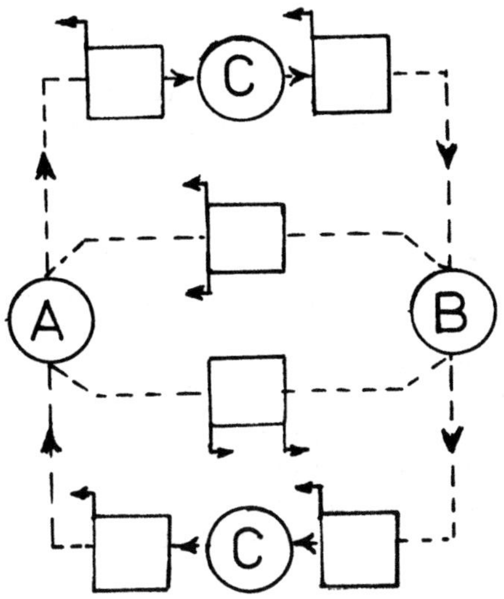

Fig. 38

There is only one case for negative feedback opportunities of B, C, D, E, etc. against A. This case concerns the possibility that A violates or attempts to violate their Immunity to be placed in a new legal relationship with A. We excluded here the general principle that A should not use his property, right *in rem* or other absolute right in order to harm others, because this principle is usually elaborated in differentiated Duties of A. We also excluded here the incidental Power-Liability relations with prospective buyers and other candidates for A's proprietary position. A now has negative feedback opportunities if B, C, D, E etc. do not act in accordance with their Duty not to interfere, or No Right to interfere, with A's absolute right, or their Disability to place A in a new legal relationship with them in respect to such a right.

The relations between A and the object of his property, right *in rem* or absolute right is *not* a law-bound unit, because these relations do not concern B, C, D, E, etc. If A owns a good, either movable, or real estate, then he forms with this property a *game*-bound unit distinguished from the complex law-bound unit which he makes with B, C, D, E etc. relative to this property. A similar game-bound unit can be formed by A and a good to which he has no title whatsoever, e.g. a good which he has stolen. On the other hand, if a good belonging to A has been stolen, then indeed the game-bound unit made by A and the stolen good is dissolved, but A retains in principle his position as an owner: A's position in the law-bound unit with B, C, D, E, etc. is not changed. The same applies to rights *in rem* or absolute rights, and to all cases in which possession is lost.

(III.C.3.b) Cybernetic properties of Law-bound Units. The cybernetic properties of law-bound units may be summarized as follows:

1) They have always an organized system for internal control, although such a system can be weak in effectiveness, such as e.g. systems limited to conclusions of law.
2) Some of them may be in their turn a servomechanical partner in a law-bound unit; this is legal personality.
3) They may display features of growth.
4) Some of them have the capacity to reproduce themselves.
5) Servomechanical partners in law-bound units may generally be replaced unless the patterns of expectations or desired behaviour are intended to be related to exclusive partners.
6) Patterns of expectations and desired behaviour can be replaced in law-bound units by other such patterns, if the purpose for which the law-bound unit was intended can be attained in a better way following the new patterns.
7) Within the framework of a greater law-bound unit smaller law-bound units may be replaced, inserted, or fall out and not be replaced, either without fundamentally affecting the coherence of the greater law-bound unit, or even slightly affecting this coherence.
8) Some of them can mould their final cause anew.

Ad 1 and 2 (Internal and external control)

The first and the second property have been treated in *(III.C.3)* and (*III.C.3.a*); legal personality will be treated moreover in *(III.C.4)*.

Ad 3 (Growth)

Law-bound units displaying features of growth do not

follow the growth of the human beings in which they participate, nor the increase of the value of a thing which forms part of it, but they grow by increase in coherence, which might be described as growing juridically.

In the course of time contracts may be reinforced by a more precise or a more detailed description of what had been agreed earlier without any changes in an obligation as such. Such a reinforcement may occur by a new contract, by a judicial decision or by a new law. This means a clarification or an amplification of the law-bound unit's patterns of expectations and desired behaviour, and this implies that the possibilities of correcting deviations from this desired pattern of behaviour are increased.

Law-bound units may also grow in another sense, which is also an increase in coherence, viz. by the growth of the relevant knowledge of the men who participate in it. If someone who participates in such a servomechanism, has no notion of his Rights and Duties in the juridical relationship in which he is involved, then the servomechanism which this relationship embodies as its desired pattern of behaviour may have little coherence. If e.g. a creditor has no idea how to force an unwilling debtor to pay, i.e. how to provide for efficient negative feedback, then the law-bound unit is not able to reach its purpose, the debt's payment, because of lack of coherence. If the creditor however becomes aware that the best thing he can do is to consult a lawyer, then soon a growth in the servomechanism's coherence may be established.

Ad 4 (Reproduction)

Reproduction of law-bound units does not need to coincide with biological reproduction.

If a farmer's cow reproduces itself, then it is possible to say, that the law-bound unit composed by the farmer and all who should respect his ownership of the calf, has reproduced itself as soon as the calf is *nasciturus*; the juridical reproduction occurs here before the biological.

If however a married couple reproduces itself, then there is no reproduction of the juridical servomechanism which is embodied in the married couple. What are reproduced, are the law-bound units in which anyone participates from the moment of his conception or his birth, however not law-bound units constituted by the parents together, but only those which comprise one of the parents. So a law-bound unit with fundamental rights of women as a pattern of expectations in which the mother participates, may similarly reproduce itself in respect of the daughter, but it cannot be reproduced relative to a son. Reproduced from either father or mother but not both are the law-bound units which comprise someone's legal relations with respect to his position as a subject of law.

Reproduction of law-bound units also occurs at the creation of legal persons: reproduced here are in any case law-bound units relative to a legal person as a legal subject.

An example of reproduction of a law-bound unit, which is not related to biological reproduction, may be found in that which can be effected by a chain-condition. If I sell my car to A, then I may stipulate not only that A will drive me with this car once a week to a cinema, but I may stipulate as well that if he, A, sells the car to another, C, that his conditions of sale to C stipulate that C will have exactly the same obligations towards me, as A had. By this stipulation I achieve that C will not only convey me regularly to the cinema, but that, if he sells the car to D, D also will have an obligation to convey me to the cinema and to stipulate similar conditions when in his turn he sells the car, etc., etc. From the moment that the car is transferred to a new buyer a new law-bound unit is created, embracing a relationship between the actual proprietor and myself and it is replaced by another one from the moment that the car is sold.

Ad 5 (Replacement of servomechanical partners)

It depends on the purpose for which the law-bound unit strives by means of the games between its servo-mechanical members, whether these can be replaced or not. A law-bound unit with respect to a certain marriage has among its purposes to provide a legal framework for the marital relations between two pre-determined individuals. If either one of the partners falls out, then replacement is only possible by creation of a new law-bound unit. A law-bound unit, however formed, by a debtor and a creditor and having among its purposes that a certain sum is paid, may undergo a replacement of both debtor and creditor. It may be a matter of indifference to the debtor whom he pays and the creditor may be indifferent as to who fulfils the obligation.

Ad 6 (Replacement of patterns of expectations and desired behaviour

A law-bound unit comprises natural or legal persons

only in certain legal relationships. Such relationships are created with the intention of reaching a certain jural aim; the attainment of this aim, e.g. that one of the parties may exercise a Power with respect to a Liability of the other party, is intended to follow the lines of certain patterns of expectations and desired behaviour.

Selection now of the correct patterns is difficult for the layman. If the wrong patterns are selected, then there is a real danger that the intended jural purpose is not attained and that undesired consequences result. In such cases a legal system may permit a wrong selection to be converted into a right one. This conversion is a transformation of a void legal act into another legal act which is valid. Thus in Roman Law the *Senatusconsultum Neronianum* regulates that a void legacy should be considered as the best possible type of valid legacy, if such is permitted by its contents *(1)*. The Supreme Court of the Netherlands decided that the void legal act should contain elements of the valid legal act *(2)*.

We see here that a law-bound unit's intended purpose can mould anew its patterns of expectations and desired behaviour.

Ad 7 (Replacement, insertion or falling out of law-bound units within greater law-bound units)

Replacement of law-bound units can be considered from two angles. In the preceding paragraphs we considered it from the point of view of its internal servomechanical partners. We may also consider such a replacement from the angle of the complexes in which law-bound units share.

Within greater complexes law-bound units may not only become replaced, but new law-bound units may be inserted and law-bound units may disappear without being replaced. In all these cases the coherence of the greater complex may, but will not necessarily be affected by such changes.

A State's legal system may not limit the number of law-bound units composed of e.g. buyers and sellers, but as soon as its courts are inundated with negative feedback activity relative to this species of law-bound units with the result that the courts cannot fulfill their other tasks, then we see a trend towards decrease in coherence of the complex law-bound unit, the legal system, while the average number of law-bound units made by buyers and sellers may remain constant.

On the other hand the quantity of certain law-bound

units may increase without affecting the legal system in this way, and this might even be accompanied by a decrease of cases in the courts relative to this kind of law-bound unit, which is a trend towards an increase in coherence of the legal system.

When considering a complex law-bound unit only one question is important: to what extent is its own coherence affected; and this includes the attainment of its own purposes, when law-bound units from which it is composed are replaced or fall-out, or when new law-bound units are inserted.

Replacement of law-bound units in any case occurs if the original law-bound unit has satisfied its purpose and is succeeded by a new one. If there is no succession, then there is no replacement, only a falling-out of the original law-bound unit.

Ad 8 (Moulding anew of final causes)

Moulding anew of final causes in law-bound units occurs if patterns of expectations and desired behaviour are modified or supplemented or replaced in such a manner that the law-bound unit's purpose is changed.

If such a change in purpose is reached by a complete change of the patterns of expectations and desired behaviour, then it is doubtful, whether we have a replacement of law-bound units or a moulding anew of a law-bound unit's final cause. The criterion here may be, whether the creation of new game rules is concurrent with a continuation of the game or whether the original game is broken off and succeeded by a new game.

So is e.g. renewel of a debt a continuation of a game with new game-rules: conditions of payment and interest may change, but the original debt is causally related to the new debt.

On the other hand transformation of a contract of rent into a contract of buying is a succession of jural games: the buyer's obligation to pay and the seller's obligation to deliver are not caused by the rental conditions, even if the rental contract provided the renter with certain advantages or preferences in the case of an offer of sale.

Changes of purposes do not occur in law-bound units without changes in the game, except when the game is not only a means to attain a purpose, but is also itself a purpose.

The distinction between these two types of law-bound

unit - the game as a purpose or only as means of reaching a purpose - corresponds to a distinction between the jural relationships which they embody. The following distinctions between jural relationships can be made:

1) The manner in which something is performed is of the same importance as that it is performed.
2) The manner in which something is performed is less important than that it is performed, although not unimportant.

It is relationships of the former kind which may be comprised of law-bound units which can mould anew their final causes. Their structure is, even without opportunities to mould final causes anew, of stronger nature than that of the second; they have better chances to reach the purpose of performance, because also the way of performance is already a performance and therefore controlled by negative feedback opportunities.

The second group indeed requires less formalism so far as the manner of performance is concerned, but the manner of performance is not already performance itself and therefore relatively difficult to subject to negative feedback control.

An obligation to pay cash is of the latter group, an obligation to pay by instalments is of the former.

Whether final causes in law-bound units can indeed be moulded anew depends however not only on the distinction discussed here, but also on the negative feedback opportunities for which a legal system provides in this respect.

Thus a complex law-bound unit like a State's legal system has among its ends, to provide for adequate negative feedback in the law-bound units composed of those over whom the State has jurisdiction. A special group of these law-bound units are those concerned with property *(3)*; provision for negative feedback opportunities with respect to the law-bound units in which legal relations between owners and non-owners are patterns of expectations and desired behaviour, is therefore a purpose of the legal system: the game played within the legal systems relative to the negative feedback in these law-bound units is now this provision for negative feedback opportunities. In other words: the game is here the purpose.

Protection of owners and non-owners depends upon the value attributed to property. Two extreme principles are possible: "property is sacred" and "property is theft". Various intermediate points of view may appear at different times and under different circumstances, like "property is neither sacred, nor theft", or "some property is sacred, some property is theft".

Modern industrial societies all show an increasing limitation of the advantages connected with ownership and a decrease in the limitations attributed to non-owners who have an interest in what an owner does or does not do with his property.

So the patterns of expectations and desired behaviour in law-bound units composed of owners and non-owners are changing. The legal system has to provide for negative feedback opportunities relative to these changed patterns: protection of non-owners is a game and a purpose which increases in importance, while protection of owners decreases in this respect; final causes in these law-bound units are moulded here anew.

Similarly, within the legal system we find those games which are particular negative feedback provisions for law-bound units of owners and non-owners subject to changes. These games are also purposes of the legal system.

The games or purposes in law-bound units relative to protection of owners and non-owners therefore, by changes caused by changing attitudes towards property, also mould a final cause anew in the law-bound unit of which they are components, viz. a State's legal system.

(III.C.4) The Theory of Law-bound Units applied to Legal Personality

(III.C.4.a) The nature of the Legal Person. The basic structure of legal persons has been described in *(III.C.3.a)* We described legal personality as a law-bound unit's capacity to be a servomechanical partner in a greater law-bound unit.

This conception deviates from the two main issues in the question of how it is possible that a legal person is a subject of law.

The earliest solution was that a legal person is a fiction. This idea originated from Canon Law. Pope Innocentius IV decided at the Lyons *Concilium* in 1245 that it was not possible to excommunicate an *universitas* or a *collegium (1)*. The canonists and post-glossators invented with respect to *universitas* qualifications such as *persona repraesentata, persona ficta, nomen intellectuale,* or *nomina intellectualia et anima carentia*. Pothier described the corporate body as an *"être intellectuel" (2)*. Savigny thoroughly analysed the concept of the legal person as a fiction *(3)*. He related this concept to incidental use of fictitious persons in Justinian law of succession *(4)*.

The legal person as a servomechanical partner in a law-bound unit, and as a law-bound unit itself, is not a fiction. In *(III.C.3.a)* the basic structure has been explained of the juridical relations which it can have and this structure does not differ from that of juridical relations of natural persons. Both natural and legal persons are in this conception servomechanisms which can play games within the framework of law-bound units.

The conception of both natural and legal persons as servomechanisms is more closely related to the later of the two main issues in the problem of explaining how a legal person is a subject of law. This is the conception, upheld by Otto von Gierke (1841-1921), that a legal person *(5)* is not a "dead abstraction" (*"Begriffsding"*), needing representation by other persons, but a living being, who as such is willing and acting" *(6)* and who "has the capacity to transform what he has been willing into acts" *(7)*.

Gierke considered the life of this being from the point of view of neovitalism *(8)*: "The mystery of life screens itself with the mystery of organism. We do not know what life really is, but this does not allow us to dissociate the image of life (*"Begriff"*) from science. For we know, that life exists. We are also able to describe and to limit the phenomenon of life. *In this way we form ("bilden") an image ("Begriff") of life, with which we operate both in natural sciences as well as in moral sciences (9)*.

However, wherever we place life, we find a bearer of life, which exhibits particular features. We notice that it is an ordered entirety, taking in and secreting parts, maintianing itself by efficient co-operation of the actual parts, of which the unity, constant in the change of parts and working in their performance of labour, does not coincide with the sum total of the parts. The real essence of this unity in plurality is hidden from us. But this does not allow us to eliminate the subjects of the processes of life from science; for their existence is certain. We also have the capacity to establish the specific properties of the bearers of life and to describe them. So we form *("bilden")* an image *("Begriff")* of the bearer of life and we use for this purpose the designation *("Bezeichnung")* of "organism", which designation points to the particular structure of the enlivened entirety. This image is as equally applicable to science as any other image which has been obtained by just abstraction from recognized facts, consequently adequately expressing contents of reality".

Gierke was not of the opinion that biological and juridical organisms have a common structure; he stated that just as all biological creatures have a structure in common, also juridical organisms are characterized by a common juridical structure *(10)*. This juridical structure is a system of law-rules by which the inner life of the juridical organisms is ordered *(11)*. Gierke called this system that of *"Sozialrecht"* (social law) with the purpose of distinguishing it from the *"Individualrecht"* (individual law) which is the system for regulating the external relations of both natural and legal persons.

Gierke's theory has great merits. The way in which Gierke indicated the notion of a legal person as an image was entirely in accordance with a cybernetic approach. In the light of later development of cybernetics it was a just decision to apply basic principles concerning external features of organic life in biology to juridical organisms. However, because neovitalism could not explain processes of life with the help of the actual laws of science, it was impossible to discover similar internal structures among biological and juridical organisms.

With cybernetics actually claiming that biologic organisms and human communities do have similar internal structures in common, it is now possible to proceed on the road which Gierke was only able to follow in its initial stage.

The question, whether a legal person is a living being or a fiction becomes irrelevant in the concept of legal persons as servomechanisms. They have their cybernetic structures in common with living organisms and as operationalized systems of law-bound units they have a common nature with living beings as well as fictitious abstractions.

(III.C.4.b) The basic structure of foundations. The crucial point of a theory on legal personality is the question whether it has the capacity to provide for a satisfactory explanation of the nature of foundations.

The Continental institution of foundation is a legal person settled by deed or last will, in which property is separated and assigned to a trustee or committee of trustees in order to take charge and to dispose of it to the benefit of a non-profit purpose.

Its medieval origin is to be found in separations of property for pious causes (churches, convents, hospitals). Foundations were devoted to Roman Catholic saints or to the Holy Ghost; the spiritual being to whom a foundation was devoted was considered as the owner of the separated property. Such conceptions however became impossible under the influence of Reformation and Renaissance *(1)*. In point of fact: the foundation is conceived either as an owner itself or as property without an owner. In this respect the concept of foundation deviates from that of corporations, where the separated property is owned by the persons who separated it, like the members of an incorporated society or the shareholders of a limited liability company.

The foundation's main distinction from the Anglo-Saxon charitable trust is that Common Law consideres a trustee as a legal owner and that Equity considers a trustee of equitable interests as an equitable owner who should perform his trust as conscientiously as if he is a legal owner; a Continental foundation's trustee is not owner of the separated property, but only administrator. The historical roots of the concept of a trustee's ownership are embedded in 13th century England where the "poor brethren" of the Mendicant Orders reconciled their holy vows to poverty with the ownership of real estate by having lay persons own land to the "use" or "need" of their work *(2)*.

Of the concepts of the foundation itself as owner of the separated property and that of property without an owner the former is correct so far as the external relations of the foundation are concerned: the beneficiaries receive money from the foundation, which is represented by the trustees. The concept of property without an owner is indeed correct relative to the foundation's internal structure - neither settler nor trustees own the separated property - but it comprises only half the truth.

The idea that property is separated and assigned to trustees in such a way that neither settler nor trustees are owner of that property is suggestive of the presumption that between the settler, or his heirs if a foundation is created by last will, and the trustees, all legal relations are ended as soon as the property has been legally transferred to the trustees. This presumption is indeed correct as far as legal relations are concerned with respect to the property's transfer, *but it overlooks the issue, that by the transfer new particular fundamental jural relations originate between the same parties*. These relations are Disability-Immunity and No Right-Privilege relations relative to the transferred property between respectively the settler, or his heirs, on one side and the trustees on the other side *(3)*. A founder (F), or his heirs, and a committee of trustees (T) make therefore, when a foundation has been created, relative to the separated property a law-bound unit of the following structure:

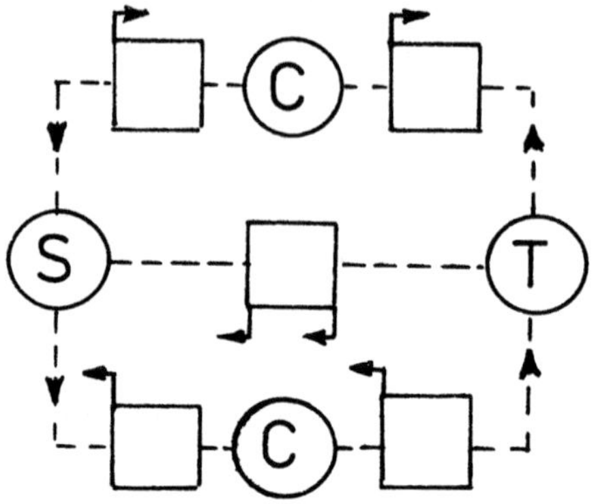

Fig. 39 (S=Settler
T=Trustee)

This law-bound unit can, like any other legal person, be a servomechanical partner in another law-bound unit according to figure 40 on the next page.

We may conclude, that in the conception of legal personality of law-bound units there is no fundamental distinction between the foundation and the other legal persons. There is only a particular internal distinction of fundamental jural relations, relative to the property separated, between the two involved parties.

(III.C.4.c) The basic structure of State and Sovereignty. The structure of States is fundamentally that of legal persons which has been treated in *(III.C.3.a)*. In its essence it resembles more a Continental style foundation than a corporate body *(1)*.

The two servomechanical partners in the State are, very simply, the sovereign on one side and the subjects on the other side. The subjects form a group of which the members have equal jural relations *(2)* with the sovereign, although subdivisions among them, e.g. civil or military servants, may moreover stand in particular jural relationships to the sovereign.

Sovereignty in this connection should be understood as a logical function. Except for the cases of absolute monarchism *(L'État c'est moi)* or dictatorship, sovereignty

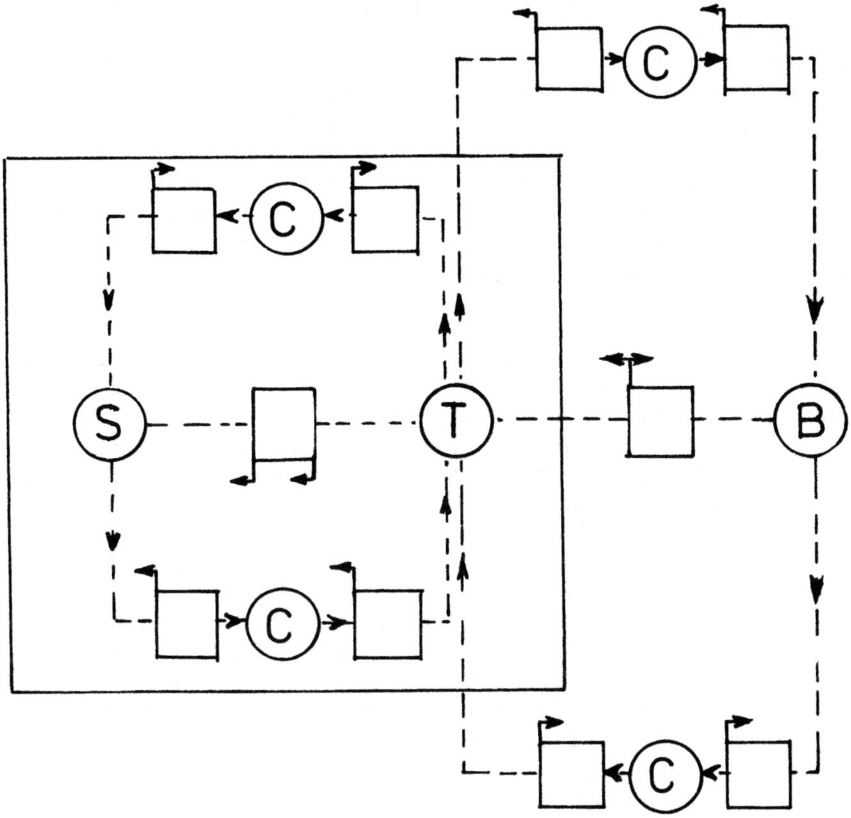

Fig. 40 (S=Settler
T=Trustee
B=Beneficiaries or others)

is shared between a monarch or a president, a governmental college, particular magistrates or colleges of magistrates, a parliament and those subjects who are qualified as citizens *(3)* of the state and who have a Privilege or even a Duty to vote in elections for parliament *(4)*. The quality of subject, on the other hand, may be attributed as well to a sharer in sovereignty when acting as a private person.

It is the sovereign who represents the State, both internally against the subjects and externally against other states and legal or natural persons, subject or not.

The fundamental jural relations between sovereign and subjects are of all the eight types and are too many to treat here *(5)*. A few general remarks should be made however.

So far as the property is concerned, which is transferred by the tax-paying subject to the sovereign *(6)*, there are fundamental relations between subjects and sovereign relative to this property which are almost similar to the internal and external fundamental jural relations of foundations. Also here we see internally, separated property without ownership and externally property at the sovereign's disposal *(7)*.

Although decisions about expenditure of taxes in a demoncratic state are generally controlled by the tax-payers or by persons on their behalf, is it not possible to consider these persons as being in the same position as the members of an incorporated society or the share-holders of a limited liability company. The reason for this is that those who act as controllers of tax expenditure act in their quality of sovereign and not as owners of the State - as such can be considered the subjects - while the members or shareholders of corporate bodies act as owners of such a body.

The internal and external structure of States can be represented according to figure 41 on the next page.

Distinction of subjects in internal components of the State and external partners depends on the quality in which they have jural relation with the sovereign. If the relations concerned are those which all subjects have to the sovereign, e.g. duties to pay taxes, rights to protection of their person and goods, then there is an internal relationship. This also applies to groups of subjects who have particular relations with the sovereign, e.g. a Privilege to use another language than the majority of subjects. If however relations are concerned in which a subject acts as a private person, e.g. by selling goods to the State, then there is an external relationship.

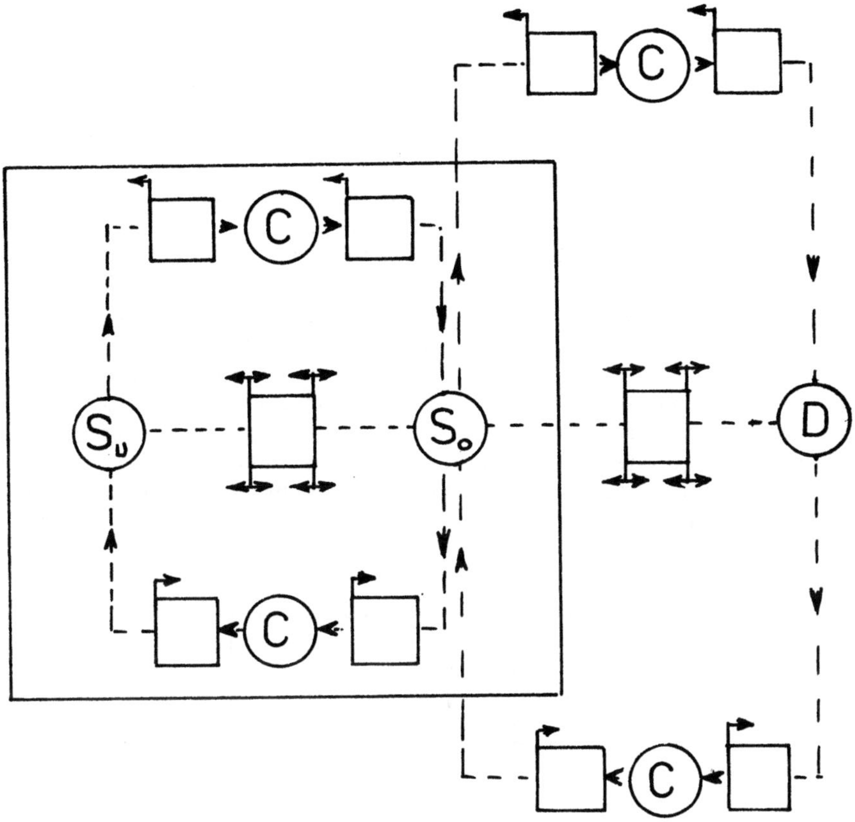

Fig. 41 (Su=Subject
So=Sovereign
D =External parties
(other states, legal or
natural persons, subjects and non-subjects)

(III.C.4.d) Sovereignity in constitutional States. The structure of a sovereign can be considered as that of a law-bound unit, composed of law-bound units comprising jural relations between persons who share parts of sovereignty and individuals in a quality of bearer of a part of sovereignty on one side and the formal head of the State on the other side.

In constitutional States sovereignty is shared between a monarch or a president and the responsible ministers or secretaries of a State. In the structure of the sovereign described here however all other bearers of sovereignty stand at the moment of exercising it in a similar relation to the monarch as the responsible ministers or secretaries of state. Just as the British and Dutch monarchs form the institution of the Crown with the members of government, so e.g. are citizens, in their capacity as voting citizens, sovereign together with the head of the state.

The structure of a sovereign can therefore be represented in the following scheme:

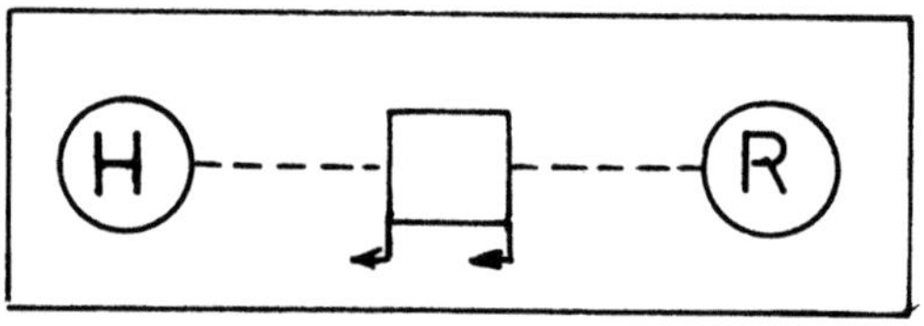

Fig. 42 (H=Head of the state, monarch, president
R=1) Responsible ministers or secretaries of state
2) Voting citizens
3) Particular magistrates or particular colleges of magistrates

Combination of the figures 41 and 42 results therefore in the following basic structure of constitutional states:

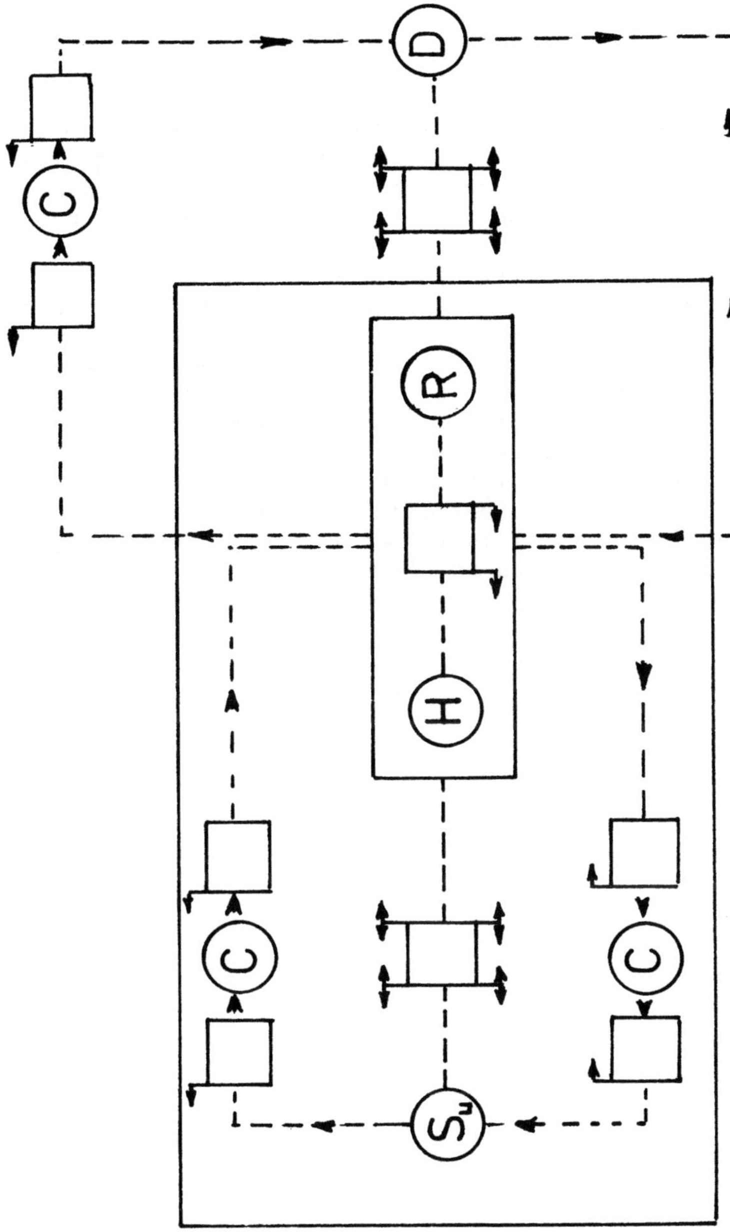

Fig. 43

(III.C.4.e) Organizations of States. States can be members of supra-national and of international organizations.

In supra-national organizations sovereignty from the States is transferred to representatives of the organization in such a way, that the member-states or the subjects of member-states can be considered as subjects of the organization.

In international organizations states co-operate together for a common purpose without transfer of sovereignty. Here the member-states cannot be considered as subjects of the organization; subjects of member-states in this quality can become bound by decisions of the organization; they are not subjects of the organization.

Supra-national organizations have therefore a basic structure with much similarity to that of a State, while international organizations have more resemblance to an incorporated society. This latter also applies to U.N.O., which will be dealt with in *(IV.E.6)*.

IV. A conception of legal evolution

(IV.A) THE BASIC PRINCIPLES OF LEGAL EVOLUTION

(IV.A.1) Introduction. Law is one of the greatest performances of civilisation; no-osphere cannot be imagined without legal frameworks holding human societies together and providing tracks along which their future existence can be maintained and improved. The human individual cannot have in a human society, if he trespasses beyond the limits imposed upon him by certain legal prescriptions. A society cannot persist if it does not guarantee to the individual certain areas of freedom to do as he pleases; freedom from certain limitations which society itself and others might impose upon him, and opportunities for a life as meaningful as possible.

We have seen in *(III.B.6)* and *(III.B.6.a)* that evolution in no-osphere is an increasing control over itself and an increasing independence of changes in the complex game-bound unit which is no-osphere itself, caused by such increases or by contradistinguished decreases in game-bound units by which no-osphere is composed.

Among the game-bound units are the law-bound units. If legal evolution is possible, then it can only be evolution related to law-bound units: they are the only game-bound units in the legal area.

There now arises one problem which should be discussed first. Law comes to us either as a body of abstract rules or as concrete applications of such rules. What now should be considered as the area of evolution: the law-book or daily legal practice? In other words, where do we really find the subjects of legal evolution?

(IV.A.2) The Subjects of Legal Evolution. Law is a construction of the human mind. It is a body of legal information stored in the human mind and in repositories of information (statute-books, case-collections, commentaries); sometimes the human mind is the only source of information on law (unwritten law).

The human mind is also the place where legal information

is digested and transformed, not only into new law, but also in the concrete applications for which law is intended. It is also in the human mind, that concretely applied law is experienced. Concrete application of abstract legal information can be seen as operationalisation of this information.

Law-bound units which are not operationalised belong to the world of legal information. Their persistence depends on the ways by which they are preserved and the problems concerned with this are by no means different to those relative to the preservation of any other information. Their development depends on the digestion of information in appropriate law-making systems.

Such law-bound units cannot function independently *(1)*; they do not operate as servomechanical structures, but are only information about these structures; it is information of this nature which is operationalised in legal practise; operationalised law-bound units are the reality of juridical life, and it is such law-bound units which are part of the no-ospheric game-bound unit. It is therefore only operationalised law-bound units which may be subject to evolution in the sense of our normative description of this notion.

In certain cases law-bound units never become operationalised. This occurs for instance when a new law is not applied. It is clear that such law-bound units cannot attribute anything to no-ospheric evolution by an activity of their own. As stored information however they might be useful some day in the creation of other law-bound units, which become operationalised indeed.

Law-bound units can in certain respects be compared to species in biology. There we saw that evolution can be considered cybernetically as evolution of a game-bound unit composed of a species and its environs *(III.B.5)*. A species is either a collection of all living beings of similar forms or such a form itself. The form or archetype is abstract information, but the collection itself is a collection of such forms which are operationalised. Learning of a species, by means of Darwinian selection, in the sense as Wiener describes it *(2)*, is only learning by such operationalised forms; forms which are not operationalised cannot learn.

Collections of similar operationalised law-bound units can better be compared to game-bound units of a species and environment. Such collections can be considered as law-bound units themselves if the similar operationalised law-bound units of which they are composed are derived from a common archetype or abstract form. This common archetype can be compared with the common genetic information of a species. Among similar law-bound units this archetypal information may only be transmitted from generation to generation if a succession of generations is due to reproduction of law-bound units *(3)*.

Creation and also dissolution of law-bound units is however not generally related to the reproduction of law-bound units and can better be compared with spontaneous generation and dissolution without progeny. In these cases it is similar archetypal patterns which with any new creation are selected anew from a common source of information by the creators of law-bound units.

(IV.A.3) Selection in processes of Legal Evolution.
We have seen in *(III.B.6.a)* that no-ospheric evolution occurs by means of selection among game-bound units and that this selection is a learning game of no-osphere, the game-bound unit of mankind and its environs. This selection is a selection among game-bound units in which the patterns of desired behaviour are determined by human values. Among these game-bound units are law-bound units.

We have described law-bound units as formal devices in *(III.C.3)*; their patterns of expectations and desired behaviour are not related to human values from this formal point of view. This formalization does not exclude the fact that their expected and desired behaviour are always patterns for human behaviour and that they are therefore so constituted that the realization of certain human values is part of the games within them. It is however not the case, that any human value, protected in this way, is a value in accordance with the ethical criterion, the criterion of evolution's interest, which has been developed in *(III.B.6.d)*. Law-bound units can therefore only contribute to evolution of no-osphere in exactly the same ways as any other game-bound unit, viz. by operation in a process of selection. Also law-bound units operate in such a process of selection:
1) by a decrease in coherence;
2) by their dissolution;
3) by an increase in coherence;
4) by their creation.

Everything that has been said about selection among game-bound units in no-osphere in *(III.B.6.a)*, selection and information on human values in *(III.B.6.c)* and human values as stimulating forces in no-ospheric evolution by lineate effects or by side effects in *(III.B.6.d)*, applies as well to law-bound units.

Decrease in coherence, dissolution, creation and increase in coherence of law-bound units can all, either mediately or immediately, affect no-osphere and either cause a greater coherence of the game-bound unit of mankind and environment, or cause a decrease in no-ospheric coherence. E.g. creation or reinforcement of particular legal advantages for adherents of a particular religion are advances if this religion was suppressed, but may be regressions if these advantages are not available to adherents of another religion who are in need of similar advantages. Dissolution or weakening of such discriminating legal advantages, which is dissolution or weakening of the law-bound units in which these advantages are patterns of expectations or desired behaviour, may ultimately lead to a greater coherence in no-osphere.

Selection among law-bound units leads to a survival or regular recreation according to a surviving archetype of operative images of law-bound units in which the patterns of expectations and desired behaviour are in accordance with the ethical criterion of evolution's interest. The role of this criterion in legal evolution will be discussed in *(IV.B.2.c)*, *(IV.D.1)* and *(IV.D.2)*.

(IV.A.4) A Normative Description of Legal Evolution. Within the framework of the cybernetical conceptions developed here relative to evolution and legal phenomena, there are three requirements which a normative description of legal evolution should fulfil:

1) Accordance with the normative description of no-ospheric evolution, given in *(III.B.6)*;
2) Accordance with the conception of selection between operative images of law-bound units as a learning-game within the game-bound unit composed of mankind and its environs, developed in *(IV.A.3)* jo *(III.B.6.a)*;
3) Accordance with the ethical criterion of evolution's interest, developed in *(III.B.6.c)*;

These three requirements are met in the following description:

Legal evolution may be interpreted as an increase in coherence of the game-bound unit composed of mankind and its environs, due to a learning process during which law-bound units may be created or increased or decreased in coherence or may be dissolved, and which may also cause by side-effects similar processes with respect to other law-bound units.

The first and the second requirement can easily be detected in the description. The third requirement, in accordance with the ethical criterion, is met, so far as the first part of the description is concerned, in the description of legal evolution as no-ospheric evolution, i.e. evolution of the game-bound unit of mankind and its environment. This requirement is also met in that part of the description where it is stated that greater coherences of law-bound units may be side-effects of the process of learning or selection: the learned data are applied in these law-bound units because they appeared to lead to evolution of no-osphere and therefore a similar result may be expected in comparable circumstances.

Notice that in this description legal evolution is not by itself evolution of a local, national or international legal system. Increases in coherence of a local, national or international legal system are only legal evolution, if they answer to the normative description of legal evolution, i.e. if no-ospheric evolution might be the result of this. Increases in coherence of legal systems in e.g. fascist states are therefore not legal evolution.

(IV.B) THE MAIN RELATIONS BETWEEN LEGAL EVOLUTION AND EVOLUTION IN NO-OSPHERE.

(IV.B.1) The effect of Legal Evolution in No-osphere. It follows from our normative description of legal evolution that a decrease in coherence or a dissolution or a creation or an increase in coherence of one single law-bound unit, e.g. a law-bound unit composed of two parties in a special jural relationship, is already legal evolution, if the requirement is met that no-osphere's greatest game-bound unit might be affected by an increase in coherence, mediately or immediately. It is therefore of less importance, whether in a group of similar law-bound units, only one, a few, the greater part or the complete group affects no-osphere, provided it is at least affected to some extent.

The possible immediate effect on no-osphere will be firstly seen in law-bound units with patterns of expectations and desired behaviour derived from the Law of Nations, international civil law, or international penal law. Legal patterns related to a national law system like legal relations relative to philantropy, well-being, religion, science, education, culture and civilisation may also belong to law-bound units immediately affecting no-osphere.

Examples of mediate effects on no-osphere by legal evolution can be found in the history of standardisation of legal relations by means of standard-contracts, their adoption in a national law, their adoption in another national law or in international treaties. Regulations are here involved which have developed from practice between a few persons in regularly recurring situations. One of the oldest examples is the *Lex Rhodia de iactu* (D.14,2,1).

It is only possible for no-osphere to be affected mediately or immediately if it is accepted that information relative to a created or dissolved law-bound unit or a law-bound unit increased or decreased in coherence reaches human individuals with opportunities to be a link in a possible chain extending from the concerned law-bound unit to no-osphere's greatest game-bound unit. In point of fact this condition will be fulfilled in most parts of the world thanks to the modern means of communication and research in the social area. Only isolated communities, or cases where legal information is consciously withheld, will probably not meet this condition. This means that almost any information on creation, dissolution or growth of law-bound units may affect no-osphere at least mediately, by side-effects. The working of possible side-effects on game-bound units with desired patterns of behaviour relative to human values has been discussed in *(III.B.6.d)*. This also applies to law-bound units; a law-bound unit's patterns of expectations and desired behaviour are related to the realization and protection of legal values, which are nothing but human values realized or protected by rules of law. The role of human values in legal evolution will be discussed in *(IV.B.2)*ff.

(IV.B.2) The role of Legal Values in Legal Evolution.

(IV.B.2.a) Legal Values and Human Values. A human value can be considered as a relation between man and his environment; man and environment build it together.

In this relation man is continuously attempting to find valuations and to give sense to his environs. These attempts to give sense are attempts to make objects valuable as objects worth pursuing or not. These attempts are never completely succesful, because of the fact that tensions always exist between subjective and objective valuations.

Objectivated valuations are subjective values made objective. Such are the legal values. E.g. in penal law we find that the human values protected by it are formulated as acts liable to punishment. From the measures of punishment we can judge the respective cadres of these values.

The first to study human values was Aristotle *(1)*, who elaborated in his Nicomachean Ethics a theory of ethical values or virtues. The nature of human values was studied later in the South-Western German school of Neokantianism, especially by H. Windelband, H. Rickert and E. Lark, of which the latter was the first to put forward a theory of legal values. Building on the work of Rickert it was Max Weber (1864-1920) who investigated the role of values in science and society and, placing their essence in faith, arrived at a "polytheism" of values. Max Scheler (1875-1928) was the first to develop a phenomenological conception of values: it is only by means of intuition that a value can be surveyed; values are indeed to Scheler of an objective nature and arranged in an objective order, but the objective world to which they belong is a world of ideas in a sense related to Plato's conception. Nicolai Hartmann (1882-1950), who enlarged the work done by Aristotle and Scheler, defended the impossibility to arrange values in a certain order because one should take the power of values or *Wertstärke* into account. Gustav Radbruch (1878-1949) sought for a solution of these relativisms with respect to legal values, because relativism recognizes ultimately any subjective value as a human value, also nazi-values. He formulated therefore material points of view, by which fixed limitations can be put with authoritarian arbitrariness. The main point of view is that of human rights as a condition for free ethical decision *(2)*. Helmut Coing (born 1912) integrated certain basic values from a value conception inspired by that of Hartmann within his concept of a Natural Law directed towards the typical nature *(Natur der Sache)* of human social relations.

We distinguished in *(III.B.6.e)* human values in ethical, aesthetical and technological values, all human values however being ultimately based on ethical values. Legal values are human values of which the realization is organized by law.

(IV.B.2.b) Legal Values and Law-Bound Units. Legal values are comprised by legal norms. This means that they can be found in that part of law-bound units, where a relation of Hohfeldian nature is expressed with respect to a certain performance. The cadres of values can be derived by comparing negative feedback opportunities of law-bound units, realizing related values.

It is doubtful whether all legal values are reducible to units as small as the smallest possible fundamental relations by which they can be expressed. A value like the idea that man should keep his promises indeed lies at the base of many jural relationships *(1)* and finds expression as a game-rule in the most complicated entireties of law-bound units as well as in the most simple ones, for example that formed by a donor and a receiver relative to a legally promitted gift.

Legal values are often conditioned by time, place and circumstances. Private property is an illustrative example of a legal value with varying contents. Determining the patterns of expectations and desired behaviour in law-bound units they determine formal lines of development in successions of law-bound units with similar purposes, however not necessarily developments in coherence of law-bound units: these are firstly determinated by the attitude of the persons forming them and by the negative feedback opportunities.

(IV.B.2.c) Legal Values and the Ethical Criterion. In *(III.B.6.e)* we developed the criterion of no-ospheric evolution's interest as an objective ethical criterion for human values. In this conception it is this criterion which is also a touchstone for legal values. It is not in the character of this criterion to force legal and

other human values into static dogmatic systems, but it can be a criterion for establishing whether a certain object should or may be pursued, or not. In this respect the ethical criterion leaves room for other autonomous sources of values, like religious faith, but it places limits on ideas contrary to no-ospheric evolution's interest: crusade and djihad equally are not in accordance with evolution's interest.

The ethical criterion itself is not a value, but a touchstone for values. It designates no-ospheric evolution as the highest human value. We can find this highest human value represented in three high ranking legal values: the human individual, no-osphere as a whole, and the processes of no-ospheric evolution; no-ospheric evolution as such can therefore be considered as the highest legal value.

No-ospheric evolution is however not only a legal value, but also a source of legal values. The legal values of the human individual and of no-osphere as a whole are sources of values already recognised, although not yet completely realized, in law; the processes of no-osphere however are sources of legal values which are not actually recognized in law.

We will discuss now in the following paragraphs the main legal values arising from no-ospheric evolution.

(IV.B.2.d) The Individual as a Legal Value and as a Source of Legal Values. No-osphere's evolution is evolution of mankind as a whole. Mankind is composed of individuals. It follows therefore that the individual has certain values from the point of view of no-ospheric organization. We have seen how Spencer and Teilhard de Chardin have each tried to formulate these values in a conception of fundamental human rights *(1)*. This means an attribution of legal values to the individual. In our conception of no-ospheric evolution an ethical criterion is included in which increases of no-osphere's coherence or at least absence of increases in no-ospheric disorder are posed as standards for human behaviour.

There are certain acts against human individuals, which decrease their coherence. Such acts, often made crimes in ordinary law, cause by their perpetration, decreases in coherence, not only in the victims, but also in the game-bound units to which these belong and ultimately they cause increases in disorder in no-osphere.

Law being, as it has been argued in *(III.B.1)*, the main device against threats of increases in disorder in no-osphere, it is by means of law, that the individual can be protected, and by means of this protection no-osphere. It is for this reason that we consider protection of the individual by means of human rights statutes as being very closely connected with our conception of evolution. These connections will be discussed in *(IV.E)*. The individual himself is in this way not only a legal value, but also a source of legal values because fundamental human rights have the capacity to determine the structure of legal systems. The individual may moreover be a source of legal values, in that he succeeds in introducing a particular idea, related to certain human values, into a legal system as a legal value.

(IV.B.2.e) No-osphere as a Legal Value and as a Source of Legal Values. The human individual as such cannot exist without his environs. Generally his environment comprises other individuals and to a certain extent his existence even depends on the relations which he maintains with these individuals. In fact nearly all human beings are involved in a network of relationships, or of game-bound units, of all kinds, extending over the whole area of no-osphere.

The individual cannot but be interested in a no-osphere where threats of increases in disorder, if not disorder itself, are driven back as far as possible. Legal protection of no-osphere may counteract that part of threatening disorder, which is due to human causes or which can be prevented by man. Attempts to provide such a protection are evident in the Law of Nations, which is directed towards a regulation of relations between States in times of peace and war.

No-osphere as a legal value can be found in those regulations of the Law of Nations, where crimes perpetrated against it are declared liable to punishment. So we find in article 6 of the Charter of the International Military Tribunal at Nürnberg, annex to the London Agreement of 6th August 1945 signed by representatives of the U.S.A., the U.K., France and the U.S.S.R., a formulation of crimes which can be considered as crimes against no-osphere.

These crimes are:

a) *Crimes against peace*: "..... planning, perpetration, initiation, or waging of a war of agression, or a war in violation of international treaties, agreements or assurances, or participation in a common plan or conspiracy for the accomplishment of any of the foregoing".

b) *War crimes*: "..... violation of the laws or customs

of war. Such violations shall include, but not be limited to murder, ill-treatment or deportation to slave-labour or for any other purpose of civilian population of or in occupied territory, murder or ill-treatment of prisoners of war or persons on the seas, killing of hostages, plunder of public or private property, wanton destruction of cities, towns or villages, or devastation not justified by military necessity".

c) *Crimes against humanity*: " ..... murder, extermination, enslavement, deportation and other inhumane acts committed against any civilian population, before or during the war, or persecutions on political, racial or religious grounds in execution of or in connection with any crime within the jurisdiction of the Tribunal, whether or not in violation of the domestic law of the country where perpetrated".

The Nürnberg Tribunal declared that its Charter is the expression of International Law at the time of its creation. It explained that crimes against peace and war crimes were already crimes under International Law before its Charter was created; so far as crimes against humanity were concerned the Tribunal was unable to "make a general declaration that the acts before 1939 were crimes against humanity within the meaning of the Charter" *(1)*. But the Tribunal indeed considered inhumane acts, committed after the beginning of the war in 1939, which were not war crimes as committed in execution of, or in connection with, the agressive war as crimes against humanity *(2)*.

This latter is due to the fact that Art. 6c of the Charter is a compromise between two opposite principles, viz. that of a State's freedom to treat its subjects as it wishes, and that inhuman treatment by a state is forbidden and should, if necessary, be punished at international level because such treatment affects *the international community*.

The principles of the Nürnberg Trial were not only applicable to individuals with an official position as organs of the State (Charter of the Nürnberg Tribunal, Art. 7), but as well to individuals in their private capacity, like Julius Streicher, who was sentenced to death because of his activities as editor of the anti-Semitic weekly "Der Stürmer".

It is for this reason, that according to international law, crimes against humanity are not only crimes of state *(3)*. We are therefore allowed to establish a crime against humanity as soon as individuals or gangs like the Ku Klux Klan or the Maffia terrorize a population and actually prevent its social, economic or cultural development.

Another regulation for the protection of no-osphere by international Law is the Genocide Convention of 9th December 1948. The convention describes in Art. II genocide as:

"any of the following acts committed with intent to destroy, in whole or in part, a national, ethnical, racial or religious group, as such:

a) Killing members of the group;
b) Causing serious bodily or mental harm to members of the group;
c) Deliberately inflicting on the group conditions of life calculated to bring about its physical destruction in whole or in part;
d) Imposing measures intended to prevent births within the group;
e) Forcibly transferring children of the group to another group".

Differences between the Genocide Convention and the Nürnberg Charter are:

1) The Convention protects a group against destruction, the Charter also protects against other kinds of persecution.
2) The Charter protects individuals, the Convention protects national, ethnical, racial and religious groups.
3) The Charter protects all who are persecuted for political reasons; the Convention does not apply to political groups, although it is possible to bring certain political persecutions under the formulation of genocide.
4) Cultural genocide, i.e. suppression of anything by which a group's spiritual life expresses itself, such as destruction of monuments or libraries, or prohibition of a group's language, is not genocide in the Convention's sense. It can however be considered as an inhumane act committed against a civilian population and therefore as a crime against humanity acoording to the Nürnberg Charter.

Actually no-osphere is not only in want of more appropriate negative feedback opportunities relative to the principles of the Nürnberg Charter and the Genocide Convention, by which ultimately human integrity is protected, but it is also in need of a world-wide protection of the human environs by International Law.

No-osphere is not only a legal value but also a source of legal values. The principles relative to the protection of individuals, of groups and of the human environment can be traced back in national legal systems and in bilateral or multilateral treaties between States. Some of these will be discussed in *(IV.E)*.

(IV.B.3) The processes of No-ospheric Evolution as a Legal Value and as a Source of Legal Values.

(IV.B.3.a) Introduction. If processes of no-ospheric evolution are disturbed or do not occur at all then there is no no-ospheric evolution and the result of this is an increase in disorder. Continuation of these processes in the most appropriate way is therefore a high ranking human value. Actually this human value as such is not protected by positive law, but certain processes which are part of the fundamentals are recognised as legal values. These legal values can be found in regulations concerning the conservation of certain biological processes in the human environment, in protection provided in family law to human procreation, in special protection of women and children by labour-laws and laws of war, in regulation by laws of education and in measures for promoting health of body and mind.

The fundamentals of no-ospheric evolutionary processes themselves however are not as such protected by law. This is due to the fact that opinions on what are the fundamentals are still changing. It is moreover doubtful whether protection of such fundamentals, basic principles as they are and therefore rather abstract notions, can be realized by means of legal formulations relative to certain acts or forbearances.

We will investigate now the fundamentals of the processes of no-ospheric evolution, and see whether these processes are subjected to general principles and whether these principles or some of them can be described as legal values.

(IV.B.3.b) Regularities in processes of No-ospheric Evolution. Understanding the processes of no-ospheric evolution is understanding the presumed regularities in these processes.

We have met several conceptions of regularity in theories of social evolution. These have been discussed in *(I.B.3.a)* and preceding paragraphs. Among these we found mechanicistic explanations of social evolution like those of Morgan and Tarde in *(I.B.2.a)* and *(I.B.2.d)*, and psychological approaches, like those of Wundt *(I.B.3.a)*, Ratzenhofer *(I.B.3.a)* and Ellwood *(I.B.1.c)* and *(I.B.2.b)*. We found ideas that social evolution is determined by creation of new information (invention, both technological and cultural) and transmission of information in the theories of Morgan, Tarde, Ratzenhofer and Ellwood. Conceptions fitting into a cybernetical explanation were moreover found in the theories of Tarde (dialectics), Ratzenhofer (dynamic network of reciprocal relationships between individuals) and Ellwood (web of intercommunication).

It seems impossible however to separate evolution in human society from that in biosphere, although distinction between these two notions is necessary. With the aim of taking a stand in regard to no-ospheric evolution I have therefore to treat no-ospheric processes in their relation to those in biosphere. When accepting Teilhard de Chardin's division between biosphere and no-osphere one should be aware of the facts that not only within these spheres is the working of evolutionary principles determined by time, place and circumstances, but that moreover within both spheres equal terms for evolutionary principles might cover notions which are only partly equal in the other sphere; such terms are especially those of struggle for life, mutation and life-impulse *(élan vital) (1)*.

In this respect special attention should be devoted to the notion of mutation. Charles Darwin and Herbert Spencer always considered the transformation or mutation of species, caused by natural selection, as an active adaptation to the environs according to the theory of Lamarck.

Lamarckian adaptations correspond in no-osphere to mutations which might be met in the shape of people, who, either voluntary or by force, have adapted themselves to a different culture or elements of a different culture to that by which they were moulded. This process, called acculturation in sociology, may concern both individuals and societies.

There is further the generally accepted theory in biology of spontaneous mutations, which has been affirmed by successful experiments. Corresponding to such De Vries mutations we find in no-osphere spontaneous or casual incidents, which may lead to changes in culture or culture elements, or to the arising of new culture elements or cultures. Incidents of this kind were e.g. the decision of St. Paul *(2)* to preach the gospel to the gentiles, or the discovery of the American continent by Columbus when sailing westward.

Moreover, in relation to a society there are changes in

basic cultural elements, which could be called mutations, because they are changes in its features, e.g. changes in society's leading men and leading ideas *(3)*.

No-ospheric mutations are, as are spontaneous de Vries mutations, not always to be considered as symtoms of evolution. The destruction of the Aztec and Inca cultures in the 16th century may thus be established as a casual incident, but not as a constructive one *(4)*.

No-ospheric mutations may occur independently of other evolutionary phenomena; their effect may be both favourable as well as disturbing to the evolutionary working of these phenomena.

Natural selection, although not offering an explanation anymore for *all* the facts of evolution, has remained recognized as the driving force behind the development of the same species. Eminent scientists of our time such as Julian Huxley and Norbert Wiener agree with the opinion that natural selction is the sole or main method of biological evolution *(5)*.

As regards biospheric evolution it seems that Bergson's criticism of the theory of natural selction is sound. Also his explanation of evolution as caused by a dynamic final cause seems, with the exception of Bergson's statement that life and God are one and the same, acceptable to me as a just starting point, but not as the only one. We have moreover noticed the structural co-ordination between a cybernetically directed servomechanism and Bergson's notion of creative evolution, which is both life's entelechy and the entelechy's realization *(6)*.
Life's entelechy - the life-impulse *(élan vital)* - has the function of a desired pattern of behaviour; this means that life's entelechy comprises a world of information. The behaviour which is realized is life or the phenomenon of creative evolution. Life's final causes are moulded anew when life proceeds: this means that information is received by which the desired pattern of behaviour is changed, for new information changes the meaning of information that will be received later.

At present we are not yet sufficiently familiar with organic processes to establish exactly where and how in organisms information received is digested and carried back; that life of cells and individuals can be interpreted as cybernetic processes has been demonstrated by a.o. S.T.Bok *(7)*. If indeed the principles of cybernetics are applicable to all dynamic processes in nature, then Bergson's vitalism might be considered as being in conformity with the principles published in the year 1948 by Norbert Wiener in his "Cybernetics" *(8)*.

Wiener described Darwinian selection as a learning process *(9)*. This is an explanation of the working of selection, but not of its purpose. It is nevertheless possible to see an element of finalism in this approach, if we include learning of purposes in the process of learning. One may also consider finalism as complementary to mechanicism, finalism being an explanation of appropriateness and mechanicism of causality *(10)*. Our conception of no-ospheric evolution as an increase in coherence of no-osphere by greater control over itself and greater independence of changes within itself is finalistic: no-osphere itself is its own final cause.

We must now investigate Teilhard de Chardin's theory of psychic energy as the driving force behind evolution. The problem is, whether this theory is acceptable as a further development after Bergson's description of creative evolution as the self-conscious energy of free activity, realizing the potentials it already possessed in its origin. Undoubtedly there is a close affinity between creative evolution or self-conscious energy and psychic energy. Teilhard de Chardin however commenced his philosophic thinking at the point where Bergson arrived at his final conclusion *(11)*.

Teilhard de Chardin's notion of psychic energy is entirely different to that of psychic energy or libido which was developed by Carl Gustav Jung (1875-1961). Taking the term libido from Sigmund Freud (1856-1939), who only used it for designating the sexual drive in both its restricted and extended sense, Jung understood by psychic energy the total force which pulses through all the forms and activities of the psychic system and establishes a communication between them. Jung had in mind a concept similar to that in physics, where energy is experienced specifically as motion and force, when actual, and as a state or condition when potential. Actually psychic energy is reflected in specific psychic phenomena as drives, wishes, will, affect, performance; potentially it is manifested a.o. in specific acquisitions, possibilities, aptitudes, or attitudes. Psychic energy is to Jung finalistic, for the psyche is to him a self-regulating system, based on the regulative function of opposites in the sense as taught by Heraclite. These opposites are to Jung the directions of progression and regression. So may intellectual efforts and negative emotional reactions succeed each other. Jung strictly confined this conception to the area of psychology, upholding the right of biology to present its own concepts concerning vital force *(12)*.

Jung's finalism seems more related to that of Driesch than to Bergson's finalism, but nevertheless it is an anticipation of cybernetics by its explanation of self-regulation in a self-regulating system by the regulative function of the opposites, viz. progression and regression, which might be considered as playing a game, in the sense of modern theories of game, with psychic energy.

Teilhard de Chardin avoids just as Bergson, dualism between mind and matter. Both emphasize that higher organic beings are of increasingly complex structure, but Teilhard de Chardin teaches that there is always some *"complexité"*, also in inorganic nature. It is on this base that Teilhard de Chardin states that psychic energy is centripetal, accumulating in the direction of a more complex and *concentrated* condition, at certain moments of *crisis concentration* crosses evolutionary thresholds, and at present drives man towards a super-collectivation.

Here, at least as regards the pre-vital phase and biosphere, Teilhard de Chardin's ingenious vision does not seem contradictory to cybernetics and other results of science, but science nevertheless does not provide sufficient evidence for its accordance with reality *(13)*. So far as Teilhard de Chardin's conclusions as to no-osphere are concerned, I hope to demonstrate in *(IV.B.3.f)* that the trend towards a cultural unification of mankind, even apart from psychic energy as in Julian Huxley, is only acceptable as one of the trends in mankind's development *(14)*, and that this trend would lead to a dead end if it were the only one.

This rejection makes it impossible to accept Teilhard de Chardin's outlook on future human collectivation within a super-organism as a natural consequence of further evolutionary development. Moreoever, recognizing Teilhard de Chardin's emphasis on the necessity that one should only enter superorganism by free-will, I am afraid that the individual within super-organism will no longer possess one of his greatest opportunities: the possibility to choose and decide for himself. Surely, there is at present no society, where these possibilities can be fully realized, because in certain respects one has always to reckon with others, but within a superorganism opportunities existing at present will be made to disappear, *especially the possibility of free choice between good and evil,* whatever the subjective notions of these terms may be. In my opinion this would not mean evolution in no-osphere, but a greater step backwards.

Among the regularities in no-ospheric evolutionary processes are included, besides of course the regularities treated here above, all those in processes which are related to increases in coherence of game-bound units, viz. to reception, digestion and negative feedback of information relative to the internal and external games, to game-rules as desired patterns of behaviour and in certain cases patterns of expectations, and to a continuous struggle against threats of disorder as part of the games.

No-osphere is however not only a game-bound unit, it is also a very complex entirety of game-bound units. The relations between game-bound units within this entirety are complex, but we may distinguish among them trends towards divergency.

We will treat these trends and their relations in the next subdivisions; it is among the relations between these trends that we shall discover a number of human values and legal values.

(IV.B.3.c) Subjects of Trends of No-ospheric Evolution. Trends of evolution can be described as prospective results of games within game-bound units.

Trends of no-ospheric evolution are always prospective results of games within the game-bound unit of mankind and environs. These games can be played by other game-bound units which are part of this entirety and by individuals within the framework of game-bound units which they make with their environs, other individuals included.

The human individual can to an important extent, perhaps even completely *(1)*, be considered as the greater part of a servomechanism, which is composed by his body, soul, mental tools and physical tools. Among the mental tools we should understand man's abilities, knowledge, experiences, opinions and conscience; among man's physical tools, the goods directly used by him. This servomechanism we might call the human personality *(2)*; it is servomechanisms of this nature which play games with their environs and which form the human parts of game-bound units.

We shall discuss in *(IV.B.3.d)* and *(IV.B.3.e)* trends of no-ospheric evolution respectively within and between individuals. Trends between individuals are trends of games within game-bound units composed of human personalities. This conception makes it possible to distinguish among the same individuals between various and even opposite trends; any of these trends being a prospective result of games within differentiated game-bound units.

Trends within the individual are prospective results of games within the servomechanism of the human personality. Also here various and opposite trends can be distinguished if we distinguish within the human personality between game-bound units composed of the physical-psychical servomechanism of body and soul, subjectively experienced as "I", on one side and man's mental and physical tools on the other side.

Other game-bound units of which the trends of the internal or external games are decisive in processes of no-ospheric evolution are the cultural and subcultural areas to which mankind's individuals belong. This conception is closely related, although not similar, to the opinion, sustained by Teilhard de Chardin and Julian Huxley, that in no-osphere there is not so much a struggle for life between individuals leading to natural selection, as a struggle between cultures, leading to the world's cultural unification *(3)*.

Taking the opposite view it can be said that in every kind of civilized society certain kinds of competition occur between its members, although at present not generally for survival any longer, but e.g. for a better situation, more possessions, esteem by the neighbours etc. There is no doubt, that such competitions may stimulate society's progress; on the other hand however there is a great danger that by such competitions individuals who could have stimulated society's progress will be made victims of society instead of its masters.

Before treating "cultural" struggles I want to distinguish between cultures and cultural areas. I may describe culture or civilization as a set of mental properties belonging to a group of human beings and embracing their common patterns of behaviour, their common means of communication and their common historical traditions; culture is therefore common information *(4)* and means of communication.

A cultural area may be described as a group of human beings with a common culture. So within a cultural area a distinction can be made between man and culture, but not a separation. A cultural area might be differentiated into sub-cultural areas, just as a culture might be divided into sub-cultures. Cultural areas moreover are led by men, but men are in their turn led by ideas, while ideas again are dependent upon men for their execution. So the leading elements of culture areas are units which embody both leading men and ideas. The notion of struggle between cultures seems to me therefore less serviceable and I prefer to use the notion of struggle between cultural areas.

Cybernetical is a cultural area a game-bound *(5)* unit embodying a group of men and the common culture belonging to them, in which the common patterns of behaviour are desired patterns of behaviour, the common historical information is stored in the individual brains of the members of the group, the games consist of happenings in which the common patterns of behaviour and historical traditions are existentially experienced as common frames of reference and in which negative feedback is possible towards internal or external forces which threaten to disturb the activities or games of the group as such. Within this game-bound unit it is game-bound units composed of leading men and ideas which collect information of importance to the cultural area and decide on its digestion and feedback. These game-bound units of leading man and ideas embody one or a few individuals with leading qualities and with ideas concerning the world around them, including the culture to which they belong and possibly other cultures. As game-bound units they not only make for a certain control and independence over themselves, but they are moreover directed towards control over their own cultural area and sometimes towards control over other cultural areas as well.

Cultural areas may be divided both horizontally and vertically. A horizontal division of cultural areas leads to sub-cultural areas, as e.g. the present Normand and Breton sub-cultural areas as part of the French cultural area. A vertical division of cultural areas leads to pressure groups like e.g. religious organizations, trade-unions, political parties, great concerns; pressure-groups may extend themselves over different cultural areas. To sub-cultural areas and pressure-groups the same cybernetical principles are applicable as in respect to cultural areas.

Cultural area and state are never altogether identical, even if they comprise the same people, cover the same territorial area and are controlled by the same leading unit of men and ideas; the state's servomechanical structure is in its essence that of a law-bound unit *(6)* and this is not the case with cultural areas.

A cultural area might be greater than a State's area, like e.g. the French cultural area, which extends over a much greater territory than that of the French republic; a cultural area might also be smaller that a State's territory, if a State has cultural minorities

When cultural areas are struggling, then their leading game-bound units composed of man and ideas decide on negative or positive feedback of political character.

If now for this process a State's servomechanism is used, provided that this servomechanism is not used in the same way by another cultural area , then state and cultural area are in political respect one and the same. It is therefore in conformity with political reality to introduce the notion of state-cultural area as the operative image of a State and a cultural area which are politically identical. Such a political identity does neither exclude the fact that the concerned cultural areas is not the only one within the state's realm, nor that it has extensions outside the territory of the state.

A singular cultural area might further embrace different States as e.g. in 19th century Germany and Italy. We also meet cases of singular states embodying different cultural areas, like e.g. present day's Switzerland and Belgium. This situation is close to that of one state embracing a number of sub-cultural areas, which together make a cultural area, like e.g. the Netherlands.

Leading game-bound units of man and ideas are of course never separated from the cultural area to which they belong, but cultural areas should be considered in relation to such units, as the more stable element in time, for men and ideas may be subject to successive alterations of a sometimes rapid nature. A curious example in this respect is Germany, where we see within one generation a fair number of different game-bound units of leading men and ideas over the same cultural area: corresponding to the period of Emperor Wilhelm II, the Weimar-Republic, the Third Reich, the allied military governmental organization and the two present German states; here the development has even led to a replacement of one cultural area by two cultural areas at the same time.

Nazi-Germany could only exist by grace of the leading ideas of National-Socialism combined with the leading person of Adolf Hitler; the Soviet-Union could only arise thanks to ideas of Marxism in combination with the personality and ideas of Lenin; the United States of America could only arise in the 18th century thanks to the ideas of human rights in combination with a number of eminent scholars who led the movement for independence *(7)*. In other areas it is often an idea of democracy combined with the leading statesmen; sometimes it is just the economic interest of a very small minority or pressure-group which is the ruling idea, in combination with rulers guided by self-interest or pure lust for power.

Struggles between cultural areas may in point of fact in some cases result in integration of originally separated cultural areas. So the struggle between the cultural area of the Cherokee-Indians and that of modern America resulted in a successful integration of the Cherokee-Indians within the American cultural area *(8)*.

Among other tribes of the American Indians however the contact with Western men has led to a reinforcement of their own cultural area, like e.g. among the Pueblos and among the Iroquois; among other tribes indeed this contact is now leading to unification, not however with the modern Western cultural area, but towards an integration of American Indian cultural areas into a new one: this is the movement of Pan-Indianism *(9)*.

Trends among cultural areas are just like those within and between individuals directed in several ways towards convergency and divergency. The nature of such trends and the legal values originating from their position will be discussed in the next subdivisions.

(IV.B.3.d) Trends within Individuals. Within an individual various forces can be seen which conflict with each other, and this conflict is a threat of disorder, which can however be mastered by reason. The threat of disorder can be considered as a divergent complex of forces, the mastering power of reason as a convergent force. But there are also within the individuals powers at work which the individual cannot possibly always keep under control, like intuition, instincts, complexes. Domination of such a force may be dangerous to the individual and lead to his physical or psychical destruction. Man is therefore appointed to provide, consciously and unconsciously, for an equilibrium between the powers within him. The impulse to reinforce himself against a life-long threat of disorder by mastering the internal powers is a driving force towards increase in coherence within the individual. This impulse may be identified with the life-impulse or creative evolution, described by Bergson as the self-conscious energy of free activity, realizing the potentials which it already possessed in its origin *(1)*.

I may draw attention to the fact that in this respect the self-consciousness of free activity is of the same nature as consciousness of the individual human being; Bergson attributed consciousness to all phenomena of creative evolution; human consciousness is situated at the top of the ascending line of vital phenomena.

The individual therefore who acts according to the impulse to reinforce himself for the mastery of the internal powers within him, achieves these acts by the grace of the self-conscious energy of *free* activity which realizes potentials already possessed by him in his origin as a purpose of realization. In other words: the life-impulse makes man strengthen himself in order to control the internal powers within him, *whether he wants to or not.* This means that the equilibrium between the powers within the individual, as one of the conditions for human existence, is achieved partly independently of his free will and therefore *partly independently of rules prescribing his behaviour*, viz. rules of law or public morality; it is partly a biological-physical process.

Domination of convergency over divergency within the individual is not only a condition for human existence, but also for no-ospheric evolution, which is dependent for its continuation, on human beings.

As a human value we can consider the biological-psychical processes which contribute to the domination of convergency over divergency in individuals. Recognition of these processes as legal values can be found in catalogues of human rights as regulations guaranteeing man adequate medical facilities, appropriate food and corporeal integrity *(2)*.

So far as the acts of reason in this respect are concerned, there is no legal system imposing upon man a duty to use his reason in order to control the divergent forces within him. As protection of recognised legal values however legal relations forbidding and penalizing attempts to commit suicide might be considered.

Prohibition of euthanasia has an aspect of almost similar nature. Although here mainly the idea is reflected that all human life should be protected, it is also here that a relation can be established with a presumed Duty of somebody who is seriously ill to struggle intelligently against divergency within him and not to ask for euthanasia.

Such an almost similar aspect can also be found in prohibition of abortion for non-medical reasons. This prohibition mainly refers to protection of the *nasciturus*, but is has also some relatedness to a presumed Duty of a mother to have the good sense to keep threats of internal divergency under control.

These prohibitions cannot apply to conditions of extreme emergency *(3)*. Control of internal divergency is then only possible if there is free entrance to the way out. Such conditions are for suicide and abortion those of the concentration camp, for abortion moreover any serious threat to the mother's life, either by illness or by violence, and for euthanasia a serious bodily suffering during an incurable illness.

(IV.B.3.e) Trends between Individuals. The individual is in his relation to other individuals subject to converging and diverging trends; the former are directed towards unification of all men within a certain cultural area or within one world society, the latter towards separation from and reinforcement against other individuals or groups of individuals, either organised or not.

Neither convergent nor divergent forces between individuals are limited to individuals of the same sub-cultural area or the same cultural area: convergent forces also exist between individuals of cultural areas which reinforce themselves against each other; on the other hand divergent forces may also act between individuals of converging cultural areas and sub-cultural areas. Individuals are often disposed to identify themselves with the cultural area which is their own, and this means that they adopt towards individuals of other cultural or sub-cultural areas, the attitude of their own area towards these other areas. One may see this especially in the case of either armed or cold war, when hostility towards the individuals of the enemy is cultivated, either spontaneously as a result of hostile acts by the enemy, or artificially by means of propaganda especially directed to that purpose.

Convergent trends among individuals may sometimes lead to the rise of new sub-cultural areas and even new cultural areas. Such a trend is only convergent within the new area but in relation to the original cultural and sub-cultural areas it may be divergent. So the present North American and Latin American cultural areas originated from converging forces among immigrant individuals, driven from their home-countries by diverging forces within these countries.

Among the specific human convergent forces we find feelings of sympathy and compassion; a special role is played in evolution by the convergent force of sexual attraction, and not only because of its function in humanity's biological survival; but also divergent trends act among individuals. There are among human beings feelings of antipathy and hatred and there is an innate desire for agression.

Lack of sufficient resources may lead to stimulation of diverging as well as converging forces; this is more intensified among individuals than among cultural areas where generally the leaders do not suffer personally from such a deficiency. If human needs are not satisfied a competition may arise, or even a struggle for life; human needs moreover can be artificially enlarged by means of "hidden persuaders" and this may result in a possibly hopeless struggle for a life with more and more possessions and comfort.

Lack of sufficient resources may create convergency by the conviction that property might be reached in a comparatively short time by means of mutual assistance and co-operation. In this respect a role may also be attributed to inclinations to live in harmony with the environs, including other individuals; these inclinations can be considered as reactions against threats of disorder within game-bound units which the individual shares with his environs; environmental disorder may be a cause of internal disorder within the human personality and the life-impulse may therefore stimulate negative feedback against this threat.

The trends towards divergency between individuals are potential dangers to no-osphere. Impulses towards mutual reinforcement and polarization cause throughout the world the game-bound units composed of antagonist individuals and their outside world to decrease their control over themselves and their independency of changes in themselves. The chance is also greater, that divergent forces cause explosions of such game-bound units, if they are not counteracted or mastered by converging powers. For the higher the tensions to which an individual is subjected, the more the possibility increases that he will not act any longer in accordance with reason, but will follow the intuitive and instinctive impulses within him, even if this would mean self-destruction. The diverging evolutionary trends among individuals are therefore, contrary to those among cultural areas *(1)*, not in themselves directed towards an everlasting struggle against disorder. But the diverging trends between individuals will be directed towards such an everlasting struggle as long as they are controlled. Mastering powers may in this respect be not so much provided by uncontrolled converging forces among diverging individuals, as by an authority *(2)* above the individuals: the leading unit of man and idea above the cultural area to which they belong, or above another cultural area which in fact wields power over them.

So between controlling and controlled powers, tensions are at work and they are destined to remain together within an unstable equilibrium: the divergent forces among individuals are a continuous challenge to the controlling powers for vigilance, and this may in its turn be a challenge to the controlled powers for finding new ways to escape the control.

Groups of individuals and authorities above them thus make, relative to the divergent trends among them, game-bound units in which the games consist of acts of control, by an authority, of the divergent trends among the individuals. If the desired equilibrium of a necessarily unstable character is maintained, then this is maintenance of the game-bound unit. Decreases in instability mean here increases in coherence of the game-bound units and these increases may mean no-ospheric evolution.

Possible increases in coherence of such game-bound units are however strongly threatened by dangers of disorder. If e.g. a state's magistrates are not successful in maintaining an equilibrium between divergent forces among its subjects, polarisation may follow; violence, suppression of groups of the population, chaos and ultimately the state's disappearance may be the result.

It follows from the necessity to control the divergent trends among individuals that human values are represented in institutions intended for that purpose.

Human values are also represented in the convergent trends among individuals. They deserve protection if they are threatened by divergency and it may be in the interest of no-ospheric evolution to organize games from which better results are to be expected than without organization.

It is in the States as organizations that we find represented as legal values, human values comprised in both the divergent and convergent trends among individuals; a State's organization is intended to provide for control over divergency among its subjects and to organize convergency between them. It is especially the State's legal system, by which this is realized *(3)*. E.g. penal law and penal procedure law provide control over divergency; civil law and civil procedure law control divergency and organize convergency; public law provides both.

Control over divergent forces among human individuals and protection of convergent trends among individuals are therefore legal values, protected in provisions of national and international law relative to the integrity of states and their governmental, legislative and judicial machinery.

(IV.B.3.f) Convergent Trends between Cultural Areas. We saw in *(IV.B.3.c)* examples of contacts between different

cultural areas which resulted in varying trends:
1) Integration of a cultural area by another one (Cherokee-Indians).
2) Integration of distinguished cultural areas into an entirely new one (Pan-Indianism).
3) Reinforcement of cultural areas which prefer to remain separated from a contacting cultural area (Pueblos, Iroquois).

The first and the second trends are indeed directed towards unification, but, with regard to the first trend certainly and to the second trend possibly, at the cost of previously existing cultural areas; these trends are therefore not directed towards multilateral impregnation on diverged lines *(1)*. The third trend in any case is not directed towards unification *(2)* of the world.

It is not possible to deny that the second and the third trends may result in a greater control over themselves and greater independence of changes in themselves of existing or newly developing cultural areas. Whether such advances are according to no-ospheric evolution's interest depends on the concrete situation. The world's peaceful unification is actually already unattainable because of the reality of the third trend.

But what would happen, if trends of the third kind came to an end and the world reached according to the first or second trend or both, a stage of unification? This would mean the end of competition between different cultural areas, because there would be left only one cultural area, embracing the whole world.

Within this cultural area there would be no more threat of disorder from the side of the vanished separated cultural areas, and this would mean an increase in coherence, and even a cumulative increase because of the better opportunities to fight other threats of disorder in human world society by the best possible co-operation. The outcome of this would be a world where the problems of food production, over-population, environmental pollution, exhaustion of mineral resources and poverty might be solved and where perhaps any human material and spiritual need could be met by application of affluently extant technological devices. E.g. education as it occurs now in schools and families would be replaced by transmission of all desirable information by means of the hypodermic syringe.

Teilhard de Chardin expected, as the outcome of convergency, mankind's unification in "point God-Omega". This solution, if attainable - we have stated our reasons for rejecting this conception in *(IV.B.3.b)* - would anyhow mean the end of humanity's existence on earth or any other heavenly body which might be colonized in future. We do not know whether this is in accordance with or exactly opposite to any regulation of cosmic order.

The end of humanity might however not be the result of a world where all material and spiritual needs can be satisfactorily met by anyone in any situation. It is indeed very probable that such a world will be subject to a great threat of degeneration of the features which we see everywhere among the *"nouveaux riches"*, but this is a threat of disorder which can be counteracted.

Convergency of humanity into one cultural area may be in the interest of mankind, if the threats of disorder are adequately met. No-ospheric coherence and no-ospheric disorder should then find an unstable equilibrium, in which no-osphere has attained its optimal coherence and controls disorder. This would mean an end to no-ospheric evolution, because greater control over itself and greater independence of changes within itself are then causes of greater disorder. It would however imply the continuation of no-osphere as a game-bound unit of dynamic character and a human existence in prosperity.

It is impossible to predict now whether this converged Utopia will indeed emerge. This convergency is anyhow not as absolute as Teilhard de Chardin's and divergent trends among individuals remain as group threats of disorder. Disorder itself would indeed increase, but we have seen in *(III.B.1)* that within systems of living beings and environment the increase in disorder might be counteracted by a rearrangement of the environs to the effect of evolution of such systems.

In the present stage of no-ospheric evolution its trends towards convergency of cultural areas are a human value. They appear to us as a legal value in the form of international institutions for worldwide co-operation between States, like the United Nations Organization and its specialised agencies *(3)*.

(IV.B.3.g) Divergent Trends between Cultural Areas. Both Pierre Teilhard de Chardin and Sir Julian Huxley see only one trend in no-ospheric evolution, that towards unification, and I treated in *(IV.B.3.c)* this trend as a possible result of contacts between cultural areas.

Trends towards unification are however not the only results of such contacts. I referred in *(IV.B.3.c)* jo *(IV.B.3.f)* to reinforcement of cultural areas which prefer to remain separated from a contacting cultural area.

Two possibilities can be distinguished here: cultural areas reinforcing themselves alone and cultural areas which unify themselves in a negative attitude towards another cultural area.

Trends of separated reinforcement may cause contacting cultural areas to reinforce in their turn. Such a reinforcement will, however, cause the separated cultural areas to reinforce again, and this will cause a further reinforcement on the other side, etc. Such a reflexive mutual reinforcement or polarization accumulates tensions between the different cultural areas, and this might lead to an explosion in the shape of a military conflict, but the more mutual reinforcement continues, the better the separated cultural areas might enter into a certain belance of terror. If one party wants to destroy the other, then there will be no surviving cultural area. This stage has now been reached between the great nuclear powers. Between less reinforced cultural areas conventional military conflicts still seem possible, and also between a less advanced party and a nucleur power, because other nuclear powers may consider use of nuclear weapons as an attack on their own.

Military reinforcement is however only one possibility of reinforcement between polarized cultural areas. Economic, scientific and cultural reinforcement are other directions of mutual reinforcement, and it depends on the actual situation which direction will prevail. So if there is no military conflict, the situation of mutual reinforcement may range between a cold war and a friendly competition. This kind of struggle for life may remain peaceful, not only because of fear for mutual destruction, but also because the different kinds of reinforcement often can only be realized, paradoxically, by means of exchange of goods and knowledge between the cultural areas, which desire to remain separated from each other. So mutual reinforcement, necessary in the struggle for life between cultural areas, will generally not lead to natural selection, when an equilibrium exists between the cultural areas. If such an equilibrium is missing, then natural selection indeed may follow, as can be seen in the destruction of the aboriginal Aztec and Inca cultural areas by the Spanish *conquistadores*.

An equilibrium between divergent forces among cultural areas is more in no-ospheric evolution's interest than natural selection; from such an equilibrium convergency may some day result, while in the case of natural selection the eliminated cultural area can never again contribute to no-ospheric evolution.

Divergency among cultural areas is a threat of disorder in no-osphere. Provision in an equilibrium between divergent cultural areas is therefore control over threats of disorder by a convergent force.

An equilibrium between divergent trends among cultural areas is a human value. As a legal value we can find it in international agreements, either bi- or multilateral, for the peaceful solution of conflicts between states and in all conventions relative to humanization of warfare, as well as in international institutions like U.N.O., the International Court of Justice, the International Red Cross Committee.

(IV.B.3.h) Trends of Velocity. Up to this point no-ospheric evolution has been treated as a result of interaction between convergency and divergency or between divergent forces among each other. The question may now be discussed whether for the continuation of no-ospheric evolution it is necessary to regulate its velocity.

No-ospheric evolution's velocity is not a uniform motion, but was earlier uniformly accelerated: each new idea or invention opens the door to more new ideas or inventions, but only if there are sufficient means of communication and of accessibility to stored ideas. If there are no means of communication and information at all, then indeed evolution may follow a uniform motion or may not occur at all.

What would the invention of making fire have meant to humanity if there had not been the possibility of the unknown inventor informing others of his discovery? But this is not all; even if others would have been informed about the techniques of making fire the use of newly discovered fire might have remained restricted to religious rites. If this had been the case, there could have been a challenge of sufficient intensity to break the taboo on using the new invention. Such a diverging power might have arisen by an accidental violation of the taboo, followed by the experience that this violation remained unpunished. This adventure might have been communicated to others who in their turn might have enjoyed the same experience.

In this way only a rupture with traditions could have opened the way for using the new invention for practical purposes and thus furthering progress along the road of no-ospheric evolution. The taboo could also have been broken merely by the overwhelming power of the dire necessity to make fire, or to die. Breaking of the taboo might not only have meant promotion of advance in the world of techniques, but also in that of religion, as can be seen e.g. in the influence of the Prometheus-story on Greek mythology.

If however in an isolated or autarchic society new ideas are not able to cross the barrier of traditions, then such a society could indeed continue its existence as long as the traditions within this society are significant to its members. But such a society will always stand in a weaker position as soon as contacts arise with cultural areas where ideas prevail which have the capacity to destroy the significance of earlier traditions. Therefore it is in the interest of each cultural area to renew continuously its traditions and to strive after traditions which not only do not impede the practising of new ideas, but which also in themselves are not in contradiction with such ideas. It is moreoever in the interest of each cultural area to take this action with the greatest possible velocity, for otherwise it may weaken or even lose its position amidst other cultural areas.

So it seems in the interest of each society that the velocity of no-ospheric evolution becomes promoted, and we find that for such promotion it is necessary to assemble an easily accessible set of stored ideas and sufficient means to communicate these.

Promotion of evolution's velocity seems also to be in the individual's interest. For this means to him that the game-bound units in which he is a servomechanical part obtain greater control over themselves and greater independence of changes within themselves. Promotion of evolution's velocity might in this respect even protect the individual against an *in concreto* threatening downfall.

On the other hand however it might sometimes be more in the individual's direct interest if he remains bound to his ancestral traditions and does not share in evolution. But, as explained above, the society to which he belongs must promote evolution's velocity for reasons of self-preservation. This means a conflict within this society, causing the parties involved to reinforce themselves against each other and this may cause the authorities above them to provide for an adequate equilibrium.

Promotion of no-ospheric evolution's velocity may therefore lead among individuals to a rupture with ancestral traditions without replacement by another way of behaviour of significance to them. This means that the price of evolution might be human victims. A human sacrifice is however a price beyond evolution's interest, because each human being as a set of stored information and as a means of communication, is to be considered, in each stage of his life, as a vehicle or at least as a potential vehicle of evolution *(1)*, and because the individual's society is interested in the fastest possible evolutionary development. Society therefore has, when trying to keep its own evolution in balance with that of other societies, also to look for an equilibrium between its own development and that of its members. The latter equilibrium can be promoted by not only providing for an accessible set of adequate knowledge and sufficient means for the communication of this knowledge, but also by educational provisions aimed at making this knowledge each individual's mental property. Promotion of the spreading of knowledge however has to occur prudently in order to prevent the above explained conflictive situation between society's leaders and those who desire to honour the ancestral traditions. Such a prudent promotion of education, adult education included, is in the interest of society and its members, and it will give to society's evolution the optimal possible velocity.

The requirement of an equilibrium between velocities of evolution of contacting societies is also in the interest of evolution of no-osphere: any human society comprises in its individuals the vehicles or potential vehicles for the promotion of no-ospheric evolution.

It is therefore a human value that underdeveloped countries are helped by developed countries. This human value becomes a legal value by provisions in this respect in National and International Law.

Such help consists in regular transmission of resources without contra-performances of similar economic value. Whatever the economic implications of such transmissions, they will be of little permanent effect if the information transmitted is insufficient to enable the individuals of underdeveloped countries to collect and build up adequate reserves of knowledge, communication and research. A human value is therefore that in a cultural area, transmission, spreading and reception of information is free.

This human value can be realized in the legal values of collection of any information which is stored in receptacles of information (books, tapes, movie-pictures) and of spreading information by any technical means of communication. These legal values can be formulated as Privileges; they have as mirror-image a No Right of the State or any other public or private body or any individual to intervene in this collection or spreading of information *(2)*.

Realised as legal values we find these freedoms only as freedom of printing without censorship in constitutional law. The other means of communication, like radio, TV or cinema, have generally not yet entered the constitutional area. This is due to the fact that their use involves problems different to that of the press, like e.g. the dangers of monopolization and abuse *(3)*.

Formulation of Privileges to collect and to spread information also applies to the educational area; they comprise the Privilege of parents to give their children an appropriate education and a Privilege of professional educators, to educate and teach according to one's own conviction *(4)*.

These legal values are derived from the requirements concerning no-ospheric evolution's optimal velocity. These requirements embody however more human values than free transmission, spreading and reception of information. We found equilibrium between velocities of growth of cultural areas and equilibrium between application of new information and application of ancestral traditions to be two other values.

These two latter values can indeed be expressed as a legal value in a Right-Duty relation between subject and government, in which it is a government's Duty to its subjects to provide these two equilibria. This legal value can therefore be considered as a pattern of expectations and desired patterns of behaviour in law-bound units composed of subjects and government. This means that in this conception the subjects should be entitled to certain negative feedback opportunities towards the government.

It is therefore from the requirements of an equilibrium between velocities of growth between cultural areas and of an equilibrium between applications of new information and ancestral traditions that we find a legal value in which is implied (in the negative feedback opportunities of law-bound units comprising government and subjects) the principle of democracy as organised control over the government by the people *(5)*.

Because the two latter requirements concerning no-ospheric evolution's velocity can now be realized by legal value in which governments have Duties to perform towards their subjects, and may be controlled in respect of these performances, it follows that within this framework governments should act according to Law.

This is now actually possible in States where the principle of Rule of Law is a fundamental of the constitution *(6)*. This principle is therefore implied, as well as that of democracy, in legal values derived from the necessities of equilibria between velocities of growth between cultural areas, and between application of new information and application of ancestral traditions.

(IV.C) AN ONTOLOGIC CONCEPTION OF NORMS.

(IV.C.1) Reality and Polarity. Recent investigations into the nature of Taoism have indicated that a surprising similarity exists between the concept of Tao and the understanding by modern philosophers of the nature of reality *(1)*. Tao or reality can be described as polarity between "actuality" and "potentiality".

This relation of polarity is in its essence that of a tensional field between two different conditions in a mutual relationship: the potential before realization is the actual after realization. Another concept of polarity is that between what is and what ought to be, or between *Sein* (to be) and *Sollen* (ought). This polarity concerns the relation of norms to reality.

The conception of evolution, as it has been explained in this book *(2)*, is based on a third form of polarity, namely between order and disorder. It will appear in the following subdivisions that these three kinds of polarity can be brought together into a broader conception of reality.

(IV.C.2) Potential and Actual Being. The conception of polarity between "actuality" and "potentiality" has led to the hypothesis *(1)* that everywhere in the universe "energy exists in two states - quiescent and active, and passes easily from one to the other". Quiescent energy is indescribable, but non-existent; it has potential existence which is demonstrated by the emergence or spontaneous creation *(2)* and activity of energy.

"There is paradoxically an aspect of being and an aspect of non-being in both states: the creative power or energy in its potentiality is as much a *reality* (ens in potentia), as in its state of actuality. On the other hand, the state of actuality may be regarded as a non-being, *from the viewpoint of potentiality*, as an *absence* of it (ens in absentia): it has already reached its realization, it can only decay and pass away, i.e. 'return to the root' which is the immense reservoir op potentialities" *(3)*.

Notice that this mutual relation of absence is only relative. During the time that potentiality is realized into actuality both obtain. Potential being and actual being can therefore occur separately, or together; they cannot however be jointly non-occurring, for this would mean that there is non-existent reality. The relation between potential and actual being is therefore not so much one of mutual negation, but a relation of subcontrariety.

(IV.C.3) The Being of "Ought" (Determinative Being). The ethical criterion and other moral rules belong, together with law-rules, to the world of norms or desired patterns of human *behaviour*.

Norms are obligation-norms if they are to the effect of an ought and they are permissive norms if they are to the effect of a may, i.e. to a permission or a privilege in the sense of Hohfeld.

We have seen in *(II.D.2.a)* that a Right-Duty relation may be considered as a primitive with respect to the other three fundamental jural relations. These three relations are therefore in this conception logical modi of the relation Right-Duty.

We have discussed these four modi in their logical interrelatedness in *(IV.3)*. All four however belong to one logical world, that of "ought" of desired patterns of behaviour and of patterns of expectations. It is possible to consider this logical world of "ought" as a modus itself. As such it can be considered as a modus of being, viz. determinative being.

The relations between "is" (Sein) and "ought" (Sollen) are a fundamental problem of philosophy and legal philosophy. The question is, whether one can deduce an "ought" from an "is". If this were possible then we could deduce law-rules from pure facts. Hume was the first to consider the problem and he declared that one can never deduce an "ought" proposition from a proposition about an "is". Kant analysed the problem in various works of his critical period and taught that the moral order of "ought" is independent from the physical order of being. Kelsen emphasized in his works a similar opinion and considered the State as a sociological "is" from which it is fundamentally impossible to deduce any rule of law or morality. Recently the problem has been thoroughly studied again by Franz Achermann *(1)*, who established: *"Vom realen Sein gibt es keinen Schluss auf das Sollen"*, or "ought" cannot be deduced from real being *(2)*. Real being is to Achermann what in *(IV.C.2)* was understood by actual being *(3)*.

If now the conclusions reached by Hume, Kant, Kelsen and Achermann are correct - and we have no reason for doubt - and if we were correct in the preceding paragraph in establishing a relationship of subcontrariety between actual and potential being, and if we assume that there exist four logical modi of being, related to each other as A-, I-, E- and O-propositions of Aristotelian logic, instead of the two in Taoism and instead of the three discussed now, then we may conclude, that "ought" or determinative being is negation of potential being: if it were negation of actual being, it would have been possible for Achermann to deduce it from "real being". This conclusion also means, that "ought" or determinative being superimplies actual being.

"Ought" as negation of potentiality should be considered as determinativeness. It embodies both physical-causal determinativeness. It embodies both physical-causal determinativeness and willed determinativeness. The former ought is the ought of the laws of nature, mathematics and logic; the latter ought is the ought *in* norms for human behaviour *(4)*. Both oughts express a relation to the question whether something should be, regardless whether it indeed occurs. It is therefore for this reason that we called this reality determinative being.

That determinative being superimplies actual being, means that a world of physical-causal rules or of norms for human behaviour has no sense if there is no world of actual being, but a world of actual being may exist without determinativeness.

Application in concreto of a modus of "ought", or of a physical-causal law, is transformation of determinative being in the form of information into actual being. It is at the same time transformation of potential energetic being into actual energetic being.

Creation of "ought" is transformation of potential information on a modus of "ought" into determinative information of "ought". This process has no corresponding occurrence in the physical-causal world: creation of norms or desired patterns of behaviour and patterns of expectations depends on the human will; physical-causal laws cannot be created, they exist as determinative being.

"Ought" in the sense of determinative being has no mirror-image, in the way that a jural Duty is related to a Right and a moral Duty to a moral title. These Duties are modi of "ought" and concern behaviour of man towards somebody else within a fundamental jural or moral relationship of Hohfeldian nature; "ought" as determinative being concerns the very existence of these relationships themselves. The four modi of "ought" are subjective reality *(5)* with an objective nucleus, "ought" itself is objective with a subjective nucleus: there is always an objective element in what subjectively is experienced, and there is always a subjective element in the interpretation of objective reality.

That "ought" in the sense of determinative being has no mirror-image can also be seen in the physical-causal laws, which determine patterns of physical-causal occurrences and their mirror-images of patterns of expectations relative to such occurrences, while these laws themselves are only determinative with respect to these patterns.

(IV.C.4) The Being of Normlessness (Indeterminative Being). The fourth norm of reality, to which we referred in *(IV.C.3)*, stands in a relation of negation to actualized being, in a relation of contrariety to determinative being and in a relation of superimplication to potential being. This form of reality is indeterminative being. To this form of reality belongs disorder as has been discussed in *(III.B.1)*.

Indeterminative being stands in its physical-causal essence at the beginning and at the end of any other modus of being. In its primeval stage it has much similarity with chaos in Greek mythology, however not as a primeval void, but as an absence of any regularity and regulation. This is in the moral and legal area a stage of normlessness, in which neither desired patterns of behaviour or norms, nor patterns of expectations exist. It comprises however a form of general permissiveness, in which anything whatever is permitted, unrestricted by any modus of "ought".

In its final stage indeterminative being is that of absolute disorder *(1)*. This is actual being transformed into complete disorder and determinative being, which is in its essence that of information, transformed into its absence.

The fact that indeterminative being superimplies potential being means that normlessness superimplies the existence of potential norms or modi of "ought". This corresponds to the fact that from the existence of such potential norms it does not logically follow that there exists normlessness.

(IV.C. 5) The Four Modi of Being as Conditions of Energy and Information. The four *modi* of reality which are developed here can be placed in a square of opposition as follows:

DETERMINATIVE BEING

INDETERMINATIVE BEING

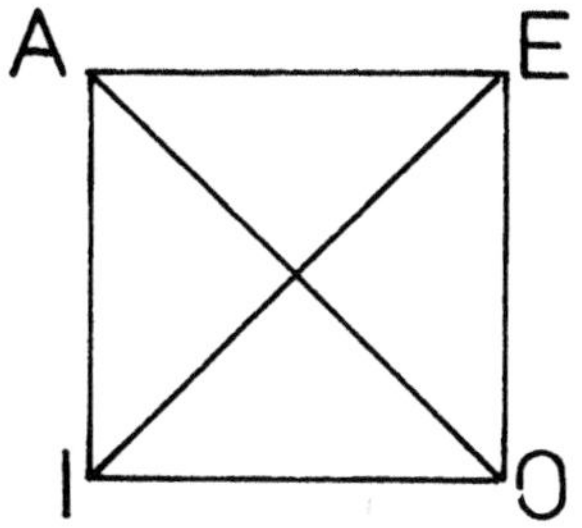

ACTUALIZED BEING

POTENTIAL BEING

Fig. 44

These four *modi*, considered separately, are only *modi* of the objective world, both of man's external environs as well as man's internal psychic world. It is not possible in reality to separate completely the four modi of being from each other. This is due to the fact that being in its potential and its determinative form is being of information.

Potential being is a reservoir of unselected information and determinative being is a reservoir of selected information. Both forms of information can only exist on a conveyance, which necessarily should belong to the actual world. Actualized being in its turn is being, which is kept coherent by either energy, or information or both: the information concerned is selected information in the determinative area. Indeterminative being may be either chaos or absolute disorder, but is not only a pre- or post-energetic disorder: also unselected information belongs to the indeterminative area in the form of unlimited permissiveness of all things whatsoever.

This interrelatedness of forms of being is no reason for not making the logical distinctions which have been made here. Taoism upholds that any form of being has a nucleus of opposite being within it. A well-known example is the conception that everything of female (ying) nature has a male (yang) nucleus, and vice versa. Similarly we can say here that the two forms of informative being (potentiality and determinativeness) each have an energetic nucleus, while energetic being (actuality) as well as pre- and post-energetic being (indeterminativeness) each have a nucleus of informative nature of respectively selected and unselected information.

We will summarize now the main points discussed here

in the following scheme.

DETERMINATIVE BEING

Selected information:
Physical-causal laws;
modi of "ought" or
desired patterns of human
behaviour and patterns
of expectations.
(*energetic nucleus:*
actualized bearers of selected
information)

INDETERMINATIVE BEING

Pre-energetic chaos:
Post-energetic disorder:
Physical-causal, moral
and juridical normlessness.
(*informative nucleus:*
unselected information:
unrestricted permissiveness)

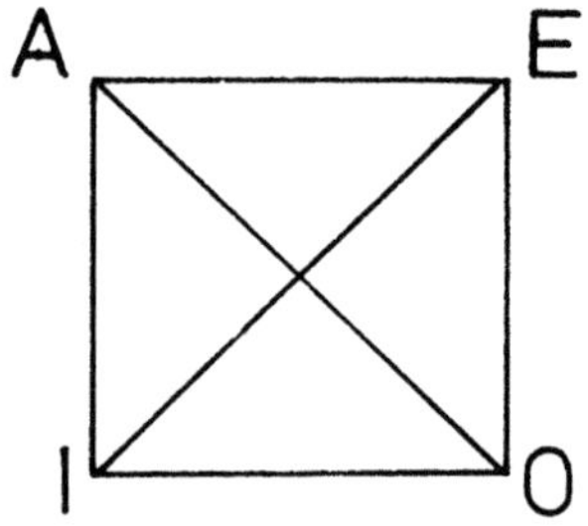

ACTUAL BEING

Energetic reality:
Physical-causal reality
objective human behaviour.
(*Informative nucleus:*
selected information:
physical-causal laws;
norms or modi of "ought" or
desired patterns of human
behaviour and patterns of
expectations)

POTENTIAL BEING

Unselected information:
Subjective human imaginations; potential modi
of "ought" or desired
patterns of human behaviour and patterns of
expectations.
(*Energetic nucleus:*
actualized bearers of
unselected information)

Fig. 45

Between the different conditions of being we can see the following tensional fields, in which a modus of being is transformed into another condition. These fields correspond with the relations of superimplication, negation and subcontrariety in traditional logic:
E-O: creation of potentiality, processes of imagination,

subjective human existence.

O-I: Tao, creation of energetic coherences, subjective human existence.

O-A: selection of information, creation of norms for human behaviour and corresponding patterns of expectations, subjective human existence.

A-I: creation of informative coherences, subjective human existence.

I-E: struggle against threats of disorder, subjective human existence.

So far as creation of potentiality in the physical-causal area is concerned, we still know too little of the origin of energy to say whether there is indeed transformation of a hypothetic chaos into potential energy and transformation of potential energy into actual. But so far as information is concerned, psychology has developed notions of reservoirs of unselected information by C.G. Jung's concepts of collective unconsciousness and personal unconsciousness *(1)*. What indeed happens when contents of unconscious areas are transformed into potential being by the process of imagination is still not clear. But transformation of subjective human imaginations, which are potential being, into forms of determinative or of actual being, is the creative essence of conscious human existence.

(IV.C.6) Being of and Being in Hohfeld's Relationships. The four fundamental Hohfeldian relations are the basic forms of patterns of expectations and desired patterns of behaviour, related to each ohter as mirror-images.

As far as they are objective information, they belong to the area of determinative being: in their determinative stage they can be perceived as rules of law or morality and they are perceptible as human behaviour in their actualized stage.

As far as they are subjective information, i.e. as far as somebody is himself a party in either one of these four relations, any party is in such a relation also a party in that one of the four other Hohfeldian relations to which the former is logically connected by superimplication, subimplication or subcontrariety. Parties in a Right-Duty relation are also parties in a relation Disability-Immunity; parties in a relation No Right-Privilege are also parties in either a relation Disability-Immunity or a relation Power-Liability, etc.

Existentially this means that a party in a Hohfeldian relation actually finds himself at one and the same instant of time within a field of tension, formed by two Hohfeldian relationships which are related to each other by subcontrariety or implication.

From a *subjective* point of view we may consider now the four Hohfeldian relations as conditions of being of similar nature as those isolated in *(IV.C.5)*. This may be illustrated as follows:

Determinative being
Right-Duty

Indeterminative being
Power-Liability

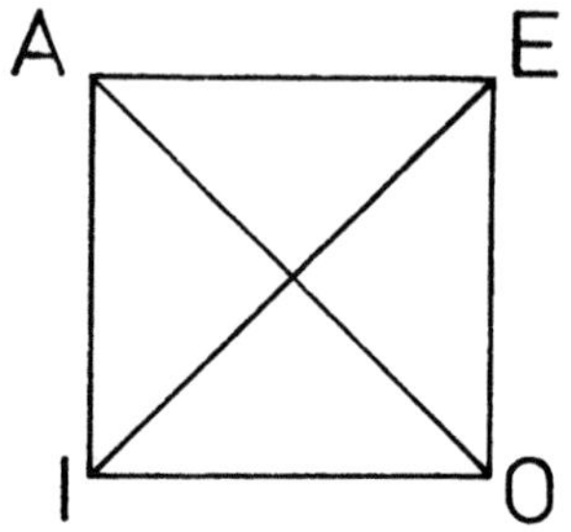

Actualized being
Disability-Immunity

Potential being
No Right-Privilege

Fig. 46

Although the four Hohfeldian relations are all determinative being from an objective point of view, it is only the relation Right-Duty which can be taken as determinative being when considered subjectively: only here one experiences as determined what should be done or what may be expected.

In a subjective conception, to be party in a Power-Liability relation is experienced as indeterminative being: there is no determination whether the Power will be exercised or not. To be in a relation No Right-Privilege is experienced as potential being. This relation expresses the absence of a Right-Duty relation but may be turned into its negation; so has a Privilege in the sense of liberty, the potentiality to become restricted by determinative Duties.

Parties in a relation Disability-Immunity find themselves in a situation of actualized being: the party with a Disability experiences his absence of a Power, and the one with the Immunity experiences his Immunity against the exercise of a Power by the other party.

Parties in Hohfeldian relationships actually experience themselves to be at one and the same instant of time in one of the fields of tension E-O, O-I or A-I as long as they remain standing in the same relation towards each other. However, at the same instant that, with respect to the same performance, parties enter into new Hohfeldian relationships, i.e. at the moment of transformation of a Disability-Immunity relation into a relation Power-Liability or vice versa, or at the moment of transformation of a relation No Right-Privilege into a Right-Duty relation or vice versa, parties experience themselves to be in a field of tension I-E or O-A.

These latter fields of tension are only distinguished from the former three by a criterion of time. At one and the same instant of time one can only experience an existence within one Hohfeldian relationship *(1)*. Within the fields of tension E-O, O-I and A-I, where one can remain for minutes or for years and years, one finds one's position alternating any microcosmic moment between Power and No Right, or No Right and Disability, or Disability and Right, or Liability and Privilege, or Privilege and Immunity, or Immunity and Duty. Within a field of tension of the nature O-A or I-E however, there indeed occur alternations of fundamentally similar nature, but only at separated microcosmic moments in which Hohfeldian relationships are turned into their contradiction. Here parties may experience a certain position in a Hohfeldian relationship for years and years; then suddenly during a microcosmic moment these postions are turned into their negation and this situation may continue again for years; it is only during this microcosmic moment that one can be in a field of tension O-A or I-E.

Although one is often able to foresee or to remember this moment, it seems incorrect to say that somebody who foresees or remembers this alternation finds himself in a field of tension O-A or I-E: if somebody foresees or remembers his existence in a field of tension then he is actually not there.

The position of the four Hohfeldian relations as subjective information is that of an intermediate stage between these relations as objective information in their stage of determinative being and their actualized stage in the form of human behaviour. This intermediate stage belongs to the field of tension A-I between actualized and determinative being.

(IV.D) AN ONTOGENIC CONCEPTION OF NORMS

(IV.D.1) The Ethical Criterion as Determinative Being. The ethical criterion belongs to the determinative form of reality.

It is of physical-final nature, because it formulates the basic principles for continuation and improvement of mankind's existence. The only alternative to its application is the end of the terrestrial human world. Its form can be compared to that of directions for use of instruments. These instruments are the potential modi of "ought": the potential desired patterns of behaviour and their mirror-images, the potential patterns of expectations.

The ethical criterion now is a touchstone used in the selection between potential modi of "ought" for establishing which of these may be transformed into determinative being and which not. As such it is a criterion in the creations of rules of law and of morality, without being of the nature of a rule of law or morality itself: it is not the expression of a modus of "ought", but it forms a part of determinative being as a physical-final condition for human existence.

The ethical criterion has no similarity with the basic norm *("Grundnorm")* in Kelsen's theory of pure law. The *"Grundnorm"* is in that conception a formal notion at the base of a logical system of law; it has itself no specific contents but it should answer to the requirement that it is the expression of truth; law and its *"Grundnorm"* belong to the order of "ought" *(Sollen)*, which is conceived as distinguished from "being" *(Sein)*.

The ethical criterion however, is, as far as its contents are concerned, not determined by the casual system of law to which it is related, but by the universal necessity that man should promote evolution of no-osphere, as we have seen in *(III.B.6.e)*; moreover the ethical criterion does not depend upon rules of law, but rules of law depend on the ethical criterion.

The ethical criterion belongs indeed, as well as the *"Grundnorm"*, to the world of "ought" *(Sollen)*, but we have seen in *(IV.C.3)*, that this world of "ought" is not distinguished from that of "to be" *(Sein)*, but is a modus of it in the form of determinative being.

The ethical criterion has further, possibly except for its contents, no similarity with the categorical imperative, formulated by Immanuel Kant a.o. as : "Act in this way, that you always use humanity at the same time, either in your person or the person of anybody else, as a purpose, never only as an instrument". The categorical imperative is an autonomous command which takes effect by virtue of itself; it is not supported by arguments; Kant is said to have stated: "I only believe in the starry sky above me and the categorical imperative within me". The ethical criterion, however, obtains its force by virtue of the arguments treated in *(III.B.6.e)*; it is indeed good to believe in it, but such a faith is not necessary because this criterion is based on reason.

The ethical criterion cannot, like the concept of "ought" to which it belongs, be represented in four modi. It can only serve as a touchstone, if it is formulated as as Duty. No Privilege-situation can be imagined, where this Duty is absent; no Liability-situation can be imagined where this Duty can be changed; but it seems correct to say that this Duty implies an Immunity against such changes.

The ethical criterion is not a pattern of desired behaviour, like a law rule or a rule of morality, but it is a criterion for such patterns. Its formulation as a Duty does not mean that it is a Duty in the sense of law or morals; it is a model, an example, with the help of which law and morals can be conceived and tested.

The individual, who finds himself in a situation in which no law rule or rule of morality for a certain case exists, is not instructed by the criterion precisely what to do or not to do, but provided with a touchstone by which he can conceive for himself a pattern of desired behaviour.

Although formulated as a Duty the ethical criterion is therefore not a Duty itself. Consequently the ethical criterion is not a pattern of desired behaviour - except for its conception as a model - and it is for this reason that the ethical criterion does not correspond with a pattern of expectations, like a Duty with a Right - except for a conception as a model for such a pattern. This latter model is exactly the converse of the former. By it one may conceive the contents of Rights and moral titles; the individual can in situations to which no norms apply, use it in order to discover which behaviour he may expect from others, provided that these persons would have conceived *in concreto* for themselves a pattern of desired behaviour in accordance with the ethical criterion.

Although application of the ethical criterion by an individual is always a subjective experience, the criterion itself can only be experienced as an objective phenomenon. Its nature is that of determinative being and its transformation into actualized being passes first through objective patterns of desired and expected behaviour in the determinative area (rules of law and morality) and secondly through subjective patterns of desired and expected behaviour (having a Duty, a Right, a Power, a Liability, etc.) into actual human behaviour.

Application of the ethical criterion occurs therefore in field of tension A-I; in field of tension O-A however it occurs as well. In the latter fields are potential modi of ought, viz. the potentials of law and morality selected from the area of potential being and transformed into rules of morality and law. This subject will be treated in the following paragraph.

(IV.D.2) Applications of the Ethical Criterion in the making of Law. Both law and public morality have, within the framework of no-ospheric evolution, their own places as stages of development. Both are in game-bound units desired patterns of human behaviour; a game-bound unit embodying rules of public morality has reached such a control over itself and independence of changes in itself that it, contrary to law-bound units, is able to provide for this control and independence without official formulation. This does not mean that rules of public morality represent a higher stage of evolution than rules of law; comparison in this respect between these two kinds of rules for human behaviour can only be made when using the description of no-ospheric evolution as criterion.

Rules of public morality may become rules of law when the game-bound unit to which they belong loses its ability to provide for control over itself and independence of changes in itself; rules of law may in their turn become rules of public morality when a law-bound unit loses its need for official formulation of its pattern of expectations and its desired pattern of behaviour *(1)*.

I will illustrate this with a few examples. In societies with a very small amount of traffic on the roads, this traffic might be able to proceed without any rule as to keeping to the right or to the left. With a growing amount of traffic on a few roads a pattern of behaviour might develop as negative feedback in respect to each of those roads separated, in the shape of a special rule for keeping either to the right or the left, and this may merely be a rule of public morality because there is not yet much need for official formulation. Different rules as to keeping to the right or the left on different roads, may however, with still increasing traffic, result in a decision of a public authority on a uniform system of road-behaviour. The actual game-bound units composed of man and road, with rules of public morality as desired pattern of behaviour, have lost their control over themselves and their independence of changes within themselves; they now require the help of official formulation of a common desired pattern of behaviour. Official formulation - and promulgation - and the need for public coercion, together make the game-bound units with rules of public morality switch over into law-bound units.

But a servomechanism embracing juridical relationships may in its turn develop such a control over itself and independence of changes in itself, that it is able to exist without any official formulation and without any need for official coercion: this we may see e.g. with betrothal in modern societies, where the rules concerning this institution pass over from the realm of law to that of public morality.

If man now is involved in a relationship with servomechanical properties, without any rule of behaviour at all, neither a rule of law nor a rule of public morality, it is by means of a double use of the ethical criterion that firstly a need for help by such a rule may be established, and secondly what kind of help should be given. So with regard to public morality it may first be established that a rule is necessary without official formulation and official coercion and the second stage is the selection from potential rules followed by non-official formulation and making public of the rule *(2)*. With regard to law *(3)* it is firstly necessary to establish that a rule is wanted based on official formulation and need for official coercion, and secondly to determine which potential formulation and which potential coercion are the best.

Using the ethical criterion as a touchstone in the making of legal rules implies moreover that it has the function of law's entelechy, when law is considered as a phenomenon extending itself in time. This means that the notion of evolution's interest is to be considered as a factor by which potentials are actually realized, which law in the course of time has developed from its origin; realization of these potentials by means of the criterion of evolution's interest is then law's *causa finalis (4)*.

Transformed in cybernetical notions this doctrine implies that a legislative servomechanism - this is a servomechanism comprising among its pattern of behaviour, rules of procedure for the making of new law rules - is not only intended for the purposes of control over itself and independence of changes in itself, and that of behaviour as formulated in the rules of procedure, but also for the twofold application of the ethical criterion.

A legislative servomechanism first establishes whether a certain behaviour is desired or not, and if so, which particular patterns are desirable. For conceiving a law rule the legislative servomechanism now has to assemble information concerning the potentials which law in the course of time has developed from its origin *(5)*. It selects *(6)* apparently appropriate potentials *(7)* and applies them to all the patterns of behaviour which at first sight might appear desirable by giving these patterns strict juridical formulations. Hereafter the ethical criterion is used as a touchstone for the solutions found and the best solution is selected *(8)*; if a solution cannot be found in this way, then the ethical criterion is used for arranging law's potentials anew according to the requirements of the situation, until a suitable solution is found *(9)*. Such a new arrangement of law's potentials might give the impression that new potentials have emerged; actual creation of new potentials however depends on the structure of the legislative servomechanism's pattern of behaviour. A legislative servomechanism should not only be directed towards the purpose of creating new law with law's existing potentials, but also to law-making with legal potentials which it still has to develop.

This development may occur in such a way, that the information which the servomechanism receives is digested by means of arrangement among law's potentials; this arrangement implies an integration of new information within law's potentials in such a manner that the meaning of the information concerning law's potentials is changed. This process may produce new potentials of law, not existing at an earlier time. The new potentials are indeed related to earlier potentials, but not more than a biologically mutated individual within a species remains related to non-mutated individuals within the same species. This moulding anew of law's potentials, of which the realization is law's final cause, is nothing but the final cause being moulded anew *(10)*.

I will illustrate this process with an example. Our present law rules are all based on the idea that the human individual is determinated to die at a certain moment. Modern biophysicists are however searching for a realization of corporal immortality *(11)* by freezing the incurably ill until such time that medical science has the capacity to heal them *(12)*. It is clear that present day laws of succession, family law or insurance law, are inadequate for meeting such a future situation; adaptation might also appear necessary in relation to other areas of the legal system. New legal rules then might be developed by comparing the requirements of the new situation with those of the old situation, formulating general distinctions between both kinds of requirements and lastly applying the general distinctions found in old legal principles applicable in the earlier situation. This process is, as far as it leads to a remodelling of the old principles *(13)* to new ones, nothing but the moulding anew of law's potentials.

A similar example can be found in the emergence of the medieval law rule, that a serf becomes a freeman after living for one year and one day in a town *(14)* (*Stadtluft macht frei* - town air makes free). This rule could not develop until towns existed; the rule was necessary for promoting immigration into a town, because its lord was interested in the creation of a strong municipal community for enforcing his political position against his vassals, or because a town's burghers were interested in enforcing their position against their town's lord. Two potentials of medieval Germanic law were moulded anew in the making of this rule.

The first potential may be found in the juridical proverb *Luft macht frei* (air makes free). This proverb is an expression of the principle of territoriality, which began to flourish when the Carlovingian empire fell apart. According to this principle a person's rank was determined by the law of his place of settlement and not by that of his birth-place *(15)*. This principle was formulated by posing that it is the air above the place of settlement, viz. the real estate to which he is entitled, which determines a person's rights *(16)*. Freedom may thus be considered as an accessory of the real estate to which an immigrant became entitled within the territory of the municipality.

Here now we find the connection with the second potential, which may be found in the ancient Germanic law of prescription for possession of real estate; the usual term of limitation covered one year and one day; the prescription was both acquisitive as well as extinctive *(17)*.

It is now possible to state that it is the ethical criterion which, by means of a legislative servomechanism, actually realizes the potentials which law in the course of time has developed from its origin, and that this realization is law's final cause; it is also the ethical criterion in this conception, which has the capacity to mould law's final cause anew. So the ethical criterion is indeed an impulse propelling law's development in the direction to which it points and so it is law's entelechy.

The cybernetical conception law's development may however not only fit in with that of Bergson's creative evolution; it may also fit in with Hegel's dialectics.

Law, public morality and state are, according to Hegel, manifestations of *"Völkergeister"* (national minds), and these *"Völkergeister"* are in their turn realizations of the *"Weltgeist"* (the world's mind) *(16)*. *"Völkergeister"* may correspond to cybernetical machinery like state-culture areas; the *"Weltgeist"*, which only exists within and by the *"Völkergeister"*, may correspond to the servomechanisms of the international community.

Law develops itself in the dialectics of history; law's dialectics are according to Hegel, development and immanent progress. This immanent destination can now be noticed in a legislative servomechanism, where the digested data concerning law's potentials form the thesis, the antithesis being formed by new information concerning social changes. Arrangement of the new information amidst the data concerning law's potentials and thus creation of new potentials, is the synthesis *(19)*, from which new legal rules result *(20)*.

Hegel himself was convinced that all law is positive law: it can only derive its form and force from legislation by the State; its contents are determined by the historical development of the national disposition and by the necessity of application *in concreto (21)*. We agree with this conception so far as the contents of national law are concerned and are of the opinion that a corresponding concept may apply to those of the Law of Nations. We do not accept legislation by or on behalf of State as the only source of law's form and force, but prefer to consider as law any regulation provided with either one of negative feedback opportunities (2), (3) and (4) discussed in *(III.C.2)*.

(IV.E) FUNDAMENTAL HUMAN RIGHTS AS A DEVICE OF LAW IN THE STRUGGLE AGAINST NO-OSPHERIC DISORDER AND IN THE PROMOTION OF NO-OSPHERIC EVOLUTION

(IV.E.1) Introduction. In *(III.B.1)* and *(IV.B.2.d)* we referred to law as the main device in the struggle against disorder in no-osphere. Law can be considered as a body of patterns of expectations and of desired patterns of human behaviour with systems of negative feedback in order to correct deviations from these patterns. Its main task is to prevent disorder in ordered societies and to turn disorder into order.

Law can be used to keep society static by using it only as an instrument against threats of disorder. Then societies do not increase their coherence, but only maintain it. Law can be used as well in order to increase societies' control over themselves and independence of changes within themselves.

Evolution of the human world as a whole is therefore dependent on legal provisions. We have seen in *(III.B.6.e)*, *(IV.B.2.c)* and *(IV.D.1)* that the ethical criterion of no-ospheric evolution's interest is necessary to serve as a touchstone for legal values and the legal provisions comprising these.

In *(IV.B)* we isolated a number of actual legal values which are to the effect that fundamentals of no-ospheric evolution are made to patterns of expectations and desired patterns of behaviour in the form of legal provisions. These legal values appeared to be related to the integrity of no-osphere as such, the integrity of processes of no-ospheric evolution, and the integrity and harmonious development of the individual, of States and of international institutions.

In other words: these legal values appeared to be concerned with protection of no-osphere and the individual in their interrelatedness. In this interrelatedness it is the individual who is the one through which no-osphere strives for control over its coherence. Ultimately these legal values are values of the individual: they concern *himself* and his no-osphere *(1)*.

In *(IV.B.2.d)* we discussed the individual as a legal value and in *(IV.B.3.h)* we argued that the individual is a vehicle or at least a potential vehicle of evolution of societies, because of his society's interest in the fastest possible development. This latter also applies to the individual's position in no-osphere.

Human contribution to no-ospheric evolution is made by those who establish new ideas. Indirect contribution may be provided by those who execute new ideas, those who provide for information which might be useful in the creation and execution of new ideas and by those who as an active or passive challenge, might inspire others to establish new ideas. This means that each individual has at least one or other quality which contributes to evolution; so e.g. anti-social persons or sufferers from mental illness play in their qualities a role of challenge which might stimulate further evolution. This challenge might act in two directions: by making the persons involved able to make an active contribution, either directly or indirectly, to evolution, and by finding ways for the prevention of the phenomena to which the persons involved are subject. Each individual is therefore valuable to evolution and this requires a general attitude of equal honesty towards all living human beings.

(IV.E.2) Minimal Standards for Protection of the Individual and his Environs. In *(IV.B)* we considered legal values as fundamental from the point of view of the principles of evolution in no-osphere; in the next subdivisions we will consider how most of these values can be and indeed are conceived from the individual's point of view as minimal standards for protecting him and his environs. Such minimal standards, relative to man, can be and to certain extents indeed are realized by means of fundamental human rights conceptions, while, so far as protection of the human environment is concerned, analogous conceptions are being developed.

These minimal standards which we will treat, are only fundamental principles of protection; their role is to provide man with a basic jural device by which he is placed in a position where he can meet the challenges of threats of disorder and necessity of no-ospheric evolution, by developing adequate and flexible juridical and social economical instruments of scientific and political nature.

This conception means that the minimal standards discussed here are not catlogues for fundamental rights of man and environment, but only a starting-point for formulations of such catalogues or improvement of such instruments already in existence. We will not attempt such formulations here, because these formulations involve various specific problems not pertinent to the framework of this study *(2)*.

(IV.E.3) Protection of Human Life. It follows from the individual's position as an actual or potential contri-

butor to no-ospheric evolution, that protection of all human life is necessary *(1)*.

Although protection of all human life generally is in evolution's interest the possible need for a few exceptions to this fundamental principle is also in evolution's interest *(2)*. The simplest case in this respect is that of a person who has seriously endangered the evolutionary servomechanism and whose imprisonment would not be a sufficient safeguard against his possible future activities in this respect. Taking the life of such a person is therefore permitted and required when there are very serious reasons to assume the existence of such future dangers; *previous* activities in this respect are however not alone a reason for the death-penalty, for evolution's interest is better served by reintegrating criminals into a normal way of life than by killing them.

More difficult is the case of incurable patients who must suffer tremendous pain before passing away. It is true that their suffering might be challenges to evolutionary developments but on the other hand it is not in evolution's interest that man should be aware of his coming death without the tranquillity which is necessary for preparing and concentrating on this very important happening. Closely related with these latter cases are those of persons who have lost consciousness and who have no hope of recovery, even although their physical life might continue for years. Evolution's interest in both kinds of cases requires a right for the individual to decide on the way he wants to die: either naturally, or naturally with the relief of drugs, or by means of euthanasia. This however does not imply the right of suicide, for it is in evolution's interest to deny such a right *(3)*; there is in this respect no difference between making an end to one's own life and that of others.

The most difficult cases are however those in which human life can only be protected by the sacrifice of human life. Since it is in evolution's interest that all individuals are treated equally in this respect, the only solution might be that in such cases the number of persons involved is used as a criterion, i.e. that as few individuals as possible would be sacrificed for the benefit of as many as possible. This criterion might be useful only however as a starting point, for it does not answer the question how the persons to be sacrificed should be selected. Sometimes we see in this respect a set pattern in regularly recurring situations. During shipwrecks it is usual to save women and children first. This rule indicates that those must be sacrificed first who may be assumed to have the greatest responsibility for the situation in which they find themselves. This latter criterion might however be in conflict with the former, viz. that of the number of individuals involved. This is e.g the case when during a delivery a choice has to be made between saving the child or the mother. This conflict cannot be solved when taking one of both norms as the greater one. The criterion of evolution's interest now requires the highest integrity of human relationships: evolution's interest however also requires that the individual is treated on an equal basis with other individuals *(4)*, independently of the relationships in which he is involved, provided that these relationships are not contrary to evolution's interest. The conflict seems insolvable, unless we introduce a third criterion, namely that evolution's interest requires that men are free from fear. Evolution's interest is thus better served when creation of progenity occurs without fear of non-survival of the delivering person; the one to be delivered being unable to have any fear at all.

This criterion is unsuitable for justification of any abortion on non-medical grounds: evolution's interest requires the greatest possible protection of all human life and exceptions to this rule can only be accepted when they are intended for the greater assurance of this protection *(5)*.

So human life's protection is the most basic human right which can be established in the interest of no-ospheric evolution. But protection of human life alone is not sufficient for assuring no-ospheric evolution's continuation. Positive law has also to provide for protection of the integrity of the areas in which human life has to develop, as well as for security that this development is as favourable as possible. These areas are the human personality, and the human environs. We will discuss their protection in the next two subdivisions.

(IV.E.4) Protection of the Human Personality. In the preceding paragraph we concluded from the basic requirement of human life's integrity that a condition for its fulfillment is integrity of the human personality.

The human personality *(1)* does not only comprise man as a living organism, but a servomechanism, composed by his body, soul, mental tools and physical tools. Among the mental tools we should rate man's abilities, knowledge, memories, opinions and conscience; among man's physical tools, his private possessions and the goods used directly by him which are common or public property, or do not belong to any particular person as e.g. the air which the individual inhales *(2)*.

The integrity of man's personality can only be realized by guaranteeing man a living not below certain minimal standards, for otherwise he cannot be considered to be a full personality as described above.

These minimal standards cannot only be limited to economical resources. This follows from the fact that the human personality requires for a harmonious development, freedom from want, fear and ignorance. Minimal standards in this respect correspond to the realizations of legal values in Rights to medical facilities, appropriate food and corporeal integrity *(IV.B.3.d)*, Rights and Privileges to collect and to spread information and Rights of control over a State's governmental body *(IV.B.3.h)*.

These minimal standards imply by themselves a state of liberty *(3)*, in which man has a general Privilege to do or not to do anything relative to which a Duty *(4)*, a Liability, Disability or a No Right is not imposed on him *(5)*.

It follows from the fact that all individuals are vehicles or potential vehicles of no-ospheric evolution, that equal treatment of all individuals in respect of religion, philosophical and political conviction, ethnic origin, race and sex, belongs to the minimal standards for protection of the human personality's integrity and development *(6)*.

These minimal standards for integrity of the human personality can of course not be met without certain necessary limitation. The principle of treatment as equals imposes the limitation that they should not violate minimal standards of protection of other persons *(7)*; just as relative to the requirement of integrity of human life, other limitations can only be justified if they are based on the criterion of no-ospheric evolution's interest *(8)*.

(IV.E.-5) Protection of the Human Environs. Protection of the human environment is not or not yet conceived in a human rights conception. We will here discuss the issues which may be formulated in such a conception.

Man's outside world is a world of space and time; its protection should therefore not only concern the present, but also extend to what remains of the past and to what might be important in future. This integrity embodies as regards the past, protection of historical data against disappearance and falsification; as to the present and the future it embraces protection of actual human societies against everything that might destroy their structure in its broadest sense, provided that this destruction is not a consequence of the construction of new structures in accordance with the criterion for no-ospheric evolution. As to the future development of human society integrity here embodies the protection against future development which may lead to such a destruction. Guarantee of the integrity of human society, both in the present and in the future should however not go so far that it extends to structures which are barriers against evolutionary development.

Integrity of both the human and the non-human world means, when applied to the aspects of history, the preservation of all historical documents, artefacts, monuments, fossils and other remains of human and non-human activity in the past.

Although evoltuion's interest requires this preservation it is possible that requirements as to the integrity of human personality or of human society need fulfilment at the cost of historical remains. How such a conflict may be solved can be seen in the case of the Assuan Dam, during the construction of which scholars and scientists from all over the world co-operated in excavating the historical remains in the area due to be submerged and transferring the temple momunments of Abu Simbel.

As to the present, integrity of both the human world means preservation of physical nature in its broadest sense: biological, geological and meteorological. The integrity of physical nature however cannot and should not be of the same absolute kind as that of the historical remains: it should however extend so far that physical nature will always be able to provide for the materials needed for human consumption and for the development of science.

This means that man is permitted and should indeed kill animals *(1)* and plants for his consumption, for his researches and also for protection of himself, but the requirements of integrity pose as limits that this should not lead to extermination of a whole species or to disintegration of a biological or geophysical equilibrium within a certain geographical area.

Integrity of the non-human world means, as regards its future aspects, a protection against actual measures which will not at the moment but certainly in future result in physical nature or parts of it being no longer able to provide for the materials for human consumption and scientific development. This means especially protection against radio active fall-out of nuclear explosions in the open air and protection against exhaustion of mineral resources.

Actually human environs as legal values are embodied in national and international provisions relative to particular geographical areas, particular threats of pollution, particular threats of exhaustion of resources and particular threats of extinction of species. The organization of a world-wide co-operation in order to control environmental crises is now in its initial stage: mankind's hope that the results of the United Nations Environmental Conference of 1972 in Stockholm will be more than just pious words seems about to be realized. Not only has a Declaration on the Environment been adopted at this conference, but also an Action Plan for the Human Environment and a Resolution on Institutional and Financial Arrangements *(2)*. Moreover by the Resolution of 15th December 1972, the U.N. General Assembly decided to establish a Governing Council for Environmental Programmes, an Environmental Secretariat and an Environment Fund *(3)*.

(IV.E.6) The United Nations Charter, the Universal Declaration of Human Rights and the European Convention on Human Rights as Instruments in the Promotion of Noospheric Evolution. Historically conceptions of fundamental human rights developed as instruments of national law *(1)* from the necessity to give the individual certain rights against the omnipotence of the State.

Since the second world war however no-ospheric evolutionary progress has been made. During this war the allied powers made, besides the preparation of special regulations for the prosecution and punishment of the German and Japanese leaders who violated human rights *(2)*, preliminary measures for the organization of a new peaceful world in which man's fundamental rights would be respected and mankind's evolution promoted. So the United States and the United Kingdom in the Atlantic Charter of 14th August 1941 proclaimed among their aims "to bring about the fullest collaboration between all nations in the economic field, with the object of insuring for all improved labour standards, economic advance and social security" and "to see established a peace which will afford to all nations the means for dwelling in safety within their own boundaries, and which will afford assurance that all men in all the lands may live out their lives in freedom from fear and want". On 1st December 1943 the same countries together with the Soviet Union, after the Teheran Conference declared on the problems of the future:

"We shall seek the co-operation and active participation of all nations, large and small, whose peoples in heart and mind are dedicated, as our own peoples, to the elimination of tyranny and slavery, oppression and intolerance. We will welcome them, as they may choose to come, into our world family of Democratic Nations". These ideas were worked out at the Dumbarton Oaks Conference between 21st August and 7th October 1944 and the Yalta Conference of February 1945. These conferences resulted in that of San Francisco between 25th April and 26th June of the year 1945 for the establishment of the United Nations Organization. Here on 26th June 1945 the Charter of the United Nations was signed; the Charter came into force on 24th October 1945. In the preamble to this Charter the peoples of the United Nations declare themselves determined "to reaffirm faith in fundamental rights in the dignity and worth of the human person, in the equal rights of men and women and of nations large and small, and ... to promote social progress and better standards of life in larger freedom". To attain the ends to which they are committed the peoples of the United Nations proclaim as one of their methods "to employ international machinery for the promotion of the economic and social advancement of all peoples" *(3)*.

One of the means of reaching this end was seen in the development of a universal declaration of human rights. The E.C.O.S.O.C. was charged with the drawing up of such a declaration; within this framework it was U.N.E.S.C.O. which had among its tasks to consult the world's leading philosophers on their opinions and suggestions concerning the rights which should be included in the new declaration. In 1947 therefore an inquiry was set up by U.N.E.S.C.O. under the leadership of its Director-General Sir Julian Huxley. In July 1947 the answers were studied *(4)* by a committee of experts under the presidency of Edward H. Carr and presented to the U.N. Human Rights Commission.

On December 10th, 1948 the General Assembly of the United Nations proclaimed "as a common guide for all peoples and nations" the Universal Declaration of the Rights of Man; this instrument, intended as a document of *ius constituendum*, states in its preamble a.o. "... the peoples of the United Nations have in a charter reaffirmed their faith in fundamental human rights, in the dignity and worth of the human person and in the equal rights of men and women and have determined to promote social progress and better standards of life in larger freedom".

The United Nation- Organization and its specialized agencies, like e.g. U.N.E.S.C.O., F.A.O., W.H.O., I.L.O.,

I.T.O., in fact together, make, as it was intended, an "international machinery" which may be considered as a servomechanism directed towards further no-ospheric evolution. So far as protection of human rights is concerned however the United Nations have not yet succeeded in the creation of a juridical servomechanism with an effective system of negative feedback *(5)*. In spite of the inadequate means at its disposal the United Nations nevertheless have been able to restrict the occurrence of infractions on human rights and to promote that human life at least obtained protection; only those who have communication with the channels of secret diplomacy know what kind of atrocities might have occurred if there had not been such an international machinery".

The principles of the Universal Declaration of Human Rights lay at the base of the only human rights declaration which belongs, at least relative to a certain geographical area, to positive international law, viz. the European Convention on Human Rights *(6)*, signed at Rome on 4th November 1950 *(7)*.

This Convention came into force on 3th September 1953, its Protocol on 18th May 1954; the right of individual application on 5th July 1955 and the jurisdiction of the European Court of Human Rights on 3th September 1958.

The principle of promotion of social and economic progress is not indeed directly mentioned in the Convention or its preamble, but it results from the Statute of the Council of Europe: in August 1949 the Consultative Assembly of the Council of Europe took the initiative which led to the present Convention, itself having reference to Art. 1 of its Statute, which proclaimed among the Council's program "agreements and common action in economic, social, cultural, scientific, legal and administrative matters and ... the maintenance and further realization of human rights and fundamental freedoms".

By the European Convention on Human Rights a juridical servomechanisms has been created in order to correct deviations from the patterns of expectations and the desired patterns of behaviour, expressed in the formulations of its human rights conception. Individuals have opportunities to complain before the European Commission of Human Rights, if all national means to find justice are exhausted *(8)*. This Commission tries to find a practical "friendly" solution *(9)*, but it will refer the case to the Committee of Ministers *(10)* if a practical solution is impossible; it can also bring the case before the European Court of Human Rights for a juridical solution*(11)*. The Committee of Ministers should find a political solution if the case is not brought before the Court *(12)* and publish, at the time of its final decision, the report of the Commission. The case can be brought before the Court by the Commission and by a State which is the High Contracting Party *(13)*.

It follows from these examples that international law is advancing towards an increasing acknowledgement of a very close connection between the ideas of human rights and promotion of social and economic *(14)* progress as one of its basic principles.

Promotion of social and economic progress is, within the framework of our conception of evolution, nothing but promotion of no-ospheric evolution.

International conventions in which States pledge themselves to promote social and economic progress in their own areas is of the same value as a contract between clergymen that they will not use bad language. For just a clergymen has a moral Duty not to curse without such a contract, it is the State which has a moral Duty, in accordance with the ethical criterion of no-ospheric evolution's interest, to promote social and economic progress even if there is no convention, the undersigning of which enforces a juridical Duty. Such a convention is however a step towards a more detailed regulation of international co-operation in the promotion of social and economic progress. This more detailed regulation can indeed now be found in the "international machinery" of the U.N.O., its specialized agencies and subsidiary bodies.

The criterion of evolution's interest being a criterion outside the area of law, it is very important that international provisions haven been developed in accordance with the commandments of this criterion: the fact that the nations who ratified the U.N.O. Charter did accept a Duty to promote social and economic progress (art. 55 and 75), has made such a promotion into a Duty of international law.

We should understand this Duty in the sense of a Duty to promote social and economic progress in international co-operation; Art. 2, sub 7 of the Charter leaves a national promotion of such a progress to the domestic jurisdiction. In other words, a State has a Duty to co-operate with other States for the promotion of social and economic progress; it has not however a Duty but only a Privilege and even an Immunity in respect to promotion of social and economic progress within its own domestic area.

A State may not however refer persistently to the principles of domestic jurisdiction in order to refuse to fulfil its duty of international co-operation in the promotion of social and economic progress, because of the sanctions discussed in the following lines.

Counterpart of a Duty being a Right, all member-States of U.N.O. have a Right against any other member-State in respect of the fulfilment of their Duty to co-operate with them for the promotion of social and economic progress of States.

They can realize this Right within the negative feedback system of this Organization: if a State, which is a member of the U.N.O. persistently refuses to assist the Organization in actions with respect to promotion of other States' social and economic progress, than it is in our opinion defendable that such a State is subject to the sanction of expulsion from the United Nations Organization (U.N. Charter, Art. 6 jo Art. 2 sub 5)*(15)*.

States which are not U.N.O.-members may in this respect be subject to the sanction, that they should not be admitted to the Organization's membership (U.N.O. Charter, Art. 4).

So far as respect for human rights is concerned, the Charter declares in Art. 1 sub 3, among the United Nations' purposes: "To achieve in international co-operation .... in promoting and encouraging respect for human rights and for fundamental freedoms for all without distinction as to race, sex, language or religion". The same principle is repeated in Art. 55 sub d and 76 sub c of the Charter.

This is not similar to a Duty to protect human rights, but States which persistently fail to fulfil their Duty to assist the U.N.O. in actions relative to the promotion and encouraging of respect for human rights and for fundamental freedoms, may be subject to sanctions which are equal to those in respect of States which do no co-operate in the promotion of social and economic progress. Of course we find here the same difficulty of the domestic jurisdiction; the Law of Nations does not impose upon a State has a Duty to promote respect for human rights within its own domestic area, but only in the international community in co-operation with other States. However just as the international community is affected if a State infringes upon the human rights of those within its jurisdiction, it is domestic areas of such States which necessarily become influenced by earnest international co-operation in the promotion and encouragement of respect for fundamental human rights. Such outcomes are the greatest events of legal evolution.

NOTES

(I.A.1) - pp. 5 - 6.

1) The word evolution, derived from the Latin term *evolutio*, simply means to unfold. Nicolaus Cusanus (1401-1464) was probably the first to use this term, viz. for indicating the relationship between a point and a line ("Linea est puncti evolutio"). Cf. Eisler (Philosophie) 177; Kuypers (Evolutie/Utrecht) 167.
An early, if not the first, application of the notion of evolution in law can be found in the title of G.A. Struve, Evolutiones controversiarium in syntagmata juris civilis, Jenae 1669. Here "evolutio" has the meaning of "unfolding" in the sense of "explanation". The term evolution connected with the idea of progress in law can be found in various descriptions of legal developments, like H. Sinzheimer, "Theorie der Gesetzgebung. Die Idee der Evolution im Recht". (Haarlem 1948), A. Pitlo, "Evolutie in het Privaatrecht" (Haarlem 1969), J. Valkhoff, "Nieuwe termen en begrippen in de rechtswetenschap", Opstellen (Verdam), or Friedmann (Theory) or in the studies of J.J.M. van der Ven on social evolution mentioned in our note to *(I.B.1.a)*.
Evolution of law, legal institutions or legal notions has in these studies a meaning of development, progress, or growth, but not in a conceptual sense. Elaboration however of the idea of legal progress within the framework of a biological or social conception of evolution was first done by Herbert Spencer: cf. *(I.C.4)* and *(I.D.2)*.
2) Cf. Raven (Ontwikkeling) 124; cf. also *(I.A.3.a)* on vitalism and neovitalism.
3) Cf. Raven (Ontwikkeling) 140 ff.

(I.A.2) - pp. 6 - 7.

1) Cf. Raven (Ontwikkeling) 149.

(I.A.3.a) - pp. 8 - 10.

1) ἡ ἐντελεχεια: το τελος ἐντος ἐχεια, having the purpose within itself; the realized potential, the cast, is also called ἐντελεχεια, but then it means το ἐντελος ἐντος ἐχεια, having the realized purpose within itself. Cf. Pauly-Wissowa, (Encyclopädie) II, 1026; Friedrich-Lübkers (Altertum) 330; Eisler (Philosophie) 174.
2) Such speculations seem however to have been current in Aristotle's time, Cf. Dampier (Science) 273.

(I.A.3.b) - pp. 10 - 11.

1) Cf. Bergson (Evolution) 45.
2) See *(IV.B.3.b)*
3) Cf. Van Melsen (Wijsbegeerte) 85 ff.

(I.A.3.b.1) - pp. 11 - 14.

Alfred North Whitehead (1861-1947), holding in this respect the same opinion as Bergson, amplified this conception with the idea, that the ultimate unit of natural occurrence is the event. Cf. Dampier (Science) 486. See also *(I.B.3.a)*, *(III.A.1)* and *(III.E.2.b)*
2) Cf. Eisler (Philosophie) 391 jo 367.
3) On Bergson's contribution to modern theories of time: Dampier

(Science) 205.

4) Bergson (Evolution) 191, 192: L'Instinct est sympathie ..... Mais c'est à l'intérieur même de la vie que nous conduirait l'intuition, je veux dire l'instinct devenu désinteressé, conscient de lui-même, capable de réfléchir sur son objet et de l'élargir indéfiniment". The origin of this idea can be traced back to Spinoza.

5) Both plants and animals are not only to a great extent liable to sexual reproduction, but this reproduction seems on both lines of evolution, in any case in its microscopic initial stage, to be exactly the same action; cf. V.J. Koningsberger, Una Quaelibet Vita (Evolutie/Utrecht) 242. Cf. also Bergson (Évolution) 67 ff.

6) Well known examples are those of human blind, whose tactile sense sometimes develops so far that they are able to "see" colours by means of touch.

7) Consciousness is therefore not a cerebral function; Bergson saw the brains as a barrier to extra-sensory perception; he emphasized the importance of research into para-normal phenomena.

8) As in the example of lacking organs in note *1)*.

9) Bergson (Évolution) 56 ff.

10) This finalism is similar to that of a cybernetic machine, instructed to change a particular purpose upon receiving further information, with a freedom to select a new purpose or even to make a new purpose on the basis of the actual data at its disposal.

11) Bergson (Évolution) 67 jo 59.

12) See Bergson (Évolution) 270.

13) As creative evolution and cybernetic machines have similar finalist features, there is much resemblance between the God-conception developed by Bergson and the ideas of Norbert Wiener, who was seriously inclined to consider God as the operative image of a cybernetic learning machine with the capacity to create other such machines "in His own image".

14) Bergson (Évolution) 294.

15) Cf. *(III.A.4.a)*.

16) Cf. *(III.A.1)* jo *(III.A.4.a)* and *(III.C.3)*.

(I.A.3.b.2) - 15 - 18.

1) Teilhard de Chardin (Verschijnsel) 44.

2) The nature of this psychic energy will be compared in *(IV.B.3.b)* with other notions of psychic energy.

3) See: Teilhard de Chardin (Verschijnsel) 71.

4) Teilhard de Chardin (Verschijnsel) 84-88.

5) Teilhard de Chardin (Verschijnsel) 216.

6) Teilhard de Chardin (Toekomst) 138.

7) This does not mean that point Omega is the same as God, but only that it is related to God, as the lowest point of a line of which the higher points represent the super natural world. If point Omega and God were identical, then Teilhard de Chardin would enter into conflict with the Roman Catholic doctrine, that man's nature does not entitle him to divine grace; "resting on God-Omega" would then imply an attribution of Divine grace as a consequence of natural processes, while the Roman Catholic doctrine considers such an attribution as always having supernatural causes, unknown to man. See Teilhard de Chardin (Verschijnsel) 267, note 1.

8) Teilhard de Chardin (Verschijnsel) 257.

9) Teilhard de Chardin (Toekomst) 148.

(I.B.1.a) - pp. 19 - 20.

1) The common elements in juridical formulations of the notion social evolution in national and international law are thoroughly investigated by J.J.M. van der Ven. He distinguished between three fundamental theses in modern differentiations of this notion: recognition of the individual, recognition of society and recognition of the State (which should provide for freedom). See Van der Ven (Evolutie/Utrecht) 38 ff., (Progrès social), (Sozialer Fortschritt heute), (Begriff sozialer Fortschritt).

(I.B.1.b) - pp. 20 - 21.

1) Barnes 194; 195 ff; 201.

(I.B.1.c) - pp. 21 - 22.

1) Barnes 862.
2) Wiener (Golem) 27 ff, 39 ff.

(I.B.1.d) - pp. 22 - 23.

1) Barnes 621, 622.

(I.B.2.a) - pp. 24 - 26.

1) Barnes 472.
2) Barnes 140, 141, 142.

(I.B.2.b) - pp. 26 - 27.

1) Barnes 140, 141, 142, 149.
2) Barnes 862.
3) A society may be described as a group of human beings, organized for the care of common affairs in a body politic, like a tribe or state. Culture or civilization has been explained in *(IV.B.3.c)* as a set of mental properties belonging to a group of human beings and embracing the patterns of behaviour, means of communication and historical traditions which they have in common. Such a group, a cultural area, may but should not coincide with a group forming a society.

(I.B.2.c) - pp. 27 - 30.

1) Barnes 142 ff.
2) Barnes 145, 146.
3) In: "One-Dimensional Man" (1964)
4) An interesting study in this connection is that of William H. Whyte Jr., "The Organization Man", New York, 1957.
5) Cf. *(III.B.3)* jo *(III.B.2)* and *(I.C.7)*.

(I.B.2.d) - pp. 30 - 31.

1) Barnes 478.
2) See *(I.C.4)*
3) If we exclude the notion of harmony. Cf. *(I.B.1.d)* in this connection with respect to Hobhouse's normative descriptions of social evolution.

(I.B.3.a) - pp. 31 - 34.

1) Barnes 220, 221.
2) Cf. Barnes 508; Aron (Pensée sociologique) 316 ff; *(I.B.3.d)*.
3) Barnes 376 ff; cf. *(I.A.3.b.1)*, *(II.E.4)* and *(III.A.1)*.
4) Barnes 862.
5) Cf. *(III.B.3)* and *(IV.B.3.h)*.

(I.B.3.b) - pp. 34 - 35.

1) In *(I.B.1.d)*
2) Cf. *(I.B.3.a)*
3) Wiener (Golem) 13, 27 ff, 47, 48.
4) Barnes 445-455.
5) Cf. *(I.B.3.e)*

(I.B.3.c) - pp. 35 - 37.

1) Cf. Barnes 862; cf. *(I.B.3.a)*
2) Barnes 544.

(I.B.3.d) - pp. 37 - 41.

1) Cf. Barnes 379 ff.
2) Van der Pot (Periodisering) 170.
3) An analogous application of Darwin's theory was upheld by Georg Simmel (1858-1918), who, basing himself on the doctrine that any organism has its own view of life according to its particular senses, taught that the true conceptions of thought are those which remain as most fitting to the species after biological selection; scientifical and historical conceptions do not teach real things, but only rational constructions.
4) Barnes 419 ff.
5) Cf. Barnes 508; Aron (Pensée sociologique) 316 ff; *(I.B.3.a)*
6) Barnes 461 ff, 468.
7) Cf. *(I.A.3.b.2)* jo *(IV.B.3.b)*

(I.B.3.e) - pp. 41 - 49.

1) The notion "Philosophy of history" (philosophie de l'histoire, Geschichtsphilosophie) originates from Voltaire ("Essai sur les moeurs et l'esprit des nations", 1765).
2) In "Die Erziehung des Menschengeschlechts" (1780).
3) Eisler (Philosophie) 246.
4) Van der Pot (Periodisering) 157
4a) Cf. *(I.C.2)*
5) In "Idee zu einer allgemeinen Geschichte in weltbürgerlicher Absicht" (1784), and "Zum ewigen Frieden" (1795).
6) So far as biology is concerned Kant stated only somewhat prudent opinions. In his "Kritik der Urteilskraft" (1790) he recognized that the nature of organism cannot be explained purely mechanically. In his "Anthropologie" (1798) he indeed suggested the possibility that man originates from animal but he restricted himself to declaring, that he could not explain how nature caused such a development. On organism in philosophy: Eisler (Philosophie) 465 ff.
7) Van der Pot (Periodisering) 65.
8) Comte's principal works in this respect are his "Cours de philosophie positive" (first ed. 1830-1842) and his "Système de politique positive" (first ed. 1852-1854). Cf. Aron (Pensée

sociologique) 81 ff; Zinn (Dreistadiengesetz) 26 ff, 72 ff, 108 ff.

9) Comte proclaimed this law as his original discovery; principal elements of this law are however already mentioned in the works of Fiore, Ibn Chaldun, Vico, Turgot, de Condorcet, Burdin and Saint-Simon, of which Comte certainly possessed knowledge. Nevertheless it was Comte who gave this law its name and provided for its greatest systematic elaboration. Cf. Van der Pot (Periodisering) 158, 160; Zinn (Dreistadiengesetz), 8 ff.

10) The idea of positivism originates from David Hume (1711-1776). It was elaborated by Comte, Stuart Mill and Spencer; neither positivism nor Comte's philosophy could however have become what they are without the work done by Sir Francis Bacon, Thomas Hobbes and John Locke.

11) Comte's ideal of a Church of Humanity has been carried out by a number of prominent positivists in England: its churches were adorned with statues of the saints of humanity, its regular services comprising among their ritual the singing of positivists hymns.

12) Barnes 544; cf. *(I.B.3.c)*

13) Cf. *(I.C.4)*

14) History is to Hegel God in his temporal development; in his spatial extension God is the same as nature.

15) See on Hegel's divisions of history in periods: Van der Pot (Periodisering) 66. Hegel considered his own time as that of the highest perfection.

16) Hegel did not devote much attention to biological evolution, seeing it not in a real, but in an ideal sense. Actually Hegel denied biological evolution with the following words: "The metamorphosis can be ascribed to the notion as such, because it alone is evolution ... it is a clumsy idea ... to regard the transformation from one natural form and sphere to a higher as an outward and actual production". Cf. Dampier (Science) 274, without references.

17) The origin of the notion of dialectics can be traced back to Heraclite; cf. the citation in *(I.C.4)*, note *1)*. Hegel's ideas on dialectics influenced a.o. the ideas of Tarde *(I.B.2.a)* and Marx. The Marxist philosopher Georg Klaus applied Lenin's elaboration of the dialectic principle to cybernetics. Cf. Klaus (Kybernetik) 66 ff, 157, 220, 226, 391. See note *19)* on this application.

18) The number of publications on Marxism is innumerable. For this analysis Tucker (Marx) and Zinn (Dreistadiengesetz) were of great value.

19) Similarities between the Hegelian principle of dialectics and the cybernetic principle of feedback (cf. *(III.A.4.a)* cannot be used as arguments for the justness of this dialectic principle; feedback is directed towards a goal, viz. a decrease or an increase in a deviation of a pattern of behaviour within an unstable equilibrium; the results of this process can reasonably be foretold. As far as I can see however the shape of the Hegelian synthesis is not actually predictable and the clash between thesis and antithesis may not always result in any synthesis at all but in destruction of thesis or antithesis or both, as well as in a situation similar to the original. George Klaus, however, reasons in fact (Kybernetik) 392 according to later developments in dialectic philosophy and bases himself on Lenin's conception that each movement, including that of thinking and its neurophysiological foundation, is both a unity of continuity and disconnection and a contradiction of continuity and disconnection: *"Nach Lenin ist jede Bewegung, auch die des Denkens und seiner neurophysiologischen Grundlage, eine Einheit von Kontinuität und Diskretheit, ein Widerspruch von Kontinuität und Diskretheit"*. (Reference to W.I. Lenin: Aus dem philosophischen Nachlass, Dietzverlag, Berlin 1960, S. 193). The examples by which Klaus compares cybernetics to modern dialectics are extremely interesting and require further investigation. Cf. note *16)*.

(I.C.2) - pp. 49 - 50.

1) Smits (Herder) 54 jo 74, 75.
2) Van der Pot (Periodisering) 182.
3) Cf. *(I.C.3)*

(I.C.3) - pp. 50 - 51.

1) Alfred Geiger also published his brother's lectures "Zur Entwicklungsgeschichte der Menschheit", Stuttgart 1871, 2nd. ed. 1878; "History of the Development of the Human Race", London 1880.
2) The idea that languages are subjected to development had already been defended by Wilhelm von Humboldt (1767-1835), who in his turn was influenced by Herder.
3) See *(III.A.4.a)*
4) Rabbi E.G. Hirsch says in the Jewish Encyclopedia: "None of the essential contentions of Judaism is vitally affected by the propositions of the evolution school. The philosophy of the Reform wing within Judaism, regarding Judaism as a growth, not a fixed quantity or a rigid law, and as still in the process of developing (tradition being its vital element), has even found corroboration in the theory of evolution".

(I.C.4) - pp. 51 - 54.

1) Heraclite (± 500 B.C.) had stated: "war is the father of all end and the king of all, and some it shows as gods, others as men; some it makes slaves, others free" (πολεμος παντων μεν πατερ ἐστι; παντων δε βασιλευς, και τουσ μεν Δεους ἐδειξε τους δε ἀνορωπους, τουσ μεν δουλουσ εποιησε τους δε ελευθερους). (Diels) Fr. 55, Hippolytus Ref. IX, 9,4 - See Kirk/Raven (Presocratic) 195.
2) See *(I.C.5)*.
3) The theory of Lamarck (1794-1829) is one of active adaptation of species to the environs in such a way, that in the course of generations adaptations become hereditary by the exercise of function. Lamarck explained evolution as an adjustment to the environs: what is used will develop and what is not used will degenerate. He stated moreover that the adaptations are hereditary. Theories of passive adaptation, like those of Buffon (1707-1788) and Eimer (1843-1898) emphasize that it is the direct moulding influences of the environs which determine the species' alterations; in Lamarck's theory it is the unique property of the species which determine how the species will adapt itself to changes in the environs.
4) This is not the opinion of K. Kuypers (Evolutie/Utrecht) 169; cf. however also K. Kuypers (Evolutie/Utrecht) 170.
5) In this work Spencer tried to reconcile science and religion, but it displeased both scientists and clergymen. Both Darwin and Spencer,

supported by Thomas Henry Huxley, were openly insulted by leading people who considered every evolutionist as an immoral monster; already in 1860 Thomas Henry Huxley had defended Darwin's theories at the Oxford meeting of the British Association against Bishop Wilberforce, who endeavoured to fulfil this important task by ridiculing the notion of evolution without any real understanding of the problem; cf. Dampier (Science) 279.

6) Spencer's mechanicism was not absolute; he was of the opinion that the ultimate concepts of physics, viz. space, time and atoms, involve inconsistencies which make it clear that the reality behind phenomena is unknowable; cf. Dampier (Science) 294.

7) The full description is: "Evolution is an integration of matter and concomitant dissipation of motion; during which the matter passes from an indefinite, incoherent homogeneity to a definite, coherent heterogeneity and during which the retained motion undergoes a parallel transformation"; "First Principles", London (1880), 396; cf. van der Pot (Periodisering) 285.

(I.C.5) - p. 55.

1) This school should not be confused with that of neodarwinism, cf. *(I.A.3.a)*

2) Cf. Dampier (Science) 280, 306, 316 ff.; Eisler (Philosophie) 180.

3) Cf. Nietzsche (Wagner) 42 jo 45. Nietzsche was disappointed in Richard Wagner for several reasons still not clear; one of these reasons being that Wagner's essence was not that of an Uebermensch, but only that of a gifted actor who was not even a German, who had only learnt to "imitate a lot of German". Nietzsche "proved" this strange concept by referring to the fact that Wagner's father, Ludwig Geyer, had been an actor and therefore an unfavourable and non-German person. Nietzsche moreover reproached Wagner for his anti-Semitism - Wagner published an anti-Semitic treatise "Das Judentum in der Musik".

(I.C.6) - pp. 55 - 58.

1) Cf. *(I.A.2.a)*, *(I.A.2.b)* and *(I.A.3.a)*; Greene (Death) 338.

2) Fischer, Evolutionisme en cultuur (Evolutie/Utrecht) 194, states only that Teilhard de Chardin influenced Huxley. See however Teilhard de Chardin (Verschijnsel) 195, where Teilhard de Chardin falls in with Huxley's statement that man is nothing but evolution which has become conscious of itself. On the relationships between Huxley and Teilhard de Chardin: J. Huxley (Essays) 186 ff.

3) Cf. *(I.B.3.c)*.

4) Cf. *(I.B.3.f)*.

5) Julian Huxley (Religion) 126.

6) I don't know whether Huxley means by "failure to unify" a lack of unification at all or a unification which we often meet in so-called primitive cultures; on the other hand modern societies have to deal with a growing number of people failing to unify the different aspects of their mental life. At present about 10% of the inhabitants of the United States need treatment at least once during their life-time because of mental disorder.

7) Julian Huxley (Religion) 186, 187.

8) The Theory of Evolutionary Humanism; see J. Huxley (Religion) 181 ff. Another contributor to this conception is G.G. Simpson.

9) Julian Huxley (Essays) 194.

10) Julian Huxley (Religion) 211.
11) Julian Huxley (Religion) 188.
12) Julian Huxley (Religion) 195.

(I.C.7) - pp. 58 - 62.

1) Julian Huxley (Evolution) 562, 564, 565.
2) Julian Huxley (Evolution) 562, 564.
3) This is distinguished from human progress which has "connotations of value as well as of efficiency, subjective as well as objective criteria"; see J. Huxley (Evolution) 567. Huxley nevertheless has tried to formulate an objective criterion for human progress in his ethical criterion; see next alineas.
4) J. Huxley gives an alternative description "a raising of the upper level of all-round functional efficiency and of harmony of internal adjustment"; (Evolution) 564, 565. Huxley refers to Spencer as the origin of the notion "greater independence"; (Evolution) 565.
5) K. Kuypers (Evolutie/Utrecht) 175.
6) J. Huxley (Evolution) 566, 567.
6) Julian Huxley (Evolution) 566, 567.
7) Julian Huxley (Religion) 209, 210.
9) Cf. *(III.C.4.a)* jo *(I.A.3.a)*
10) Cf. Wiener (Golem) 32 and *(III.A.1)*
11) Such a normative description is given in *(III.B.4)*

(I.D.1) - pp. 63 - 65.

1) Cf. note *1)* ad *(I.A.1)*
2) See *(I.D.2)* and *(I.D.3)*

(I.D.2) - pp. 65 - 67.

1) Thomas Huxley's grandson, Julian Huxley, is not of this opinion, as it appears from his theory of "Evolutionary Humanism"; cf. *(I.C.6)* jo *(III.B.6.e)*.
2) i.e. when it causes evolution according to Spencer's description of the individual or the group. Cf. *(I.C.4)*.
3) The formula of justice as developed by Spencer was first published by him in his "Social Statics" (1850). F.W. Maitland demonstrated in "Mind", vol. VIII, (1883), pp. 508-9, that the same principle had already been formulated in other words by Kant in his "Metaphysische Anfangsgründe der Rechtslehre". See on Spencer's analysis of the corresponding and different aspects of both formula: "The Principles of Ethics" (1893), vol. II, part VI, p. 437, Appendix A - "The Kantian idea of rights".
4) Cf. the French human rights-declaration of 1789, art. 4: "La liberté consiste à pouvoir faire tout ce qui ne nuit pas à autrui: ainsi l'exercice des droits naturels de chaque homme n'a de bornes que celles qui assurent aux autres membres de la société la jouissance de ces mêmes droits. Ces bornes ne peuvent être déterminées que par la Loi".
5) In the "Principles of Ethics" (1893) Vol. II, part IV, pp. 25-181. See on formulation of fundamental human rights: Van der Ven (Grundrechte); Dietze (Formulierung).
6) Cf. the Bill of Rights of Virginia (1776), art. 1: "That all men ... have certain inherent rights...; namely the enjoyment of life and liberty, with the means of acquiring and possessing property, and pursuing and obtaining happiness and safety". The U.S. Declaration

of Independence (1776) declares among man's inalienable rights "Life, liberty and the pursuit of happiness".

7) Cf. *(I.C.4)*.

8) Cf. Wiener (Golem) 5, 13, 27, 47, 48.

9) There is no objection against considering money and securities as bearers of information on goods and services representing economic values. The information concerns here the exchange-value on the market and not primarily the nominal value. The exchange-value can be calculated by means of the rate of exchange or quotation on one side and the nominal value on the other side.

(I.D.3) - pp. 67 - 69.

1) Teilhard de Chardin (Opbouw) 50

2) See *(III.C.3)* jo *(III.C.2)* for a distinction between law and morals.

(II.A) - pp. 70 - 72.

1) See *(III.A.3)*

(II.B) - pp. 73 - 76.

1) Cf. Wesenberg (Privatrechtsgeschichte) 141; Wieacker (Neuzeit) 391

2) Cf. Wesenberg (Privatrechtsgeschichte) 143

3) Cf. Wieacker (Neuzeit) 446, 447

4) Cf. Wieacker (Neuzeit) 451

5) More comprehensively in Pound (Fifty Years) 568 ff.

(II.B.1) pp. 76 - 77.

1) Cf. Windscheid (Pandektenrecht) 87 ff.

2) Pound (Fifty Years) 571 sees in Windscheid's "Können" only a power; this seems incorrect: cf. Windscheid, loc.cit.

3) Cf. Windscheid (Pandektenrecht) 89, note 3; Pound (Fifty Years) 571, 572.

4) Cf. Williams (Salmond) 261

5) Larenz (Teil) 172: "Der Begriff wurde geprägt durch Seckel in der Festgabe f. Koch, 1903, S. 205 ff".

(II.C) - pp. 78 - 79.

1) Hoebel (Man) 46 ff.

2) Cf. the critical analysis in Pound (Fifty Years) 572-576. The final rejection of all critical opinions which are due to misunderstanding can be found in Stone (Province) 115-133.

3) Cf. Radin (Restatement); Hoebel (Man) 48, 49; Williams (Salmond) 270.

4) Hohfeld (Conceptions) 64.

5) Cf. Stone (Province) 133.

6) See for the historical and philosophical sources of Hohfeld's system: Pound (Fifty years) 571, 572.

7) Hohfeld seems to have conceived his four pairs of "jural opposites" (Right versus No Right, Power versus Disability) as opposites in the sense of thesis versus antithesis. Hohfeld's scheme seems moreover to suggest that each of his four pairs of "jural correlatives" (the complementary concepts Right and Duty, Power and Liability, etc.), by which his fundamental jural relationships are represented, were intended to express a dialectic synthesis.

(II.C.1) - pp. 79 - 82.

1) Hohfeld (Conceptions) 5
2) Cf.*(II.D)*.
3) Cf.*(II.E.5.a)* and *(II.E.5.b)*; cf. also Freudenthal (Logique) 20 ff.
4) Cf.*(II.D.2.a)*.
5) A "privilege not to do" opposed to a "duty to do" and a "privilege to do" opposed to a "duty not to do" are upheld in Williams (Salmond) 270 and Fitch (Revision) 269 ff. This was not Hohfeld's intention; cf. Hohfeld (Conceptions) 47 ff. and Rosdorff (No-Revision) par. 1 and 2.
6) Cf. *(II.F.1)* and *(II.F.5)*
7) Hohfeld (Conceptions) 38.

(II.C.2) - pp. 82 - 83.

1) A number of other opportunities is treated in the following parts of *(II)*, in *(III.C)* and in *(IV.C)*; moreover, *(III)* and *(IV)* are applications of the system elaborated in *(II.E)* and *(II.F)*, in which the ideas of Hohfeld are connected with those of Bentham.
2) Hohfeld (Conceptions) 72.
3) Cf. however *(III.C.3.a)*.

(II.D.1) - pp. 84 - 86.

1) Cf. C.L. Hamblin, Elementary Formal Logic, a programmed course, London 1967, pp. 17ff., 22 ff., 34ff., 46ff.

(II.D.2.a) - pp. 89 - 90.

1) The cybernetic structure of Hohfeld's fundamental relations will be treated in *(III.C.2)*.

(II.D.4) - p. 91.

1) Hart (Concept) 92. Cf. also Ross (Directives) 91
2) Ross (Directives) 120.

(II.D.5) - pp. 91 - 92.

1) Ross, op. cit., p. 119.

(II.D.6) - pp. 92 - 93.

1) Cf. Moritz (System) 55ff; Rosdorff (No-Revision) par. 2.
2) Hohfeld, op.cit., p. 39.
3) Hohfeld, op.cit., p. 47.
4) Moritz (System) 55 ff.; Rosdorff (No-Revision) par. 2.
5) Moritz (System) 56; Rosdorff (No-Revision) par. 2.
Cf. Restatement in the Courts, Permanent Edition, Glossary of words and phrases described in the Restatement, American Law Institute Publishers, St. Paul, Minnesota, 1957, where Privilege has ambiguously been described as: "... A legal freedom on the part of one person against another to do a given act or a legal freedom not to do a given act". Cf. also Rosdorff (No-Revision) par. 2.
7) Cf. Larenz (Teil) 162.

(II.E.1) - pp. 96 - 97.

1) Rechtstheorie, 2. Band 1971, Heft 1, p. 55-66. Cf. also Rosdorff (Synthesis).
2) 'Of Laws in General', ed. H.L.A. Hart in The Collected Works of Jeremy Bentham (University of London: The Athlone Press, 1970). This work of Bentham was published in 1945 by Ch.W. Everett under the title "Bentham's Limits of Jurisprudence Defined".

(II.E.2.a) - p.97.

1) Bos (Methoden) 287 jo 85,86.
2) Raz (Concept) 52,53.
3) Von Wright (Action) 71.

(II.E.2.b) - pp. 98 - 99.

1) Cf. Russell (Philosophy) Ch. XXVI. Cf. also p. 311: "The events that happen in our mind are parts of the course of nature, and we do not know that the events which happen elsewhere are of a totally different kind". The idea that events are the ultimate units of all occurrence originates from Whitehead, who amplified in this respect Bergson's theory, that the essence of reality is becoming. Cf. Dampier (Science) 486. Cf. also *(I.A.3.b.1)* and *(III.A.1)*.
2) Cf. Čapec (Impact) 368.

(II.E.3) - p. 99.

1) Cf. Russell, op.cit. p.216.
2) Cf. Hohfeld (Conceptions) 47; Rosdorff (No-Revision) par. 2.

(II.E.5.b) - p. 101.

1) The examples of will-expressions similar to Hohfeld's liability and immunity are indeed chosen from constitutional law, but they apply as well to laws and statutes which are not constitutional.

(II.E.6.a) - pp. 102 - 103.

1) Cf. Suyling (Inleiding) I, 85 and 102 ff.

(II.E.7) - pp. 103 - 104.

1) This is clearly exposed by Miss A.M. Bos in her formalization of Bentham's systems of volitional logic. Cf. Bos (Methoden) 302, 303 jo 275 ff.
2) Cf. Bos (Methoden) 294, 295, 302 jo 187. Next to Bentham's four "aspects of the will" four other volitional propositions, all based on "Duty", are formalized there, viz. notions called "Encouragement", "Discouragement", "Non-Encouragement" and "Non-Discouragement". Miss Bos did not find however jural notions to which these concepts are identical. I cannot but see in the two former of these concepts anything else but formalizations of contracts with mutual obligations, and in the two latter formalized negations of such contracts.

(II.F) - p. 105.

1) See *(II.C.1)*.

(II.F.1) - pp. 105 - 106.

1) Also the notion Lex in the adagium expressing the Rule of Law principle Lex est Rex is a lex imperfecta. Cf. *(II.F.3)* jo *(IV.B.3.h)*.

(II.F.5) - pp. 108 - 109.

1) Cf. *(II.D.2.a)*.

(III.A.1) - pp. 110 - 111.

1) Cf. Marlet (Verschijnselen) 127; Tyrrell (Parapsychologie) 180 ff.; Tenhaeff (Telepathie) 84.
2) Cf. Jacobi (Jung) 57.
3) Wiener (Golem) 30: "... we must be aware that there are images and images. Pygmalion made the statue of Galathea in the image of his ideal beloved, but after the gods brought it to life, it became an image of his beloved in a much more real sense. It was no longer merely a pictorial image but an operative image".
4) Cf. Wiener (Golem) 31 where Wiener discusses requirements for a possible reproduction of machines by machines. Wiener posed this problem among others in the following words: "can the new and varied machine itself act as an archetype, even to its own departures from its own archetypal pattern?" (Golem) 29 - The term "archetype" was chosen by C.G. Jung for indicating the "primordial images" or "dominants of the collective unconscious", which have the structure of a "pattern of behaviour". Cf. Jacobi (Jung) 39ff. jo 57,58. Wiener did not however derive his notion of archetype from Jung; it fits in better with the notion of archetype in biology, than with the psychological notion; the archetypes of cybernetic machines and animals are not so much patterns of behaviour, but images of devices with certain desired patterns of behaviour.
5) The italics are mine.
6) Eighteenth century mechanism saw the ideal form of a machine in that of a watch.
7) Cf. Klaus (Kybernetik) 177, 178.
8) Cf. Klaus (Kybernetic) 173, 177, 350, 351, 355.
9) Wiener (Golem) 13: "Darwinian natural selection is a kind of racial learning, which operates within the conditions imposed by the reproduction of the individual". This theory is described in Golem, 27ff. Cf. also Golem, 48 where this theory is described as similar to Wiener's conception of heredity in self-reproducing machines.

(III.A.2) - pp. 112 - 113.

1) Pierce (Symbolen) 50 ff.
2) Pierce (Symbolen) 38.
3) Cf. Pierce (Symbolen) 176 ff.

(III.A.3) - pp. 113 - 114.

1) Klaus (Kybernetik) 42, 43; Frank (Kybernetik) 26, 27.
2) A bibliography on cybernetics can be found in Klaus (Kybernetik) 537 ff. Cf. also Frank (Kybernetik) 180 ff. On cybernetics and legal system: Van den Bergh (Muzen) 120, 122.
3) Klaus (Kybernetik) 41: "Kybernetik ist die Theory des Zusammenhangs möglicher selbstregulierender Systeme mit ihren Teilsystemen".

4) Klaus (Kybernetik) 34, 35. In 1963 half a year before his premature death Wiener described cybernetics as "the science of communication and control, whether in machines or living organisms". This formulation permits, unlike Wiener's earlier normative description its application in botany. Cf. Wiener (Golem) 8.

(III.A.4.a) - pp. 114 - 116.

1) See Pierce (Symbolen) 250.
2) Cf. Wiener (Golem) 30, 31, 32; Pierce (Symbolen) 250.
3) These instruments are also called receptors.
4) On negative feedback as a distinguishing mark of living organisms: Bok (Leven) 169 ff.
5) Cf. *(III.B.1)* and *(IV.C.4)*, *(IV.C.5)*.

(III.A.4.b) - pp. 116 - 118.

1) Klaus (Kybernetik) 115, refers to a publication of these authors in German, edited in Princeton, "Theorie der Spiele und des ökonomischen Verhaltens". In his bibliography - (Kybernetik) 538 - he mentions the same authors: "Spieltheorie und wirtschaftliches Verhalten", Würzburg, 1961.
2) (Golem) 15,17 ff.
3) (Golem) 17 jo 22.
4) (Golem) 25,26.
5) Cf. also Siccama (Paradox) 9 ff.
6) See on the role of game in law: Huizinga (Ludens) 111 ff, 128 ff.
7) Huizinga (Ludens) 5.
8) Huizinga (Ludens) 305, 306.

(III.B) - p. 123.

1) See *(III.A.4.c)*.

(III.B.1) - pp. 123 - 126.

1) Cf. Van Soest (Informatie) 25.
2) Cf. Raven (Ontwikkeling) 13-16.
3) Cf. Sir Julian Huxley's normative description of biological progress in *(I.C.7)*.
4) Cf. Van Soest (Informatie) 25.
5) Bok (Cybernetica) 159-161.
6) Meadows (Club).
7) Contra Meadows (Club): Polak (Contra-Club).
8) See *(IV.D.2)*.
9) See *(III.C.3)* jo *(III.C.2)* for a distinction between law and morals.

(III.B.5) - pp. 129 - 131.

1) Wiener (Golem) 13, 27 ff.

(III.B.6.d) - p. 134.

1) See on human values *(III.B.6.e)* and *(IV.B.2.a)*.

(III.B.6.e) - pp. 134 - 138.

1) Legal values and their relations to no-ospheric evolution are treated in *(IV.B.2)* ff.
2) Among the technological values philosophical values are comprised although philosophical values are also included, as well as the

religious values, among the ethical values; legal values and historical values can be considered as ethical and as technological values; technological values are only mediately related to questions of "ought" or "may", but immediately they concern the problem "how".

3) The normative description of evolution given in *(III.B.4)* is with respect to aesthetical progress, only directly applicable as far as the sensation of beauty answers to the objective criteria for such an experience as discovered by science and therefore objectively suitable as patterns for human behaviour in the creation of works of art. As far as subjective aesthetical criteria are involved, evolution can only be established at the hand of its indirect results. Thus for example, in order to determine whether pop-music represents evolution compared to the earlier kinds of popular music, a comparison has to be made between its evolutionary results, such as a possible decrease in juvenile delinquency, and its destructive effects, as for instance damage to the places where it is performed.

4) See *(I.C.7)* jo *(I.C.6)*.

5) J. Huxley (Religion) 212.

6) Important ideas concerning the relations between human existence and law can be found in Van der Ven (Existentie). It is postulated there, that the deepest and most original origin of law which can be found in man's existential unity is love, namely in the sense of a way of existence of complete self-realization in complete communication with the other. Law cannot enforce such a way of existence, but it can favour it in a twofold fashion: "by refraining from anything which might be a handicap to the existential unfolding, which man may reach in love, and if necessary by protecting and perhaps even promoting the space for this unfolding". Cf. Van der Ven (Existentie) 78.
It is possible to arrive at a similar result with the criterion of evolution's interest, for this criterion does not concern the interest of a world-embracing entirety which man has to serve, but the interest of the human individuals, which the individuals can only realize in communication with each other in their roles as components of the entirety, i.e. as human beings. The ultimate attainable act of perfect communication between individuals is an act of love; such acts may be performed if one person has succeeded in acquiring control over the fading in the channel of communication with the other; cf. *(II.A.3)*. It is a well-known fact that many people succeed in a perfect communication with others, without a conscious application of Claude Shannon's theory; it is nevertheless in evolution's interest that law promotes a decrease of fading in the greatest possible number of channels of inter-human communication.

(III.C.2) - pp. 140 - 141.

1) See *(III.C.3)* for a distinction between law and morals which is based on the distinctions between negative feedback opportunities.

(III.C.2.a) - pp. 141 - 143.

1) Cf. Grotius (Inleidinge) III,15,9.

2) Wesenberg (Privatrechtsgeschichte) 22 cf. also Grotius, Inleidinge, III,1,52 (incorrect from a historical point of view); Bynkershoek (Observationes) I, no 1005.

3) Planitz (Rechtsgeschichte) 9,10.

4) It is however not the only touchstone; modern German bona fides is therefore not similar to Justinian aequitas; cf. Wieacker (Neuzeit) 476. Modern Dutch bona fides however is, according to constant administration of justice ad Art. 1374,3 of the Dutch Civil Code, equal to the requirements of reason and aequitas; cf. also Hellema (Dwaling) 14.
5) Also Glauben has a root in ancient Germanic Law. Some of the Germanic tribes had a custom that movable property could not be followed into the hands of a third person. This rule was formulated in several adagia like "Hand muss Hand wahren", "mobilia non habent sequelam", "possession vaut titre" and also in "wo einer seinen Glauben gelassen, da muss er ihn wieder suchen"; cf. De Blécourt (Begrip) 138. Complementary to this Glauben stood of course the Treu of the "hand" which had been entrusted with the movable.
6) Hellema (Dwaling) 12; cf. also pp. 13,14. Hellema's conception of bona fides is based on Van der Ven's anthropological conception of law; cf. Van der Ven (Existentie) 67. Van der Ven considers active knowing a person and passive becoming known by a person as complementary. Hellema considers as Treu behaviour according to what someone proved to be towards the other and as Glauben the confidence that the former will act in accordance with the way in which he became known by the latter.
7) Schulz (Roman Law) 356; G.2,50.

(III.C.3) - pp. 143 - 144.

1) These negative feedback opportunities have been treated in *(III.C.2)*
2) The term "norm-bound unit" seems indeed appropriate for game-bound units in the area of morality but cannot be recommended, because S. T. Bok used it in biophysics as a term indicating servomechanisms consisting of matter, or smaller structures like e.g. proton and electron, of which there is still no certainty if they are servomechanisms or not; cf. Bok (Leven) 15, 84, 271.

(III.C.3.a) - pp. 144 - 158.

1) Cf. the enumeration in *(III.C.2)*.
2) Cf. Hohfeld (Conceptions) 96, 97.

(III.C.3.b) - pp. 158 - 164.

1) G.2, 197 ff.; UE 24, 11a.
2) H.R. 21st January 1944; N.J. 1944, 120.
3) Cf. *(III.C.3.a)*

(III.C.4.a) - pp. 164 - 166.

1) Gierke (Genossenschaftsrecht) III, 280 ff.; Saleilles (Personne) 219 ff. jo 309.
2) Pothier (Personnes) I,VII.
3) Savigny (System) II, 240 ff. See Hanenburg (Rechtsperson) 170 ff. on the 18th century philosophical background of Savigny's theory.
4) D.46,I,22; D.37,I,2; D.50,17,117.
Cf. Spruit (Plinius) 6 ff., 9 ff., 15 on the impossibility of succession by personae incertae in classical Roman Law.

6) Gierke (Privatrecht) I, 472.
7) Asser (Rechtspersoon) 67.
8) Gierke (Verbände) 21, 22.
9) The italics are mine. Gierke published these words in 1902; he still did not, unlike Wiener distinguish between operative and pictorial images, cf. Wiener (Golem) 30 ff. We now speak of operationalisation of objects or systems; cf. *(III.A.1)*.
10) Gierke (Verbände) 34.
11) Gierke (Verbände) 28 ff.

(III.C.4.b) - pp. 166 - 168.

1) Cf. De Blécourt (Kort Begrip) 60 ff.; VerLoren/Spruit (Hoofdlijnen) 131, 205.
2) Cf. Jenks (Book) 247 jo 293 ff.
3) Even before the time of Charlemagne settlers of churches reserved for themselves and their heirs a Privilege to designate the pastor of the founded church. In the early Middle Ages however settlers still considered themselves as owners of the separated property. Cf. De Blécourt (Kort Begrip) 220.

(III.C.4.c) - pp. 168 - 171.

1) Cf. *(III.C.4.d)*.
2) Cf. *(II.F.2)*
3) The British Nationality Act of 1948 declares that all citizens of Commonwealth States ("Commonwealth citizens") are British subjects. A British subject is therefore either a citizen of the United Kingdom and Colonies, or a citizen of another State of the Commonwealth. In our conception the notion of subject is restricted to persons under full jurisdiction of the sovereign.
4) In pre-feudal societies the citizens gathered in public meetings to exercise themselves the functions of ruler, legislative and judge.
5) See also *(II.E.6.a)*, *(II.F.2)*, *(II.F.3)*, *(II.F.4)*, *(II.F.5)* and *(II.F.6)*.
6) Cf. *(II.E.7)* and the example in *(II.D.2)*.
7) This applies to the Roman aerarium which was at the exclusive disposal of the Senate, but not to the Roman fiscus; the latter, although mainly spent for public purposes, belonged to the Emperor's private property. Also taxes paid in medieval feudal states became private property of the rulers.

(IV.A.2) - pp. 175 - 177.

1) Unless it can be proved that their nature is that of an "idée force"; cf. *(I.B.3.c)*.
2) Wiener (Golem) 13, 27 ff., 47, 48.
3) Cf. *(III.C.3.b)* ad 4.

(IV.B.2.a) - pp. 181 - 182.

1) Cf. Coing (Grundzüge) 13 ff., Friedmann (Theory) 197-199. References to literature on law and values in Henkel (Einführung) 236.
2) More details and literature in Zong (Radbruch); cf. also Friedmann, loc.cit.

(IV.B.2.b) - p. 182.

1) Cf. *(III.C.2.a)*.

(IV.B.2.d) - pp. 183 - 184.

1) See *(I.D.2)* and *(I.D.3)*.

(IV.B.2.e) - pp. 184 - 187.

1) (Judgment) 65.
2) Ibidem.
3) Drost (Humanicide) 347: "Laesio humanitatis constitutes the most serious crime communis iuris by reason of the official character of the offenders and the offensive nature of the deeds under the common law of peoples". We agree here with Dorst, that offenders with an offical position deserve a still more serious punishment than those who perpetrate laesio humanitatis in their private capacity.

(IV.B.3.b) - pp. 187 - 192.

1) See *(IV.D.2)* for application of these terms to legal phenomena.
2) The Bible does not mention this decision, but it does report its consequences in the Acts and St. Paul's letters.
3) Cf. *(IV.B.2.d)*.
4) See on the role of casual incidents in the developments of shapes of government: J. Huizinga (Verkenningen) 28, 31. In my opinion Huizinga overemphasizes the disturbing casual incidents, and neglects the constructive ones. This results not only in Huizinga's rejection of the notion of evolution as a working hypothesis which is suitable for the science of history, but even in a rejection of the possibility that a causal chain might exist between special historical events.
5) Julian Huxley (Religion) 191; Wiener (Golem) 13 27 ff., 47,48.
6) See *(I.A.3.b.1)*. Jural applications in *(IV.D.2)*.
7) Bok (Leven) 169, 271. Cf. also von Neumann (Computer)
8) Cf. *(I.A.3.b.1)*.
9) Wiener (Golem) 13,27 ff.,47,48.
10) Raven (Ontwikkeling) 140-153.
11) See on Bergson's influence on Teilhard de Chardin: J. Huxley (Essays)197.
12) Cf. Jacobi (Jung) 51 ff.
13) It may be well-worth comparing "psychic energy" to the later developed concept of information. Cf. the notion "idée-force" in *(I.B.3.d)*.
14) Teilhard de Chardin distinguishes, besides this trend towards unification, still another no-ospheric evolutionary trend, viz. that towards individualization and personalization of the individual, which trend is the driving force behind the trend towards mankind's unification. Cf. J. Huxley (Essays) 195.

(IV.B.3.c) - pp. 192 - 196.

1) This depends on the increase of our knowledge concerning human phenomena which at present partly or completely give the impression of not obeying the laws of causality, like extra-sensory perception and other para-psychological phenomena. C.G. Jung has developed a principle of explanation, supplementary to causality, which he described under the name of "synchronicity" as "a coincidence in time of two or more causally unrelated events which have the same or similar meaning"; cf. Jung (Archetypen) 118, 161, 182, 201 ff., 219, Jacobi (Jung) 48 ff., Jaffé (Jung) 22 ff. If such a principle indeed belongs to the cosmic order then our present ideas on reception, digestion and negative feedback of information in servomechanisms might require revision; a better understanding of "synchronicity" might result in a search for machines which are suitable for the artificial making of "synchronicitic" phenomena.

2) See *(IV.E.4)* for a more juridical description of this notion.

3) Divergency, a fan shaped differentiation of mankind into differentiated anthropological types and social communities, is seen by Teilhard de Chardin and Julian Huxley as only an initial stage of no-ospheric development; the present convergent movement is a multilateral impregnation of mankind's groups of anthropological types and societies on the diverged lines. Neither Teilhard de Chardin nor Julian Huxley seem to have given attention to the fact that in no-osphere, competition may not only result in selection, but also in divergency. See *(IV.B.3.g)* on this subject. Fischer (Evolutie/Utrecht) 196, discussing the ideas of Teilhard de Chardin and Julian Huxley in this respect, speaks of a struggle and selection between the cultures, or between the nations, classes or other groups, which are its vehicles. This differentiation seems to me similar to horizontal and vertical divisions of the notion of cultural areas which we will make in this paragraph.

4) This answers to C.G.Jung's conception of "collective consciousness"; Cf. Jacobi (Jung) 29ff.

5) Cf. *(III.B.3)*.

6) Cf. *(III.C.4.a)*.

7) Nazi-Germany and Stalinist Soviet-Russia were very close to state-individuals; present-day's one party states are generally very close to state-pressure-groups because of the preponderance of the only political party; the U.S.A. is close to a state-cultural area, however mixed with the notion of state-pressure-group as determined by either the Republican or Democratic Party.

8) See Woodward (Cherokees) 305 ff.; cf. Hagan (Indians) 151 ff.

9) This movement started ± 1890 when the Ghost-Dance religion swept across the United States as a common cult of American Indians; cf. Bailey (Messiah) 103 ff.

(IV.B.3.d) - pp. 196 - 198.

1) Cf. *(I.A.3.b.1)*.

2) Un. Decl. 24; 25 jo 5. Eur. Conv. 3.

3) Cf. *(IV.E.3)*.

(IV.B.3.e) - pp. 198 - 200.

1) See *(IV.B.3.g)*.

2) An authority above individuals is not always a converging power; it may act as a diverging power if its behaviour forces individuals to separate from the group or area above which it stands.

3) Un.Decl. 8,9,10,11,12; Eur. Conv. 5,6,7.

(IV.B.3.f) - pp. 200 - 202.

1) See note 3 ad *(IV.B.3.c)*.

2) See *(IV.B.3.g)* on possible unification among cultural areas of this type.

3) Un. Decl. 28.

(IV.B.3.h) - pp. 204 - 208.

1) Cf. *(III.B.6.c)*, *(IV.B.2.d)* and *(IV.E.1)*.
2) Eur. Conv. 10.
3) Cf. Eur. Conv. 10 (1).
4) Cf. Un. Decl. 26.
5) Un. Decl. 21 (3). Subjects entitled to such a control are citizens cf. *(II.C.4.c)*.
6) The principle of Rule of Law was formulated by Albert Venn Dicey, but its contents emerged from the constitutional struggles in 17th century England on the issue whether *Rex* is *Lex* or *Lex* is *Rex*. Cf. Jenks (Book) 136 ff. and Potter (Introduction) 148. Cf. also *(II.F.3)*.

(IV.C.1) - p. 209.

1) See Grava (Inquiry) 146-161.
2) Cf. *(III.B.1)* ff.

(IV.C.2) - p. 209.

1) Grava (Inquiry) 154, with quotations from Herbert L. Samuel, Essay in Physics (New York, 1952), p. 50 ff.
2) Spontaneous creation of hydrogen-atoms is suspected to occur everywhere in space.
3) Grava (Inquiry) 150.

(IV.C.3) - pp. 210 - 212.

1) Achermann (Sollen).
2) Achermann (Sollen) 84. This is also the base of Radbruch's conception that values cannot be deduced from being (Sein), but only from higher values. Cf. Zong (Radbruch) 28
3) Achermann (Sollen) 46 ff. Potential being corresponds to Achermann's "ideal being" ("ideales Sein").
4) This applies to ought as a primitive and therefore also to Liability, Immunity and Privilege as the four logical modi of Ought or Duty. Cf. *(II.D.2.a)*.
5) See also *(IV.C.6)*.

(IV.C.4) - p. 212.

1) Cf. the last sentence of *(III.A.4.a)*.

(IV.C.5) - pp. 212 - 215.

1) Cf. Jacobi (Jung) 8 ff., 30 ff., 71, 79, 136.

(IV.C.6) - pp. 215 - 217.

1) Cf. *(II.E.4)*.

(IV.D.2) - pp. 220 - 224.

1) In the first case rules of morality are indeed of determinative nature, but they are also potential law rules; in the second case it is law rules which, although of determinative reality, are similarly potential rules of morality. See *(III.C.3)* for a cybernetic distinction between law and morals.
2) This process occurs spontaneously in public life and the "procedure" described here does not comprise an analysis of the real psychological

and sociological phenomena which also participate in it.

3) Application of the principles here unfolded may not only occur in the making of statute-law, but also when judge-made law is created.

4) Cf. *(II.B)* ad Ihering jo *(I.A.3.b.1)* and *(IV.B.3.b)*.

5) The digestion of this information belongs to the tasks of legal history and comparative law.

6) The body of law's potentials can be compared with an index of which the meaning can be changed by alterations in the arrangement of the data which it comprises.

7) These potentials should not necessarily belong to the legal system in which a legislative servomechanism participates, as may be inferred from the reception of Roman Law in Western-European areas, when the aboriginal Germanic customary law, towards the end of the Middle Ages, was losing its adequacy amidst changing societies.

8) A corresponding process is that of *finding* law in courts relative to concrete cases.

9) This also applies to law-making in courts with certain formal competencies in this respect, like the Anglo-Saxon legal area or in Switzerland, or with only material opportunities, like the cassation courts in France, Belgium or the Netherlands.

10) Cf. *(I.A.3.b.1)*.

11) Cf. Jean Rostand in his foreword to Ettinger (Diepvriesmens).

12) Ettinger (Diepvriesmens) 19 ff, is of the opinion that even the dead may be conserved, if they are frozen very soon after their clinical death, because the dead are only temporary incurable and future science therefore might be able to cause their resurrection by healing their diseases.

13) Among old principles, which possibly need not be remodelled to new ones, might be legal regulations concerning the consequences of reincarnation, which regulations might be found in societies with a general belief in reincarnation. Christian belief in resurrection of the dead has not led to a regulation of the legal consequences of this occurrence, very probably because this resurrection is believed to occur within a world order where material and spiritual needs do not exist.

14) This conception appears for the first time in the year 1160 as a formal rule in the municipal law of Schwerin; the elements of this conception are however already emerging in provisions of the privilege for Speyer of the year 1111; see Schütze (Stadtluft) 111 jo 3 ff.; cf. also Planitz (Stadt) 116 ff.

15) The latter principle is that of personality; in the Middle Ages it was never completely superseded by that of territoriality. Cf. (Meyers) Bijdrage, 8, 16 ff, 84 ff, 88 ff; Meijers (Nieuwe Bijdrage) 61 ff; VerLoren/Spruit (Hoofdlijnen) 47, 98, 171.

16) Cf. Schütze (Stadtluft) 111, 112.

17) Cf. de Blécourt (Begrip) 166, 167; Planitz (Stadt) 117, 118 jo 389 note 23.

18) "Weltgeist" and God are to Hegel synonymous. Cf. *(I.B.3.e)*.

19) New-Hegelian legal philosophy has tried to eliminate the doctrine of dialectics. Cf. Friedrich (Rechtsphilosophie) 92.

20) In Klaus (Kybernetik) cybernetics is treated as a dialectic system.

21) Hegel (Rechtsphilosophie), 21-28.

(IV.E.1) and (IV.E.2) - pp. 225 - 226.

1) We treated corresponding ideas of Herbert Spencer and Pierre Teilhard de Chardin in *(I.D.2)* and *(I.D.3)*.

2) See Van der Ven (Grundrechte) and Dietze (Formulierung).

(IV.E.3) - pp. 226 - 228.

1) Un. Decl. 3; Eur. Conv. 2.
2) Cf. Eur. Conv. 2.
3) Cf. *(IV.B.3.d)*.
4) See *(IV.E.4)*.
5) The fundamental principle relative to the legal position of unborn children is formulated in D 1.5.7 (Paulus libro singulari de portionibus, quae liberis damnatorum conceduntur): "Qui in utero est, perinde ac si in rebus humanis esset custoditur, quotiens de commodis ipsius partus quaeritur: quamquam alii antequam nascatur nequamquam prosit". The fundamental problem relative to legalisation of abortions is the actual moment at which organic structures "in utero" are transformed from a "quod" into a "qui". Cf. also Un. Decl. 25 (2): "Motherhood and childhood are entitled to special care and assistance. All children, whether born in or out of wedlock, shall enjoy the same social protection".

(IV.E.4) - pp. 228 - 229.

1) See also *(IV.B.3.c)*.
2) Cf. Un. Decl. 12; Eur. Conv. 8.
3) Un. Decl. 3, Eur. Conv. 5 (1).
4) Un. Decl. 29 (1).
5) Cf. Un. Decl. 29 (2); Eur. Conv. 5. If a liability is imposed, man indeed retains his general privilege, but runs the risk that a legal burden will be imposed upon him later.
6) Cf. Un. Decl. 1; 2; 7; Eur. Conv. 14.
7) The origin of this principle can be traced back to Kant: cf. *(I.D.2)*. Cf. Un. Decl. 29 (2) and 30; Eur. Conv. 17 and 18; cf. however also Eur. Conv. 15 and 16.
8) Cf. Un. Decl. 29 (2) and 29 (3).

(IV.E.5) - pp. 229 - 231.

1) The methods for killing animals in this respect should however not be contrary to the criterion for no-ospheric evolution. With the same criterion solutions might be found as to problems concerning vivisection.
2) United Nations Conference on the Human Environment:
Final Documents (Adopted on June 16, 1972):
I) Declaration of the United Nations on the Environment
II) Action Plan for the Human Environment
III) Resolution on Institutional and Financial Arrangements.
Reproduced from U.N. Document A/Conf.48/41 and Corr.1, Report of the United Conference on the Human Environment, in: International Legal Materials, Current Documents, Volume XI, Number 4. July 1972. Washington (D.C.). (The American Society of International Law) 1972.
3) Resolution adopted: 229 (XXVII) Text in: Resolutions of Legal Interest adopted by the General Assembly at its twenty - seventh Session. 19 September - 19 December 1972. United Nations, Press Section, Office of Public Information. United Nations, N.Y.

(IV.E.6) - pp. 231 - 235.

1) The treaties made after World War I with respect to rights of minorities provided in international protection of minorities within the jurisdiction of vanished or newly created states.
2) Cf. *(IV.B.2.e)*.

3) The same principles are repeatedly mentioned in provisions of the U.N. Charter: art. 55 declares them as principles for the international economic and social co-operation which the U.N. Organization will promote; art. 73 lists them among the leading principles for its policy as to non-self-governing territories; art. 75 places them among the leading principles for the international trusteeship system.

4) A selection of the answers is published in "Autour de la nouvelle Déclaration Universelle des Droits de l'Homme"; textes réunis par l'U.N.E.S.C.O., Éditions du Sagittaire, 1949.

5) In 1966 the U.N. Assembly accepted two covenants on respectively, economical, social and cultural human rights and civil and political human rights; these covenants will enter into force between the States which ratified them three months after the 35th ratification; a special commission will provide facultative mediation when a State has complaints concerning the execution of one of these covenants by another State; a separate protocol provides for the individual in a right of application to the mentioned commission in respect of violation of a right attributed to him in one of the covenants by a State which undersigned the protocol.

6) Eur. Conv., Preamble.

7) This document is the framework of a law-bound unit composed of European States on one side and the European Committee of Ministers on the other side, with a negative feedback machinery comprising the European Commission of Human Rights and the European Court of Human Rights. This law-bound unit can promote no-ospheric evolution by increases in coherence of itself and by side-effects in other law-bound units composed of States and Organizations of States. In all these cases greater coherences of the no-ospheric game-bound unit may be the result.

8) Eur. Conv. 25, 26.

9) Eur. Conv. 28, 29, 30.

10) Eur. Conv. 31.

11) Eur. Conv. 32 (1), 48.

12) Eur. Conv. 32.

13) Eur. Conv. 48.

14) Cf. on juridical formulation of social evolution our note to *(I.B.1)*.

15) Art. 2 sub 5 of the Charter declares among the U.N.O.'s principles, to which art. 6 refers in respect of the sanction, that "All Members shall give the United Nations any assistance in any action it takes in accordance with the present Charter ..... ".

SAMENVATTING IN HET NEDERLANDS.

(a) Algemeen-juridische beginselen.

(a.a) Evolutie, recht en cybernetica.

Om het begrip "juridische evolutie" te omschrijven werden drie groepen problemen onderzocht:
1) Hoe dienen wij het begrip "evolutie" op te vatten?
2) Welke functie vervult het recht binnen het kader van dit begrip?
3) Hoe dient de structuur van het recht binnen het kader van dit begrip verstaan te worden?

Wij zijn er van uitgegaan dat sedert de tweede helft van de 20e eeuw de biologie, de natuurwetenschappen en de sociale wetenschappen een gemeenschappelijke beschouwingswijze aanwezig is over het sturen van objecten en systemen, nl. de cybernetica. Vanuit deze achtergrond hebben wij de begripsvorming nagegaan rond de term evolutie, zoals zich in de 19e en 20e eeuw ontwikkeld heeft in de biologie en de sociale wetenschappen. Hierbij hebben wij in het bijzonder onderzocht in hoeverre de gevonden omschrijvingen verband hielden met rechtsverschijnselen en in hoeverre de gevonden omschrijvingen zich leenden voor een cybernetische formulering.

Met name Spencer en Teilhard de Chardin hebben, ieder op hun eigen wijze, hun opvattingen over evolutie gerelateerd aan beschouwingen over de fundamentele mensenrechten. Deze beschouwingswijzen zijn gericht op bescherming van de mens als deelhebber aan en keten in het evolutieproces zoals dat op de aarde aan de gang is sedert het ontstaan van het leven.

Een andere relatie kan tussen recht en evolutie gelegd worden aan de hand van de moderne visie dat evolutieprocesen in de levende natuur het gevolg kunnen zijn van strijd tegen de altijd aanwezige dreigingen van wanorde en desintegratie. Evolutie houdt dan een vergroting van integratie in. Binnen het kader van de menselijke evolutie nu, is het recht het belangrijkste instrument, waarmede binnen en tussen menselijke gemeenschappen de dreiging van wanorde kan worden tegemoetgetreden.

Uiteraard is het subject van evolutie - datgene wat aan evolutie onderworpen is - binnen de verschillende disciplines van andere aard. Binnen de biologie is dat het species; binnen de sociale wetenschappen is het de mensheid

- ook een species -, een menselijke gemeenschap, een groep menselijke individuen; binnen de informatiewetenschappen kan men spreken over evolutie van cybernetische systemen of servomechanismen. In overdrachtelijke zin spreekt men ook wel over evolutie van groepen objecten of van ideeën. Juridische evolutie kan weliswaar in de laatste zin worden opgevat, maar voor de rechtswetenschap blijkt juist een evolutiebegrip van betekenis dat gerelateerd is met het begrip servomechanisme.

Onder een servomechanisme verstaat men een physisch, een organisch of een sociaal systeem dat zelf aan de hand van doorlopende informatie en onder veranderende omstandigheden naar een bepaald doel streeft. De ingevoerde informatie, wat deze ook zij, kan altijd omschreven worden als informatie betreffende de omgeving van het servomechanisme; het gedrag van het servomechanisme is afhankelijk van het doel waarnaar het streeft en de informatie die het bereikt over de resultaten van dit streven en over veranderingen in zijn omgeving. Voorbeelden van dergelijke cybernetische systemen zijn computers, systemen van met elkaar verbonden computers, levende wezens en gemeenschappen van levende wezens. Omschrijving van het begrip evolutie met behulp van het begrip servomechanisme is dan ook niet alleen van toepassing binnen de informatiewetenschappen, maar ook in beginsel in de biologie, in de sociale wetenschappen en in de rechtswetenschap.

Een dergelijke omschrijving werd door ons als volgt geformuleerd: *Evolutie is een toename in controle over zichzelf en een toename in onafhankelijkheid van veranderingen binnen zichzelf van een servomechanische eenheid die bestaat uit een servomechanisme en dat deel van diens omgeving, waarmede dit een spel speelt, of uit een complex van dergelijke eenheden.*

(a.b) Servomechanismen en spelbandeenheden.

Een operationeel servomechanisme is steeds voorzien van een programma, waarin een gewenst gedragspatroon is vastgelegd, waarbij - afhankelijk van het gestelde doel en de ingevoerde informatie over de resultaten van eerdere gedragingen en over gebeurtenissen in de omgeving - uit een aantal alternatieven de optimale gedraging gekozen wordt. Dit is het proces van de terugkoppeling; de alternatieven worden bepaald door een patroon van verwachtingen over het eigen gedrag en over de gebeurtenissen in de omgeving.

Men kan servomechanismen niet los zien van hun omgeving. Zij kunnen alleen functioneren door met deze omgeving volgens bepaalde spelregels een spel te spelen; vaak ook bestaat deze omgeving weer uit andere of soortgelijke servomechanismen, die op hun beurt met hun omgeving hun eigen spel spelen. De regels van het spel zijn vastgesteld in de patronen van gewenst gedrag; de spelstrategie wordt bepaald door het patroon van verwachtingen over eigen gedrag en het gedrag van de omgeving.

Een servomechanisme kan ook samen met zijn omgeving als een grotere servomechanische eenheid worden beschouwd. Men kan evenzo als servomechanische eenheid een servomechanisme samen met alleen een deel van zijn omgeving beschouwen. Een individu, een fiets en een rijwielpad vormen samen een andere servomechanische eenheid dan hetzelfde individu met een bureau en daarop een schrijfmachine. In deze beide gevallen speelt hetzelfde individu een spel met een deel van zijn omgeving, maar de spelregels verschillen. Men kan dan stellen dat één individu met delen van zijn omgeving twee verschillende servomechanische eenheden vormt, afhankelijk van de qualiteit, waarin het individu tot zijn omgeving staat. Hieruit volgt, dat één levend wezen - afhankelijk van zijn hoedanigheden - deel uit kan maken van een groot aantal qualitatieve servomechanismen. Dergelijke qualitatieve servomechanismen of "spelbandeenheden" (gamebound units) vormen de subjecten van het hier eerder geformuleerde evolutiebegrip.

(a. c) Rechtsbandeenheden.

Twee individuen kunnen terzake van een bepaalde betrekking één spelbandeenheid vormen. Voorbeelden hiervan zijn de man-vrouw relatie, de betrekking meester-leerling of de relatie tussen koper en verkoper. Ook zijn complexere spelbandeenheden voorstelbaar; bv. een gezin, een dorpsgemeenschap, een staat of de mensheid in zijn totaliteit. Deze laatste spelbandeenheid noemen wij die van de "no-ospheer" (de σφαιρα of wereldbol overdekt door dragers van de νοος of menselijke geest, die te onderscheiden is van de biospheer; de term no-ospheer stamt van Teilhard de Chardin).

Spelregels in spelbandeenheden kunnen het karakter dragen van rechtsregels. Ter onderscheiding van andere spelbandeenheden werd aan dergelijke constructies de benaming "rechtsbandeenheden" (law-bound units) toegekend. De structuur van deze rechtsbandeenheden kan omschreven worden als die van twee of meer partijen, die met elkaar een spel spelen volgens regels door het recht aangewezen ter bereiking van bepaalde doeleinden. Zo vinden we in het geval dat de rechtsband uit een koopovereenkomst bestaat, als doeleinden levering en betaling; als spelregels vinden we regelingen betreffende de rechten en van plichten van verkoper en koper. Een plicht tot prestatie kan in dit verband worden omschreven als een gewenst gedragspatroon, en een recht op een prestatie als een patroon van verwacht gedrag.

We vinden terugkoppelmogelijkheden voor het geval gedragsverwachtingen niet gerealiseerd worden, zoals bij wanprestatie of verborgen gebreken. Terugkoppelmogelijkheden gelijk bv. formele ingebrekestelling of terughouding van de wederprestatie kunnen zich tussen beide betrokken partijen alleen afspelen, maar er kan ook een derde partij, de rechter, in gemengd raken. In een dergelijk geval is de rechtsbandeenheid opgebouwd uit rechtsbetrekkingen tussen de rechter en deze partijen zelf. Het is mogelijk om iedere juridische relatievorm samen met de partijen die haar vormen, voor te stellen als een rechtsbandeenheid.

Vaak is een rechtsbandeenheid opgebouwd uit kleinere rechtsbandeenheden. Zeer duidelijk spreekt dit bij gecompliceerde structuren, zoals bv. staten; de zo even besproken rechtsbandeenheid opgebouwd uit koper, verkoper en hun rechtsbetrekkingen is ook nog van complex karakter. Een voorbeeld van een niet-complexe rechtsbandeenheid wordt gevormd door schenker en begiftigde met de tussen hen bestaande eenzijdige overeenkomst van schenking.

De complexiteit wordt enerzijds bepaald door het aantal partijen, anderzijds door het aantal rechtsbetrekkingen, waartoe de relaties tussen partijen herleidbaar zijn. Bij een simpele koopovereenkomst kan men twee rechtsbetrekkingen onderscheiden, die betreffende de levering en de betaling. Het is mogelijk te stellen dat in dit geval partijen deel uitmaken van twee rechtsbandeenheden, de één met levering als doel en de andere met betaling als doel. Men kan in dit geval echter ook stellen dat levering en betaling samen het doel vormen dat partijen trachten te bereiken. In een dergelijk geval is het praktischer om met betrekking tot deze eenheid van doelstelling ook met één rechtsbandeenheid te werken.

(a.d) Hohfeld's acht jurische grondbegrippen.

De vraag naar de bouwstenen van de rechtsbandeenheden leidt tot die naar de kleinste elementen, waaruit de rechtsbetrekking is opgebouwd. Deze vraag is sedert de 19e eeuw aan de orde geweest in de Anglo-Amerikaanse school van de analytische rechtswetenschap en in de Duitse school van het Pandektisme. Het antwoord dat uit het werk van beide scholen resulteerde in het tweede decennium van de 20e eeuw was de leer van de acht juridische grondbegrippen van Wesley Newcomb Hohfeld.

Deze leer, die o.m. zijn sporen heeft nagelaten in de door particulieren tot stand gebrachte codificaties van Amerikaans recht, biedt nog onvolkomenheden. Wij hebben getracht deze te elimineren door een synthese tot stand te brengen tussen Hohfeld's leer en de leer van Jeremy Bentham, die van de analytische rechtswetenschap de grondlegger was. Verder hebben wij, in aansluiting op het werk verricht door M. Radin en E. Adamson Hoebel, de grondbegrippen die Hohfeld onderscheidde getracht nader te preciseren. Daarbij hebben wij gevonden dat tussen de vier juridische basisrelaties, gevormd door telkens twee van Hohfeld's acht juridische grondbegrippen (t.w. de paren van "jural correlatives": Right-Duty, Power-Liability, Disability-Immunity en No Right-Privilege) logische relaties bestaan, vergelijkbaar met die tussen traditioneel-logische A-, E-, I- en O-Proposities.

Deze vier paren grondbegrippen drukken telkens één van de vier eenvoudigst denkbare rechtsbetrekkingen uit die er tussen twee partijen kan bestaan. De twee begrippen waaruit een dergelijke fundamentele rechtsbetrekking is opgebouwd kan men beschouwen als elkaars spiegelbeeld. Zo is een "Right" te verstaan als een recht op een prestatie (een handelen of een niet-handelen) en een "Duty" als de plicht tot deze prestatie van de wederpartij. Een "Power" is een mogelijkheid om in de toekomst een nieuwe fundamentele rechtsbetrekking te scheppen of om een dergelijke bestaande betrekking te wijzigen, en een "Liability" is de onderworpenheid van de wederpartij aan het risico van een dergelijke uitoefening van een "Power".

Een "Power" is hetzelfde als een wilsrecht of Gestaltungsrecht.

Een "Disability" daarentegen drukt de afwezigheid van een "Power" uit; de wederpartij heeft dan een "Immunity", d.w.z. hij heeft geen "Liability" want hij is immuun tegen gedrag van de ander in de vorm van het uitoefenen van een "Power" (die deze in werkelijkheid niet heeft).

Het grondbegrip "Privilege" drukt de afwezigheid uit van een plicht iets te doen of niet te doen. Dit ontbreken van een plicht tot zowel presteren als niet presteren kan men ook omschrijven als een vrijheid iets te doen en niet te doen, of als een recht iets te doen en niet te doen. De andere partij heeft dan een "No Right", d.w.z. hij heeft geen recht op een prestatie; hij is terzake van een bepaalde handeling door de wederpartij niet gerechtigd tot het maken van een inbreuk op diens vrijheid. Men zou dan ook een "No Right" kunnen omschrijven als een noodzaak tot dulden. Zo heeft, in het geval van een servituut, bij een recht van overpad de eigenaar van het heersend erf een "Privilege" om over het dienend erf te lopen, terwijl de eigenaar van het dienend erf te dier zake een noodzaak tot dulden, een "No Right" heeft, overigens naast een "Duty" tot dulden, een duldplicht.

Wij vonden dat de logische relaties tussen Hohfeld's vier paren grondbegrippen als volgt kunnen worden voorgesteld: (A) Right-Duty, (E) Power-Liability, (I) Disability-Immunity, (O) No Right-Privilege.

De termen die Hohfeld gebruikte om zijn grondbegrippen aan te duiden zijn weliswaar identiek met Angelsaksische rechtstermen, doch zij geven telkens slechts één van de begrippen weer, die met deze woorden kunnen worden uitgedrukt. Dit heeft verwarring gesticht. Bij pogingen Hohfeld's begrippen met Nederlandse woorden weer te geven dreigt hetzelfde gevaar. Uit het bovenstaande blijkt dat voor Hohfeld's begrippen soms onderscheiden Nederlandse bewoordingen mogelijk zijn en dat het terrein van toepassing van deze termen bepaalt welke weergave de meest geschikte is. Wij zien er om deze redenen van af om voor Hohfeld's systeem Nederlandse standaardtermen te introduceren.

(a.e) Hohfeld's grondbegrippen en de wilsvormen van Bentham.

Bentham had alle recht beschouwd als de uitdrukking van de wil van een wetgevende souverein betreffende het gedrag van personen onderworpen aan zijn gezag. Deze wil kan volgens Bentham geuit worden in vier vormen, die tot elkaar in logische betrekkingen staan op een wijze die vergelijkbaar is met de A-, E-, I- en O-proposities uit de traditionele logica. Deze vier vormen zijn (A) Bevel, (E) Verbod, (I) Niet Verbod (Verlof te handelen), (O) Niet Bevel (Verlof na te laten).

Wij hebben deze onderscheidingen van de wil onderzocht en geconcludeerd dat de vier vormen van de wil die Bentham onderscheidde in werkelijkheid slechts twee wilsvormen zijn: (1) Een Bevel, nl. om te handelen of na te laten, dus een begrip Bevel in ruime zin; (2) Een Verlof, nl. om te handelen of na te laten, dus een Verlof in ruime zin. Wij vonden bovendien, dat er nog twee andere vormen van wilsuitingen bestaan, die niet door Bentham zijn behandeld: (3) de verklaring dat een handelen of nalaten dat thans geen object is van een bezwarende reglementering dit kan worden in de toekomst (voorbeeld: een grondwettelijke regeling dat een staat bepaalde belastingen kan invoeren bij een bijzondere wet); (4) de verklaring dat een handelen of nalaten als onder (1) ook in de toekomst niet bezwarend zal worden gereglementeerd (voorbeeld: een grondwettelijk verbod om bij de wet de plicht in te voeren tot een bepaalde religie te behoren).

Wij toonden aan dat ook deze vier vormen van wilsuiting tot elkaar in logische betrekkingen staan op een wijze te vergelijken met die tussen traditionele A-, E-, I- en O-proposities: A (1), E (3), I (4), O (2) (de cijfers corresponderen met de vier wilsaspecten). Dit was mogelijk doordat deze vier nieuwe wilsaspecten als volgt identiek zijn met vier van de acht jurische grondbegrippen uit het systeem van Hohfeld: A (1) Duty, E (3) Liability, I (4) Immunity, O (2) Privilege.

Hohfeld benadrukte de tweezijdigheid van jurische relaties, terwijl Bentham deze slechts vanuit het standpunt van één partij analyseerde. Wat de positie van de andere partij, de wilsuitende souverein betreft, men kan het leerstuk betreffende diens wil als grondslag voor gedragsregels altijd vervangen door een andere conceptie die aangeeft waarom in bepaalde gevallen bepaalde gedragingen gewenst zijn. Een dergelijke conceptie is die van de Rule of Law (Lex est Rex), die juist het omgekeerde is van Bentham's uitgangspunt (Rex est Lex). In beide concepties evenwel blijft behoefte bestaan aan een buiten het recht gelegen toetssteen van objectieve aard om de uiteindelijke geoorloofdheid of gebodenheid van gedragingen vast te stellen. Een dergelijke toetssteen vonden wij in een ethisch criterium dat straks aan de orde komt.

(a.f) De juridische grondbegrippen als onderdelen van rechtsbandeenheden.

De vier fundamentele rechtsbetrekkingen kunnen ook cybernetisch beschouwd worden als onderdelen van rechtsbandeenheden. De begrippen "Right", "Power", "Privilege" en "Immunity" drukken ieder een type of klasse van verwachtingspatronen uit betreffende gedrag van de wederpartij terwijl de termen "Duty", "Liability", "No Right" en "Disability" elk als type of klasse van patronen van door de ander gewenst gedrag te beschouwen zijn. Degene bij wie een dergelijk patroon van verwachtingen aanwezig is heeft, indien het gedrag van de wederpartij daaraan niet beantwoordt, terugkoppelmogelijkheden om de wederpartij alsnog te brengen tot gedragingen overeenkomstig diens patroon van gewenst gedrag, of tot een alternatief hiervoor. Deze terugkoppelmogelijkheden kunnen gerealiseerd worden door middel van een juridische "mechanisme", maar ook zonder, bv. door middel van een informeel verzoek. Biedt de rechtsorde geen terugkoppelmogelijkheden, zoals het verkrijgen van een rechterlijke veroordeling, een verklaring van recht, of een mogelijkheid tot eigenrichting dan is er geen sprake van een rechtsbetrekking, doch van een morele relatie die voor het overige haar eigen soms zeer rigoureuse terugkoppelmogelijkheden hebben kan.

(a.g) De vier fundamentele rechtsbetrekkingen en de vier vormen van het Zijn.

De vier fundamentele rechtsbetrekkingen werden door ons ook onderzocht op hun ontologische en ontogenetische omstandigheden. Dit bracht met zich mee dat wij een visie op de plaats van gedragsvormen in de werkelijkheid moesten ontwikkelen, met name op het sinds Hume en Kant traditionele onderscheid van de realiteit in twee ordeningen, die van "Sein" en van "Sollen". Wij hebben eerst nagegaan in hoeverre er nog andere vormen van de werkelijkheid kunnen bestaan. Het resultaat was, dat o.i. de werkelijkheid zich in vier fundamentele zijnsvormen manifesteert, die met elkaar samenhangen op een wijze die vergelijkbaar is met die van traditioneel-logische A-, E-, I- en O-proposities, te weten: (A) het determinatieve zijn; (E) het indeterminatieve zijn; (I) het actuele zijn; en (O) het potentiële zijn. Al het "Sollen" valt onder het determinatieve zijn; tot het interdeterminatieve zijn behoort alles wat beschouwd kan worden als wanorde en ontbreken van normen; tot het actuele zijn behoren de feitelijke menselijke gedragingen, voorzover deze beschouwd kunnen worden als actualisering van determinatief zijn en dus niet vallen onder het gedrag dat gekenmerkt kan worden als wanorde of als niet bepaald door normen; tot het potentiële zijn rekenen we de objecten van menselijke voorstellingen - voor ons zijn hier belangrijk de potentiële gedragsnormen.

De begrippen actueel zijn en potentieel zijn hebben wij ontleend aan de gedachtenwereld van het Taoisme-zoals dit met huidige natuurwetenschappelijke opvattingen gerelateerd kan worden. Het begrip indeterminatief zijn is te verbinden met onze opvatting dat evolutieprocessen altijd het kenmerk dragen van strijd tegen dreigingen van wanorde.

De vier fundamentele juridische relaties kunnen vanuit een objectief gezichtspunt gerekend worden tot de wereld van het determinatieve zijn. Vanuit een subjectief standpunt evenwel behoort elk van de vier relaties tot een andere vorm van zijn, en wel tot die zijnsvorm, waarmede het overeenstemt naar zijn plaats in het logische quadrant. Zo wordt de Right-Duty relatie (A) subjectief beleefd als determinatief zijn (A), de Power-Liability relatie (E) als indeterminatief zijn (E), de relatie Disability-Immunity (I) als actueel zijn (I) en de relatie No Right-Privilege (O) als potentieel zijn (O).

(a.h) Een ethisch criterium gebaseerd op de beginselen van no-ospherische evolutie.

Op basis van deze ontologische conceptie konden wij ook een ontogenetische conceptie ontwikkelen met betrekking tot gedragsnormen. Bij het ontstaan van juridische of morele gedragsregels komt het eerder genoemde door ons ontwikkelde ethische criterium naar voren. Dit criterium behoort tot het determinatieve zijn, doch is geen regel van recht of moraal: het is geen patroon van gewenst gedrag en het heeft geen spiegelbeeld in de vorm van een verwachtingspatroon; het is een toetssteen aan de hand waarvan men de inhoud van dergelijke patronen kiezen kan. Het criterium houdt het volgende in: *de mens dient welbewust zodanig te handelen dat de spelbandeenheid van de mensheid en haar omgeving een grotere controle over zichzelf en een grotere onafhankelijkheid van veranderingen in zichzelf verkrijgt, hetzij direct, hetzij middelijk door cumulatieve resultaten of door neveneffecten.* De gelding van dit criterium is gelegen in het feit dat de mens deel uitmaakt van spelbandeenheden, waarin tenminste één van de spelen gericht is op een toename in samenhang van de spelbandeenheid. Vindt een dergelijk spel niet langer plaats, dan wordt de dreiging van wanorde en desintegratie, die altijd op de achtergrond aanwezig is, acuut en valt de spelbandeenheid uiteen. Dit beginsel geldt ook voor de no-ospheer, die beschouwd kan worden als een spelbandeenheid bestaande uit de mensheid en haar omgeving.

(a.i) Juridische evolutie.

Binnen spelbandeenheden gevormd door mensen is het recht het belangrijkste instrument om dreigingen van wanorde en desintegratie onder controle te houden. Deze gedachte ligt ook ten grondslag aan onze omschrijving van het begrip juridische evolutie: *een toename in samenhang van de spelbandeenheid die bestaat uit de mensheid en haar omgeving, veroorzaakt door een leerproces, gedurende welke rechtsbandeenheden kunnen geschapen worden dan wel kunnen toe- of afnemen in samenhang, of kunnen worden ontbonden, en dat ook door middel van neveneffecten soortgelijke processen teweeg kan brengen in andere rechtsbandeenheden.* Toename in samenhang van een staat als rechtsbandeenheid - d.i. versteviging van een nationale rechtsorde - is dus alleen als juridische evolutie op te vatten indien toename in samenhang van de no-ospherische spelbandeenheid hiervan het gevolg is. Voorbeelden van onmiddelijk werkende oorzaken zijn wettelijke maatregelen tot invoering van nieuwe sociale voorzieningen of nieuwe onderwijsmogelijkheden. Voorbeelden van middellijk werkende oorzaken zijn o.m. nationale of particuliere regelingen, die in de rechtsstelsels van andere staten worden gerecipieerd.

(a.j) De no-ospherische evolutieprocessen.

Bij het analyseren van de no-ospherische evolutieprocessen hebben wij de invloed op deze processen nagegaan zoals die wordt uitgeoefend door spelbandeenheden van diverse aard: de individu en zijn omgeving, de spelbandeenheden gevormd door pressure-groups of door een sub-cultuur of cultuur gekenmerkte groepering, en door spelgebonden eenheden van politieke aard, zoals staten, onderdelen van staatsorganisaties, of organisaties van staten. Wij concludeerden dat tussen deze spelbandeenheden een netwerk van spelprocessen aan de gang is in de no-ospheer, met zowel convergerende als divergerende gerichtheden; zowel convergentie als divergentie kunnen leiden tot evolutie, stilstand of terugval. Bij terugval is steeds sprake van opdringen van wanorde, terwijl ook bij stilstand het gevaar voor wanorde door degeneratie groot is. Uiteindelijk zullen de evolutieprocessen kunnen leiden tot een instabiel evenwicht tussen een mensheid onder optimaal welzijn en een omgeving waarvan de wanordedreiging onder optimale controle staat. Wij analyseerden onder welke voorwaarden deze toestand zo snel mogelijk bereikt kan worden.

(a.k) De no-ospheer als rechtswaarde.

Dat de no-ospheer zelf een rechtswaarde is valt af te leiden uit diverse regelingen van het Volkenrecht, die gericht zijn tegen handelingen die voor de no-ospheer een daadwerkelijk gevaar opleveren. Een dergelijke regeling is bv. het charter voor het Internationale Militaire Tribunaal in Neurenberg, dat de bestraffing regelde van misdrijven tegen de vrede, oorlogsmisdrijven en misdrijven tegen de mensheid die door leidende Nazi-figuren bedreven waren. Een ander voorbeeld is de Genocideconventie.

(a.l) De no-ospheer als bron van rechtswaarden.

Als delen van de no-ospheer genieten individuen, groepen van individuen en het menselijke milieu rechtsbescherming in velerlei regelingen van nationale en internationalaard.

Bescherming van de individu als deel van de no-ospheer, bescherming van het no-ospherische milieu en bevordering van no-ospherische evolutie behoort tot de doelstellingen van de Verenigde Naties. Dit blijkt o.m. uit het Charter van deze organisatie, uit de Universele verklaring van de Rechten van de Mens, uit de opzet van gespecialiseerde organen van de Verenigde Naties zoals de U.N.E.S.C.O., F.A.O., W.H.O., I.L.O., I.T.O. en de in 1972 opgerichte Governing Council for Environmental Programmes, Environment Secretariat en Environment Fund. Ook moderne Volkenrechtelijke regelingen van regionele aard kunnen op dergelijke doelstellingen gericht zijn, gelijk de Europese Conventie voor de Rechten van de mens, die de eerste regeling is welke internationaal geinstitutionaliseerde en daadwerkelijke mogelijkheden biedt tot bescherming van de individu bij aantasting van fundamentele mensenrechten.

(a.m) De no-ospherische evolutieprocessen als rechtswaarde en als bron van rechtswaarden.

Niet alleen de no-ospheer, maar ook de zich daarbinnen afspelende evolutieprocessen zijn te beschouwen als rechtswaarden. Als zodanig genieten deze processen niet alleen bescherming in wetten op nationaal niveau, maar ook middels Volkenrechtelijke regelingen. Deze rechtswaarden nu bleken op hun beurt ook weer bron van nationaal of internationaal erkende rechtswaarden te zijn. Wij vonden de volgende betrekkingen:

(1) *De no-ospherische evolutieprocessen mogen niet gestopt worden:* rechtsregels gericht op instandhouding van de biologische processen in het menselijk milieu; rechtsregels gericht op bescherming van de menselijke procreatie; voorschriften uit het oorlogsrecht en het arbeidsrecht tot bescherming van vrouwen en kinderen; rechtsregels ter bevordering van de physieke en geestelijke gezondheid.

(2) *De noodzaak dat binnen het individu convergentie over divergentie domineert:* grondrechten gericht op voldoende medische voorzieningen, op de beschikbaarheid over behoorlijk voedsel op de integriteit van het menselijk lichaam.

(3) *Tussen individuen dient controle te bestaan over divergentie en bescherming van convergentie:* rechtsregels van nationaal recht en van Volkenrecht met betrekking tot de integriteit van staten, hun rechtsorde en hun bestuurlijke en wetgevende instellingen.

(4) *De noodzaak van convergentie tussen gebieden met onderscheiden culturen*: instellingen tot bevordering van een wereldomvattende samenwerking tussen staten gelijk de U.N.O. en zijn gespecialiseerde organisaties.

(5) *De noodzaak om te streven naar een evenwicht van convergentie en divergentie tussen gebieden met onderscheiden culturen:* internationale overeenkomsten tot vreedzame regeling van conflicten tussen staten, tot humanizering van de oorlog; internationale instellingen zoals de U.N.O., het Internationale Gerechtshof, het Internationale Comité van het Rode Kruis.

(6) *De noodzaak te streven naar een evenwicht tussen de snelheden van evolutieprocessen binnen gebieden van onderscheiden cultuur, die met elkaar betrekkingen onderhouden:* nationale en internationale regelingen betreffende ontwikkelingshulp, vrijheid van drukpers, vrijheid tot verspreiding van informatie d.m.v. bioscoop, radio en televisie. Zie ook sub (7).

(7) *De noodzaak te streven naar een evenwicht tussen enerzijds de toepassing van nieuwe informatie en anderzijds het toepassen van voorvaderlijke tradities, en de onder* (6) *genoemde noodzaak:* regelingen betreffende de controle door het volk van een staat over de regering en het beginsel van de Rule of Law.

(b) Bijzondere juridische beginselen.

(b.a) Plicht en sanctie.

De vraag of een plicht altijd voorzien moet wezen van een sanctiedreiging om deze plicht tot rechtsplicht te maken werd door ons ontkennend beantwoord in onze synthese van leerstukken van Bentham en van Hohfeld. Een sanctie is o.i. in wezen hetzelfde als een plicht; een dergelijke verplichting kan omvatten het verrichten van een vervangende prestatie, het betalen van een schadevergoeding, het betalen van een boete of het ondergaan van een vrijheidsstraf. Tegenover de plicht die in de vorm van een sanctie geformuleerd is staat een recht op de vervangende prestatie, het bedrag van een schadevergoeding, het bedrag van de boete of op het ondergaan van een vrijheidsstraf. Indien een rechtsplicht altijd voorzien zou wezen van een sanctiedreiging, dan dient de sanctie op haar beurt ook weer met een sanctiedreiging versterkt te worden, en deze laatste sanctie op haar beurt eveneens, etc.

Een plicht zonder sanctiedreiging kan deel uitmaken van een natuurlijke verbintenis of van een *lex imperfecta*. Een dergelijke plicht is o.i. een rechtsplicht, wanneer men een verklaring van recht kan vragen, inhoudende dat deze plicht op één van de betrokken partijen drukt.

(b.b) Claim en actie.

Als spiegelbeeld van de plicht die van een sanctiedreiging vergezeld is, gebruikt het Angelsaksische recht de term "claim". Deze term drukt uit de aanwezigheid van een recht op een prestatie en van een rechtsmiddel tot het afdwingen van nakoming, een vervangende prestatie, een schadevergoeding, een boete of het ondergaan van een vrijheidsstraf.

Dit rechtsmiddel is de actie en deze is altijd het spiegelbeeld van een sanctiedreiging. Tegenover een rechtsplicht zonder sanctiedreiging staat altijd een recht zonder actie; een dergelijk recht heeft de wederpartij van degene die gehouden is tot prestatie op grond van een natuurlijke verbintenis of een *lex imperfecta*. Vertaling van de term "claim" met het woord "recht" is dan ook minder juist te achten.

(b.c) Natuurlijke en civiele verbintenissen.

Hohfeld beschouwde zijn begrip "Right" als identiek met "claim" en "Duty" als identiek met "plicht voorzien van een sanctiedreiging". Uit het bovenstaande volgt dat o.i. de relatie tussen "claim" en "plicht, voorzien van een sanctiedreiging" uiteen valt in twee Right-Duty relaties, nl. (1) een recht-plicht relatie en (2) een relatie actie-sanctiedreiging; deze tweede relatie is een Right-Duty relatie die supplementair is aan de eerste en niet zelfstandig voor kan komen. In wezen is de civiele verbintenis dan ook steeds uit twee fundamentele rechtsverhoudingen opgebouwd: een natuurlijke verbintenis en een verbintenis van supplementaire aard die alleen door haar aanwezigheid met de natuurlijke verbintenis samen een civiele verbintenis schept.

(b.d) Natuurlijke verbintenissen en andere "natuurlijke" rechtsbetrekkingen.

Wat wij tot dusverre gezegd hebben over het karakter van de Right-Duty relatie als natuurlijke verbintenis geldt in wezen ook voor de andere drie fundamentele rechtsbetrekkingen. Ook deze zijn in hun eenvoudigste vorm niet voorzien van een relatie actie-sanctiedreiging, maar ook zij kunnen er mee worden versterkt in de vorm van zulk een supplementaire Right-Duty relatie. Derhalve kunnen wij ook t.o.v. de relaties Power-Liability, Disability-Immunity en No Right-Privilege onderscheid maken tussen "civiele" en "natuurlijke" rechtsbetrekkingen.

(b.e) Goede trouw en cybernetica.

Het begrip goede trouw, opgevat in de traditionele dualistische zin van "Treu" en "Glauben" heeft een zinvolle plaats binnen de cybernetische structuur van de rechtsbetrekking. Iemand's "Treu" is te beschouwen als zijn gedraging overeenkomstig een patroon van gewenst gedrag en "Glauben" is het vertrouwen van de wederpartij dat overeenkomstig zijn verwachtingspatroon zal worden gehandeld door de ander.

(b.f) De absolute rechten.

Hohfeld was van mening dat juridische relaties alleen kunnen bestaan tussen mensen en niet tussen mensen en vermogensbestanddelen. In deze opvatting is eigendom van een zaak dus niet het meest absolute recht *op* een zaak, maar met betrekking tot een zaak. Wij hebben ons bij deze opvatting aangesloten doch bleven niettemin als probleem zien, hoe de betrekkingen tussen mens en vermogensbestanddeel kunnen worden verklaard. Wij vonden hiervoor een oplossing.
De gerechtigde tot een absoluut recht maakt deel uit van een rechtsbandeenheid, opgebouwd uit rechtsbetrekkingen tussen hemzelf en ieder tegen wie hij zijn absolute recht kan geldig maken; deze rechtsbandeenheid maakt samen met het vermogensobject, deel uit van een spelbandeenheid. In het geval van onvrijwillig bezitsverlies valt deze spelbandeenheid uit elkaar, maar de rechtsbandeenheid blijft intact.

(b.g) Ne bis in idem.

Wij vonden dat na uitoefening van een "Power" de "Liability" van degene tegen wie deze wordt uitgeoefend omslaat in haar negatie, nl. een "Immunity" tegen uitoefening van dezelfde "Power". Hierin ligt het beginsel besloten, dat in dezelfde instantie over dezelfde zaak niet meer dan eenmaal kan worden beslist.

(b.h) Excepties en nulliteiten.

Een verbintenis kan nietig zijn of vernietigbaar, of de nakoming kan niet of nog niet opeisbaar zijn. Bij nietigheid wordt een beroep gedaan op het niet bestaan van de verbintenis, bij vernietigbaarheid doet men een beroep op een peremptoire exceptie, bij nog niet opeisbaarheid op een dilatoire exceptie en bij andere vormen van niet-opeisbaarheid op een declinatoire exceptie. Wij vonden, voortbouwend op onze uitwerking van Hohfeld's systeem, dat tussen deze excepties en nulliteiten logische betrekkingen bestaan en wij ontwikkelden een wijze om deze voor te stellen.

(b.i) Rechtspersonen.

De vraag of de rechtspersoon een fictie is dan wel een levend wezen wordt irrelevant in het licht van de opvatting, dat rechtspersonen rechtsbandeenheden zijn, die - evenals de mens - in de vorm van qualitatieve servomechanismen zelfstandig deelnemen aan het rechtsverkeer. Zulke geoperationaliseerde systemen van rechtsbandeenheden hebben een cybernetische structuur die enerzijds tot de wereld van de levende natuur gerekend kan worden en anderzijds tot die van de fictieve abstracties.

(b.j) De stichting.

Onze opvatting over de rechtspersoon opent de mogelijkheid om ook het wezen van de stichting te verklaren. Wanneer iemand een stichting opricht, dan zondert hij vermogen af, en daarvan cerliest hij de eigendom, maar op de vraag wie dan eigenaar wordt is tot dusverre geen bevredigend antwoord gevonden.

O.i. wordt deze vraag volkomen irrelevant, wanneer wij ons realiseren, dat bij overdracht van het stichtingsvermogen aan het bestuur van de stichting, tussen dit bestuur, dat geen eigenaar wordt, en de stichter rechtsbetrekkingen ontstaan. Deze nieuwe rechtsrelaties betreffen het afgezonderde vermogen en zijn t.a.v. de stichter overerfelijk Zij omvatten een Disability-Immunity relatie tussen stichter en bestuur, inhoudende dat de stichter of diens erfgenamen aan het bestuur na de vermogensafzondering geen verdere verplichtingen kunnen opleggen ter zake van het afgezonderde vermogen, alsmede een betrekking No Right-Privilege, waarin het bestuur vrij is om met het stichtingsvermogen te handelen binnen de grenzen van het doel van de stichting, terwijl de stichter geen recht heeft om in dit opzicht van het bestuur andere handelingen te verlangen. Op deze wijze ontstaat er tussen de stichter en het bestuur een rechtsbandeenheid die in een andere rechtsbandeenheid de positie in kan nemen van partij en wel op gelijke wijze als iedere andere rechtspersoon.

(b.k) De staat.

Als rechtspersoon vertoont de moderne staat veel gelijkenis met de stichting. Ook hier zien we een afgezonderd vermogen, waarvoor geen eigenaar kan worden aangewezen, doch waarover de souverein de beschikking heeft. Dat in democratisch georganiseerde staten de belastingplichtige staatsburgers in principe na betaling condities kunnen opleggen over de besteding en ook nog bij de besteding kunnen ingrijpen vindt zijn verklaring in het feit dat zij in deze hoedanigheid deel in de souvereiniteit hebben. In hun qualiteit echter van belastingplichtige onderdanen blijven zij tot de souverein staan in dezelfde relaties Disability-Immunity en No Right-Privilege, die wij t.a.v. het stichtingsvermogen aantroffen tussen stichting en bestuur.

REFERENCES

Achermann (Sollen - F. ACHERMANN, Das Verhältnis von Sein und Sollen. Thesis Zürich. Winterthur, 1955.

Aron (Pensée sociologique) - R. ARON, Les étappes de la pensée sociologique: Montesquieu, Marx, Tocqueville, Durkheim, Pareto, Weber. Paris, 1967.

Asser (Rechtspersoon) - C. ASSER, P. SCHOLTEN en M.H. BREGSTEIN, Handleiding tot de beoefening van het Nederlands Burgerlijk Recht, I.2: Vertegenwoordiging en Rechtspersoon. Zwolle, 1954.

Bailey (Messiah) - P. BAILEY, Wovoka, The Indian Messiah. Los Angeles, 1957.

Barnes *(nom. cit.)* - H. E. BARNES, An Introduction to the history of sociology. Chicago, 1965-7.

Bergh, van den (Muzen) - G.C.J.J. VAN DEN BERGH, Themis en de Muzen. De functie van de gebonden normen in het recht. Thesis University of Amsterdam, Haarlem, 1964.

Bergson (Évolution) - H. BERGSON, L'Évolution Créatrice. Paris, 1914.

Blécourt, de (Begrip) - A.S. DE BLÉCOURT, Kort Begrip van het Oud-Vaderlands Recht. Bewerkt door H.F.W.D. FISCHER. Groningen, 1959.

Bok (Cybernetica) - S.T. BOK, Cybernetica (Stuurkunde). Hoe sturen wij ons leven, ons werk en onze machines? Utrecht, 1958.

Bok (Leven) - S.T. BOK, Het ontstaan van het leven. Utrecht, 1963.

Bos (Methoden) - A.M. BOS, Over methoden van begripsvorming in het recht. Deventer, 1967.

Bynkershoek (Observationes) - C. VAN BYNKERSHOEK, Observationes Tumultuariae. Ediderunt E.M. MEYERS, A.S. DE BLÉCOURT, H.D.J. BODENSTEIN. Haarlem, 1926.

Čapec (Impact)	- M. ČAPEC, The philosophical impact of contemporary Physics. London, 1961.
Coing (Grundzüge)	- H. COING, Grundzüge der Rechtsphilosophie. Berlin, 1950.
Dampier (Science)	- W.C. DAMPIER, A history of science and its relations with philosophy and religion. With a postscript by I. Bernard COHEN. Cambridge, 1961.
De Blécourt	- *see* Blécourt, de
Dietze (Formulierung)	- G. DIETZE, Ueber Formulierung der Menschenrechte, Berlin 1956.
Drost (Humanicide)	- P.N. DROST, The Crime of State. Penal protection for fundamental freedoms of persons and peoples. Book I: Humanicide International governmental crime against individual human rights. Leyden, 1959.
Eisler (Philosophie)	- R. EISLER, Handwörterbuch der Philosophie. Berlin, 1913.
Ettinger (Diepvriesmens)	- R.C.W. ETTINGER,(The prospect of immortality) De diepvriesmens. Kunnen wij langer leven? Met een voorwoord van Jean ROSTAND. Amsterdam, 1964.
Fischer (Evolutie/Utrecht)	- H. Th. FISCHER, Evolutionisme en Cultuur. In "De Evolutieleer na honderd jaar". Een reeks voordrachten gehouden ter gelegenheid van de Universiteitsdag op 21 Maart 1959 te Utrecht. Haarlem, 1959.
Fitch (Revision)	- F.B. FITCH, "A Revision of Hohfeld's Theory of Legal Concepts". In: "Logique et Analyse", vol. 30-40 (1967).
Frank (Kybernetik)	- H.G. FRANK, Kybernetik und Philosophie. Materialien und Grundrisz zu einer Philosophie der Kybernetik. Berlin, 1966.
Freudenthal (Logique)	- H. FREUDENTHAL, Logique mathématique appliquée. Paris, 1958.
Friedmann (Theory)	- W. FRIEDMANN, Legal Theory, London, 1967-5.

Friedrich (Rechtsphilosophie) - C.J. FRIEDRICH, (Die Philosophie des Rechts in historischen Perspektive). Rechtsfilosofie in historisch perspectief. Translated and annotated by J.A.C.J. VAN DE WOUW. Hilversum, 1964.

Gierke (Privatrecht I) - O. VON GIERKE, Deutsches Privatrecht, I, Allgemeiner Teil und Personenrecht. München, 1936.

Gierke (Genossenschaftsrecht III) - O. VON GIERKE, Das Deutsche Genossenschaftsrecht, III, Die Staats- und Korporationslehre des Altertums und des Mittelalters und ihre Aufnahme in Deutschland. Darmstadt, 1954.

Gierke (Verbände) - O. VON GIERKE, Das Wesen der menschlichen Verbände. Rektoralsrede 1902. Darmstadt, 1954.

Grava (Inquiry) - A. GRAVA, A structural inquiry into the symbolic representation of ideas. The Hague, 1969.

Greene (Death) - J.C. GREENE, The death of Adam. Evolution and Its Impact on Western Thought. Ames (Ia.), 1959.

Grotius (Inleidinge) - H. DE GROOT, Inleidinge tot de Hollandsche Rechts-Geleerdheid. Met de te Lund teruggevonden verbeteringen, aanvullingen en opmerkingen van den schrijver en met verwijzingen naar zijn andere geschriften uitgegeven en van aantekeningen en bijlagen voorzien door F. DOVRING (Lund), H.F.W.D. FISCHER (Leiden). E.M.MEIJERS (Leiden). Leiden, 1965.

Hagan (Indians)

Hagan (Indians) - W.T. HAGAN, American Indians. Chicago, 1964.

Hanenburg (Rechtspersoon) - J.J.H.M. HANENBURG, De "Rechtspersoon" in de Justiniaanse wetgeving. In: "Tijdschrift voor Rechtsgeschiedenis", XXXI, II, 1963, pp. 167-242.

Hart (Concept) - H.L.A. HART, The Concept of Law, Oxford, 1970.

Hegel - *see* p. 283

Hellema (Dwaling) - A.W. HELLEMA, Dwaling over toekomstverwachtingen. Oratie Utrecht. Deventer, 1972.

Henkel (Rechtsphilosophie) - H. HENKEL, Einführung in die Rechtsphilosophie. Grundlagen des Rechts. München, 1964.

Hoebel (Man) - E. Adamson HOEBEL, The Law of Primitive Man, A study in comparative legal dynamics. Cambridge (Mass.), 1964.

Hohfeld (Conceptions) - W.N. HOHFELD, Fundamental Legal Conceptions as applied in judicial reasoning. Edited by WALTER WHEELER COOK. With a new foreword by A.L. CORBIN. New Haven (Conn.), 1964.

Huizinga (Ludens) - J. HUIZINGA, Homo Ludens. Proeve eener bepaling van het spelelement der cultuur. Haarlem, 1938.

Huizinga (Verkenningen) - J. HUIZINGA, Cultuurhistorische Verkenningen. Haarlem, 1929.

Huxley (Essays) - J.S. HUXLEY, Essays of a Humanist. Amsterdam, 1966.

Huxley (Evolution) - J.S. HUXLEY, Evolution. The Modern Synthesis. London, 1945.

Huxley (Religion) - J.S. HUXLEY, Religion without Revelation. New York, 1964.

Jacobi (Jung) - J. JACOBI,(Die Psychologie von C.G. Jung. With a foreword by C.G. Jung. With a framework by Dr. JUNG. New Haven (Conn.), 1964.

Jenks (Book) - E. JENKS, The book of English Law. London, 1953.

Jaffé (Jung) - A. JAFFÉ, Jung over parapsychologie en alchemie. Jung's laatste jaren. Rotterdam, 1969.

Judgment *(nom. cit.)* - Judgment of the International Military Tribunal for the Trial of German major War Criminals (with the dissenting opinion of the Soviet Member),

Nuremberg, 30th September and 1st October 1946. London, His Majesty's Stationery Office, Miscellaneous No. 12, 1946.

Jung (Archetypen) - C.G. JUNG, (Von den Wurzeln des Bewusstseins). Archetypen. Den Haag, 1964.

Kalinowski (Logique) - G. KALINOWSKI, Introduction à la logique juridique. Éléments de sémiotique juridique, logique des normes et logique juridique. Paris, 1965.

Kirk/Raven (Presocratic) - G.S. KIRK and J.E. RAVEN, The Presocratic Philosophers. Cambridge, 1962.

Klaus (Kybernetik) - G. KLAUS, Kybernetik in philosophischer Sicht. Berlin, 1965.

Klug (Logik) - U. KLUG, Juristische Logik. Heidelberg, 1966-3.

Koningsberger (Evolutie/Utrecht) - V.J. KONINGSBERGER, Una quaelibet vita. In: De Evolutieleer na honderd jaar". Een reeks voordrachten gehouden ter gelegenheid van de Universiteitsdag op 21 Maart 1959 te Utrecht. Haarlem, 1959.

Kuypers (Evolutie/Utrecht) - K. KUYPERS, Het Evolutiebegrip en zijn toepassing op de mens. In: "De Evolutieleer na honderd jaar". Een reeks voordrachten gehouden ter gelegenheid van de Universiteitsdag op 21 Maart 1959 te Utrecht. Haarlem, 1959.

Larenz (Teil) - K. LARENZ, Allgemeiner Teil des deutschen bürgerlichen Rechts. München, 1972-2.

Lübker (Altertum) - F. LÜBKER, Reallexicon des klassischen Altertums. Hrsg. von J. GEFFCKEN und E. ZIEBARTH in Verbindung mit B.A. MÜLLER. Leipzig, 1914-8.

Marlet (Verschijnselen) - J.C.C. MARLET, Paranormale verschijnselen. Met een geleidewoord door J.J.G. PRICK, Bilthoven; 1957.

Meadows (Club) - D.L. MEADOWS, The Limits to Growth - A Report of the Club of Rome Project on the Predicament of Mankind. New York, 1972.

Van Melsen (Wijsbegeerte) - A.G.M. VAN MELSEN, Evolutie en Wijsbegeerte. Utrecht, 1968-2.

Meijers (Bijdrage) - E.M. MEIJERS, Bijdrage tot de geschiedenis van het internationaal privaat- en strafrecht in Frankrijk en de Nederlanden. Haarlem, 1914.

Meijers (Nieuwe bijdrage) - E.M. MEIJERS, Niewe bijdrage tot het ontstaan van het beginsel der realiteit; Tijdschrift voor Rechtsgeschiedenis, III, 1922. pp. 61 ff.

Moritz (System) M. MORITZ, Hohfeld's System der juridischen Grundbegriffe. Lund, 1960.

Nietzsche (Wagner) - F. NIETZSCHE, Der Fall Wagner. Nietzsche contra Wagner. Leipzig, 1908.

Opstellen (Verdam) - Uit het Recht. Rechtsgeleerde opstellen aangeboden aan Mr. P.J. VERDAM. Deventer, 1971.

Pauly-Wissowa (Encyclopädie) - PAULY's Real-Encyclopädie der classischen Altertumswissenschaft. Neue Bearbeitung. Unter Mitwirkung zahlreicher Fachgenossen hrsg. von G. WISSOWA. Stuttgart, 1896.

Pierce (Symbolen) - J.R. PIERCE, (Symbols, Signals and Noise). Symbolen en Signalen. Aard en werking van de communicatie. Utrecht, 1966.

Planitz (Rechtsgeschichte) - H. PLANITZ, Deutsche Rechtsgeschichte. Graz, 1950.

Planitz (Stadt) - H. PLANITZ, Die deutsche Stadt im Mittelalter von der Römerzeit bis zu den Zunftkämpfen. Graz, 1954.

Polak (Contra-Club) - F. POLAK, De Contra-club van Rome. Historische lessen en hoopvolle perspectieven. Amsterdam, 1972.

Pot, van der (Periodisering) - J.H.J. VAN DER POT, De periodisering der geschiedenis

Een overzicht der theorieën. Met een voorwoord van Prof. Dr. J.M. ROMEIN. 's-Gravenhage, 1951.

Pothier (Personnes) - R.J. POTHIER, Traité des personnes et des choses. In: "Oeuvres de Pothier, annotées et mises en corrélation avec le Code Civil et la législation actuelle par M. BUGNET. Tome neuvième". Paris, 1846.

Potter (Introduction) - H. POTTER, An historical introduction to English Law and its Institutions. London, 1948-3.

Pound (Fifty Years) - R. POUND, Fifty Years of Jurisprudence. In: (1937) 50 H.L.R.

Radin (Restatement) - M. RADIN, A Restatement of Hohfeld. In: (1938) 51 H.L.R.

Raven (Ontwikkeling) - Chr.P. RAVEN, Ontwikkeling als Informatieverwerking. Een theoretisch-biologische studie. Hilversum, 1968.

Raz (Concept) - J. RAZ, The Concept of a Legal System. An Introduction to the Theory of Legal System. Oxford, 1970.

Rosdorff (No-Revision) - L.W. ROSDORFF, Hohfeld's Theory of Fundamental Legal Concepts: a No-Revision. In: "Logique et Analyse", will appear in 1973 ed.

Rosdorff (Synthesis) - L.W. ROSDORFF, Bentham and Hohfeld: a Search for a Synthesis. In: "Rechtstheorie", 2/73.

Ross (Directives) - A. ROSS, Directives and Norms. London, 1963.

Russell (Philosophy) - B. RUSSELL, An Outline of Philosophy. (U.S.A. title: Philosophy) London, 1927.

Saleilles (Personne) - R. SALEILLES, De la personnalité juridique. Paris, 1910.

Salmond - *see* Williams.

Savigny (System II) - F.C. VON SAVIGNY, System des heutigen Römischen Rechts, II. Berlin, 1840.

Schreiber (Logik d.R.) - R. SCHREIBER, Logik des Rechts. Berlin, 1962.

Schulz (Roman Law) - F. SCHULZ, Classical Roman Law. Oxford, 1969.

Schütze (Stadtluft) - P. SCHÜTZE, Die Entstehung des Rechtssatzes: Stadtluft macht frei. Berlin, 1903.

Siccama (Paradox) - Jhr. D.G. RENGERS HORA SICCAMA, Paradox, Zwolle, 1962.

Smits (Herder) - E.J.F. SMITS, Herder's Humaniteitsphilosophie. Thesis Groningen, 1939. Assen, 1939.

Van Soest (Informatie - J.L. VAN SOEST, Informatie en Communicatie-Theorie. Delft, 1962.

Spruit (Plinius) - J.E. SPRUIT, C. Plinius Secundus en het erfrecht van zijn tijd. Een rechtshistorisch vertoog over Plinius' Epistulae V,7 II,16 en IV,10. Oratie Utrecht. Deventer 1973.

Stone (Province) - J. STONE, The Province and Function of Law. Sidney, 1950.

Suyling (Inleiding) - J. Ph. SUYLING, Inleiding tot het Burgerlijk Recht. Haarlem, 1948.

Teilhard de Chardin (Opbouw)- P. TEILHARD DE CHARDIN (*from* L'Avenir de l'homme). De opbouw van de toekomst. Utrecht, 1964.

Teilhard de Chardin (Toekomst) - P. TEILHARD DE CHARDIN (*from* L'Avenir de l'homme). De toekomst van de mens. Utrecht, 1963.

Teilhard de Chardin (Verschijnsel) - P. TEILHARD DE CHARDIN (Le Phénomène humain). Het verschijnsel mens. Utrecht, 1965.

Tenhaeff (Telepathie) - W.C.H. TENHAEFF, Telepathie en Helderziendheid. Utrecht, 1958.

Tucker (Marx) - R.C. TUCKER, Philosophy and myth in Karl Marx. Cambridge, 1972.

Tyrell (parapsychologie) - G.N.M. TYRREL (The Personality of Man). Ontdekkingen van de parapsychologie. Utrecht, 1964.

Van den Bergh - *see* Bergh, van den

Van der Pot - *see* Pot, van der

Van der Ven - *see* Ven, van der

Ven, van der (Begriff sozialer Fortschritt) J.J.M. VAN DER VEN, Zum Begriff "Sozialer Fortschritt". In: "Sozialer Fortschritt" (Berlin), Jg XI (1962), p.85 ff.

Ven, van der (Evolutie/Utrecht) - J.J.M. VAN DER VEN, "Maatschappelijke vooruitgang" als evolutionair beginsel in de rechtsontwikkeling. In: "De Evolutieleer na 100 jaar". Een reeks voordrachten gehouden ter gelegenheid van de Universiteitsdag op 21 Maart 1959 te Utrecht. Haarlem, 1959.

Ven, van der (Existentie) - J.J.M. VAN DER VEN, Existentie en Recht. Schets van een antropologische Rechtsbeschouwing. Bilthoven, 1966.

Ven, van der (Grundrechte) - J.J.M. VAN DER VEN, Grundrechte und Geschichtlichkeit. Marburg, 1960.

Ven, van der (Progrès social) - J.J.M. VAN DER VEN, L'évolution de la notion de progrès social. Rapport Général. Congrès International de Liège et Bruxelles, 20-23 septembre 1958. Association Internationale pour le progrès social /Also published in German and Dutch/.

Ven, van der (Sozialer Fortschritt heute) - J.J.M. VAN DER VEN, Was bedeutet socialer Fortschritt heute? In: "Wirtschaft und Recht" (Zürich), Bd XII (1960), p. 68 ff.

VerLoren/Spruit (Hoofdlijnen) - J.Ph. DE MONTÉ VERLOREN, Hoofdlijnen uit de ontwikkeling der rechterlijke organisatie in de Noordelijke Nederlanden tot de Bataafse omwenteling. Vijfde druk bewerkt door J.E. SPRUIT. Deventer, 1972.

Wesenberg (Privatrechtgeschichte) - G. WESENBERG, Neuere deutsche Privatrechtsgeschichte im Rahmen der europäischen Rechtsentwicklung. Zweite Auflage. Neu bearbeitet von G. WESENER. Lahr/Schwarzwald, 1969.

Wieacker (Neuzeit) - F. WIEACKER, Privatrechtsgeschichte der Neuzeit. Göttingen, 1967.

Wiener (Golem) - N. WIENER, God and Golem, Inc. A Comment on Certain Points where Cybernetics Impinges on Religion. Cambridge (Mass.) 1964.

Williams (Salmond) - G. WILLIAMS, Salmond on Jurisprudence. London, 1957.

Windscheid (Pandektenrecht) - B. WINDSCHEID, Lehrbuch des Pandektenrechts. Frankfurt a.M., 1891.

Woodward (Cherokees) - G.S. WOODWARD, The Cherokees. Norman (Okla.), 1963.

Von Wright (Action) - G.H. VON WRIGHT, Norm and Action. London, 1963.

Zinn (Dreistadiengesetz) - K.G. ZINN, Die positivistischen Evolutionsthese des Comteschen Dreistadiengesetzes. Darstellung und Vergleich mit ökonomischen Entwicklungsstufenlehren. Thesis Mainz, 1965. Mainz, 1966.

Zong (Radbruch) - ZONG UK TJONG, Der Weg des rechtsphilosophischen Relativismus bei Gustav Radbruch. Bonn, 1967.

Hegel (Rechtsphilosophie) - G.W.F. HEGEL, Grundlinien der Philosophie des Rechts. Mit Hegel's eigenhändigen Randbemerkungen in seinem Handexemplar der Rechtsphilosophie herausgegeben von J. HOFFMEISTER. Hamburg, 1962-4.

INDEX
(persons)

INDEX
(subjects)

CURRICULUM VITAE

The author was born in 1931 in Rotterdam. In Zeist he passed in 1950 his final examination at secondary school level (H.B.S.-A). During the period 1950-1951 he carried out his compulsory military service and in 1953 he passed the necessary examination in Latin, Greek and mathematics (Staatsexamen Gymnasium A) in order to take up his law studies at the State University of Utrecht, which he started in the same year. He obtained his LL.B. degree (Candidaatsexamen Nederlands Recht) in 1955 and in 1960 he passed the examination for his LL.M. degree (Doctoraalexamen Nederlands Recht).

In 1957 the author was appointed as assistant to the Institute for Legal History at the State University of Utrecht. He has been on the research and education staff of this Institute since 1961 and teaches ancient Dutch and Frisian Law, and Roman Law.

STELLINGEN

I

D. 1.18.12 bindt de Oost-Romeinse stadhouders aan de normen gesteld in de wetgeving en de appèlrechtspraak in Constantinopel en draagt hun op geen acht te slaan op hetgeen vroeger door de magistraten te Rome gedaan werd tegen de daar geldende normen in.

II

De Oud-Germaanse "Mannheiligkeit" kon eerst ontstaan toen de privé-eigendom van de grond tot ontwikkeling kwam.

III

Optekening van het Friese recht was voor koning Redbad overbodig.

IV

Van de oudste in het Fries geschreven rechtsbronnen kunnen alleen afzonderlijke bepalingen naar hun ontstaansperiode worden gedateerd.

V

De bevoegdheid van het Internationaal Gerechtshof staat niet in de weg aan overdaging door de ene staat van de andere staat voor de nationale rechter van laatstgenoemde.

VI

Een alleen door de rechtswetenschap als juist erkend richtsnoer kan nimmer grondslag wezen voor het ontbreken van materiële wederrechtelijkheid.

VII

Aan rechtspersonen kunnen grondrechten worden verleend.

VIII

Gelijk gewaardeerde menselijke waarden van dezelfde klasse kunnen als rechtswaarden positiefrechtelijk ongelijk worden behandeld.

Batch number: 10854269

Printed by Printforce, the Netherlands